At the Heart of the Reich

At the Heart of the Reich

The Secret Diary of Hitler's Army Adjutant

Major Gerhard Engel

Notes and Introduction
by
Hildegard von Kotze

Preface by
Charles Messenger

Translated by
Geoffrey Brooks

Skyhorse Publishing

Visit our website at www.skyhorsepublishing.com.

10 9 8 7 6 5 4 3 2 1

Library of Congress Cataloging-in-Publication Data is available on file.

Cover design by Rain Saukas

Print ISBN: 978-1-5107-1155-6

Ebook ISBN: 978-1-5107-1156-3

Printed in the United States of America

Contents

Maps

Maps

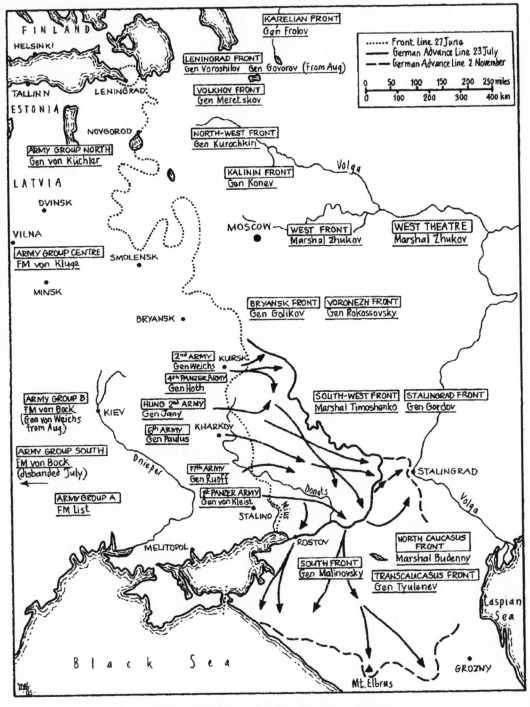

**German Attacks on the Eastern Front,
June–November 1942**

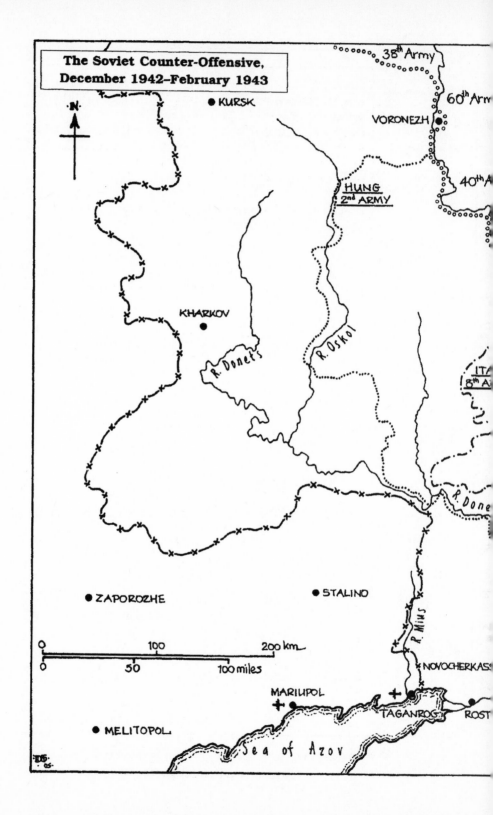

The Soviet Counter-Offensive,
December 1942–February 1943

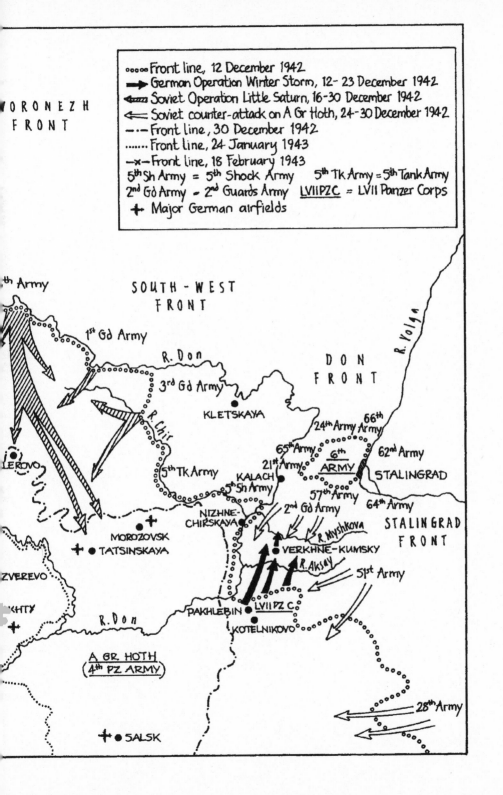

VORONEZH
FRONT

Front line, 12 December 1942
German Operation Winter Storm, 12-23 December 1942
Soviet Operation Little Saturn, 16-30 December 1942
Soviet counter-attack on A Gr Hoth, 24-30 December 1942
Front line, 30 December 1942
Front line, 24 January 1943
Front line, 18 February 1943
5th Sh Army = 5th Shock Army   5th Tk Army = 5th Tank Army
2nd Gd Army = 2nd Guards Army   LVIIPZC = LVII Panzer Corps
Major German airfields

SOUTH-WEST
FRONT

...th Army

1st Gd Army

R. Don

3rd Gd Army

KLETSKAYA

R. Chir

...LEROVO

5th Tk Army

KALACH

5th Sh Army

NIZHNE-
CHIRSKAYA

MOROZOVSK

TATSINSKAYA

ZVEREVO

...KHTY

R. Don

PAKHLEBIN

KOTELNIKOVO

A GR HOTH
(4th PZ ARMY)

SALSK

DON
FRONT

R. Volga

24th Army

65th Army

21st Army

6th
ARMY

66th
Army

62nd Army

STALINGRAD

57th Army

2nd Gd Army

64th Army

STALINGRAD
FRONT

R. Myshkova

VERKHNE-KUMSKY

R. Aksay

51st Army

LVII PZ C.

28th Army

Preface

Gerhard Engel occupied a very privileged position in the Third Reich during the period 1938–43. As Hitler's Army Adjutant, not only did he act as a liaison officer between the Reichs Chancellery and the German Army High Command (*Oberkommando des Heeres – OKH*) but, as a member of Hitler's inner circle, he was also privy to some of the Führer's innermost thoughts and concerns. His diary therefore provides valuable insights into the way Hitler thought and operated, as well as on the frictions that developed between him and the German Army.

Indeed, the Engel diary more than complements the account by Nicolaus von Below, Hitler's Luftwaffe Adjutant during 1937–45, which has already been published in English (*At Hitler's Side*, Greenhill, 2001). This is especially since Below's work was written many years after 1945. In contrast, even though, as Hildegard von Kotze's introduction points out, text was added by the author after 1945, Engel's diary has an immediacy which makes it a valuable historical document. True, the diary is fragmentary, with often several days and even weeks and months between entries – in many ways it reads like a series of snapshots. Part of the reason for this may simply have been lack of time. As von Below pointed out, being an adjutant to Hitler was very demanding and often entailed a 16-hour day. It may also simply have been because Engel did not consider that anything had happened which was of particular note. There are also entries, probably written some time after the event, in which dates and other detail are questionable. In this respect, the reader needs to exercise a degree of caution, although these anomalies do not have a significant bearing on the integrity of the diary as a whole.

Engel took up his appointment on the eve of *Anschluss* and in the wake of the von Blomberg and von Fritsch scandals. Indeed, his first diary entry, on the very day that German troops entered Austria and union between the two countries was proclaimed, records Heinz Guderian's shock over the treatment meted out to the luckless Werner von Fritsch, who had been Commander-in-Chief of the Army for four years before he was forced to resign in early February 1938.

The motivation for fabricating a homosexual affair involving von Fritsch was that Hitler saw him as an obstacle to creating a mass army imbued with National Socialism. Indeed, one of the main themes of the diary is Hitler's ranting against his generals. In particular, he accused them of having too little political understanding and of timidity. Much of this was because they considered that the expansion of the army was being carried out too rapidly and hence Hitler's allusion to the 100,000-man army mindset.

The Army's interests were also not served by the generals closest to Hitler, something which is reinforced by Engel. Wilhelm Keitel, Chief of the Armed Forces High Command (*Oberkommando der Wehrmacht* – OKW), popularly known as *Lakaitel* ('lackey') – a play on his name, seldom, if ever, stood up to Hitler, which, of course suited the latter. The same applied to Walter von Brauchitsch, who succeeded von Fritsch as Army C-in-C. This was not so much on account of a supine character, but more because von Brauchitsch had wanted to divorce his wife so that he could remarry, but she demanded a financial settlement beyond his means. He therefore agreed to become C-in-C in return for a sizeable sum of money, which put him in debt to Hitler. Furthermore, his second wife had a dubious background and he was well aware that von Blomberg's demise had been brought about by the same situation. It was therefore unsurprising that the new C-in-C adopted an obsequious attitude towards the Führer.

Engel railed against both Keitel and von Brauchitsch and, like many other officers, placed his hopes in Ludwig Beck, the Army Chief of Staff. Beck was well aware that Hitler's expansionist ambitions could lead to disaster and, once Hitler turned his eyes on Czechoslovakia, addressed a memorandum to von Brauchitsch. He warned that a German invasion of that country might well bring in the other major European powers and that Germany would find itself having to fight a major war on two fronts, a problem which had traditionally dogged German strategic thinking. His memorandum was ignored, but in spite of pleas by Engel, he would not speak directly to Hitler, complaining of his demagogic attitude. Even so, Beck did persevere with von Brauchitsch and persuaded him to call a meeting of the senior commanders. The result was that von Brauchitsch finally presented Beck's memorandum to Hitler who dismissed it as merely another example of military timidity. It was virtually the last straw for Beck. After a final row with von Brauchitsch over his failure to stand up to Hitler, he resigned in August 1938. His place was taken by General Franz Halder, who previously headed the OKH Operations branch. Hitler had initially despised Halder as a desk soldier, but did recognise his powers of organisation. Engel makes no comment on Beck's demise, but he does record his first meeting with Halder in his new post. His previous dealings with the new Chief of Staff had been stiff, largely because Halder did not trust Engel, believing him to be a Hitler toady. When Halder now displayed a pistol on his desk and complained that he was being followed it was clear that he was suffering from a persecution complex. When Engel then told him what the Reich Chancellery were thinking, Halder said he was interested only in the political aspects; his colleagues would take care of the military aspects since he had little regard for Hitler's thoughts on the subject. The final straw in Engel's eyes was the presentation by von Brauchitsch and Halder of the Army's plan for the invasion of Czechoslovakia. Hitler rejected large parts of it and demanded revisions. Neither the C-in-C nor the Chief of Staff stood up to him and the final humiliation in Engel's eyes was von Brauchitsch's public declaration of the loyalty of the Army to the Führer.

Engel does not give a view on the Munich Agreement by which Britain and France agreed not to block Hitler's annexation of the Sudetenland. However, his accounts of conversations with Hitler make it clear that the Führer was already turning his eyes to Poland and that he was clear that peace could only come once the matter of the Polish Corridor, which separated East Prussia from the remainder of the Third Reich, was resolved to his satisfaction. Likewise, Engel mentions nothing about the final dismemberment of Czechoslovakia in March 1939, although he does mention Hitler's anger at not being forewarned by Mussolini of the Italian annexation of Albania the following month. Engel also alludes little to the growing tension with Poland over the summer.

Yet, other subjects did preoccupy him. These came largely from the conversations that he had with Hitler. Religion was one and he noted Martin Bormann's unsuccessful attempts to persuade Hitler to outlaw the church. It was a subject which would come to the fore again during the war, when there was talk of abolishing military chaplains on the grounds that they were an obstacle to making the Army truly National Socialist. With regard to Crystal Night on 9–10 November 1938 Engel expressed his outrage, believing that it would incur international condemnation of Germany. He also later bewailed the purge of those of Jewish blood who were serving in the

Wehrmacht. Another topic which kept surfacing, and reflected a shared interest between Hitler and Engel, was art and Engel seems frequently to have been subjected to tirades against the evils of abstract painting. Engel also records two cases of scandal in the Wehrmacht, both involving junior officers, which came to Hitler's attention. What they reveal is that, in the aftermath of the von Blomberg and von Fritsch affairs, the high command reacted by adopting a very rigid and conservative policy on officers' marriages. Hitler, however, regarded this as mere hypocrisy. Yet, when Hitler was presented with petitions approved by OKH for reduced punishment for soldiers who had engaged in homosexual acts he rejected them out of hand, describing this 'sin of the flesh' as 'high level decadence'. (Diary entry for 15 March 1940.)

Engel says nothing of the planning for the invasion of Poland, but Hitler's address to his generals on 22 August 1939 does gain his attention. He was impressed by the calm manner in which the Führer spoke, but noted the 'mask-like' expressions of the audience. Indeed, as he shortly discovered, they were not convinced by Hitler's assertion that the British and French warnings that they would stand by Poland were a bluff. Engel was therefore furious when the senior adjutant, Rudolf Schmundt, told Hitler how enthusiastic his generals had been about his speech. The signing of the Soviet–German non-aggression pact on 23 August did, however, give Hitler a green light and he ordered the invasion of Poland for three days later. Yet, as Engel describes, Mussolini's declaration that his country was not yet ready for war created immediate confusion within the Reich Chancellery, with peace and war factions jostling for the Führer's ear and he himself unusually indecisive. In the event, it was those who advocated war, representing the Party rather than the military, who won the day and, after one postponement, the invasion of Poland was launched on 1 September 1939.

Engel's first diary entry after the outbreak of war was not until 10 September. It was not about the course of the campaign, but specifically over Hitler's frustration that von Fritsch was exercising his right as Colonel of the 12th Artillery Regiment to lead it in battle. It also transpired that von Blomberg had asked to be given a field command and it would appear that Hitler listened to Engel, who pleaded against this being done, and stated that Blomberg would only be allowed back if he divorced his wife. As for von Fritsch, he was killed by a Polish machine-gunner on 22 September. The other topics that Engel covered at the time were Hitler's determination to eradicate all Polish influence in German-occupied Poland and the creation of ghettoes for the Polish Jews. There were also complaints by the Army of atrocities being committed against Polish intellectuals and Jews but, as far as Hitler was concerned, this was a political issue and nothing to do with the military.

As soon as Poland had been vanquished, Hitler wanted to turn against France and Britain as soon as possible. His generals believed that they were about to face a far more formidable foe than the Poles. They needed time, not just to redeploy their forces, but also to assimilate the lessons from the late campaign. Again, as Engel describes, Hitler accused the Army of defensive mindedness and nearly sacked von Brauchitsch, only changing his mind because there was no obvious successor imbued with a sufficient degree of National Socialism. Intriguingly, Engel's diary entry for 6 December 1939 mentions Hitler dismissing the current plan for the invasion of the West, which was little more than a repeat of the 1914 Schlieffen Plan, except that it would take in Holland and was designed merely to secure the English Channel and North Sea coasts. While he did not come up with a new plan, Hitler did declare that the Panzers could go through 'mountains'. Yet, it was not for another two months that Hitler was made aware, after a visit by Schmundt to the headquarters of Army Group A, of the von Manstein plan. Erich von Manstein was Chief of Staff to Army Group A and had developed his plan with the support and approval of his commander, Gerd von Rundstedt. It accorded precisely with Hitler's thoughts, but went further in aiming for the total defeat of the Allied forces. According to Engel, Hitler had a personal aversion to von Manstein, although the reason is not given, but seized gratefully on his plan. OKH, whom von Manstein had pestered without success, rewarded him with the command of an infantry corps rather than a Panzer formation which had been his desire.

Engel has only one entry covering the overrunning of Denmark and Norway in April 1940, which he made after a visit to Norway during the first week of the campaign. While he himself was very impressed with the Army's performance, Hitler continued to believe that the generals were weak in their resolve. Though the invasion of the West finally began on 10 May 1940 Engel's diary remains silent until the 23rd, when he noted a telephone conversation between Göring and Hitler, in which the former declared that his Luftwaffe could destroy the British in the pocket which had been created by von Rundstedt's Panzers. Thus was planted one of the major seeds behind Hitler's so-called 'halt order' of 24 May, the other being von Rundstedt's own decision to call a temporary halt to enable his armour to draw breath and for his infantry to catch up. Göring's intervention irritated the Army and was motivated by the desire for the Luftwaffe to play a decisive role. Hitler acceded to it, seeing the Luftwaffe, according to Engel, as properly imbued with National Socialism (it had been formed, of course, after Hitler came to power) in contrast to the traditional conservatism of the Army. While Hitler stated that the Army needed to prepare for Phase 2 of the campaign, the overrunning of the remainder of France, it proved a fatal decision in that the BEF was largely able to escape across the English Channel.

In the aftermath of the campaign in the West Engel paints Hitler as believing that Britain had been so weakened that it would cave in quickly, especially after an air offensive. He was also clearly thinking of a puppet British leader with whom he could deal and the indication was that he would have liked, if it had been possible, to have had the Duke of Windsor in this role, although Oswald Mosley would have been acceptable. There is also a curious reference to Charles de Gaulle (14 June 1940). At the time of writing it is most unlikely that Hitler would have known much about the man who was about to make himself leader of the Free French, especially since de Gaulle did not make his first radio broadcast until four days after the diary entry. Engel may well have inserted this at a later date, as appears also to be the case with the reference to the sinking of the battleship *Bismarck* (28 March 1941) two months before it actually took place.

Engel makes little general reference to the Battle of Britain and the subsequent postponement of the invasion of England, but the planned invasion of Russia begins to loom large. Hitler's pretext appears to have been to prevent Britain gaining an ally, but it was vital that Russia be overcome speedily. The directive for Barbarossa was issued in December 1940 and it is noticeable that a high priority was given to preparing Hitler's field headquarters at Rastenburg in East Prussia which came to be known as the Wolf's Lair. Another key priority was securing the Balkan flank by bringing regional states into the Tripartite Pact. Hitler, however, became concerned when, in March 1941, the British began to send troops to Greece. While a contingency plan for the invasion of the Balkans (codenamed Marita) had been drawn up the previous December, Hitler now realised that, if Marita had to be put into effect, it would mean having to postpone Barbarossa from May. As it happened, a coup in Yugoslavia, bringing about its withdrawal from the Tripartite Pact, which it had recently joined, triggered the invasion of Yugoslavia and Greece in early April. Engel also confirms the Army's discomfort over the Commissar Order. In contrast, Hitler was determined that territories seized in the east were not to remain under Army control. This was reinforced by what appears to have been a vehement attack by Himmler on the Army's humane treatment of conquered populations (7 April 1941).

The April 1941 entries reveal something of Hitler's Middle East strategy. Engel records him as desperately wanting to bring Turkey into the war as an ally, something which Churchill was also pursuing. There was also the German failure in Iraq, once the revolt there had been put down. In the midst of all this was the bombshell created by Rudolf Hess's flight to Britain. This clearly stunned Hitler, although he did state that Hess's ideas were on the borderline 'between reality and madness'.

The actual invasion of Russia receives no mention until the end of July. Engel records a conversation with a Hitler uncertain over objectives – should they be political or economic? The plan with which the Germans had attacked made Moscow the prime objective, with Leningrad and the Ukraine as subsidiaries. On 19 July Hitler had issued Directive No. 33. This stated that Moscow was no longer the main goal and that Army Group Centre was to hand over the bulk of its armour to enable the capture of Leningrad and the overrunning of the Ukraine, Russia's agricultural heartland. This produced consternation in OKH, which was already complaining of unnecessary meddling by OKW. During 4–6 August Hitler visited the headquarters of Army Groups Centre and South to elicit views. He was told that Moscow must remain the priority, but rejected this. A week later orders for the transfer of armour from Army Group Centre were confirmed. Von Brauchitsch and Halder made one final attempt to get the orders rescinded, addressing a memorandum to Hitler. He dismissed it out of hand, accusing von Brauchitsch of failing to command the army and of being too influenced by the views of his subordinates. As Engel observed (21 August 1941), the Commander-in-Chief's days were now numbered.

Leningrad was duly put under siege on 4 September and attention turned to von Rundstedt's Army Group South, which created a massive pocket around Kiev. In the meantime, Hitler had had another change of heart, deciding to restore primacy to Moscow. Army Group Centre could not resume its advance, however, until the armour it had passed to von Rundstedt had been returned, but this was not possible until the Kiev pocket had been reduced, which took place on

19 September. Not until the end of the month did Army Group Centre begin to move, but by then the first of the autumn rains had fallen. Yet, Hitler was confident that ultimate victory was imminent, declaring to the German people on 3 October that Russia 'has already been broken and will never rise again'. Events during October seemed to confirm this, with a mass exodus from Moscow taking place in the middle of the month, but mud slowed the advance and it came to a virtual halt at the end of the month. The Russian winter now arrived and Army Group Centre's momentum was restored as frosts hardened the ground. Even so, according to Engel (16 November 1941), Hitler remained unconvinced that Moscow was the decisive objective.

The future of von Brauchitsch now resurfaced as an issue. It was becoming accepted within Hitler's inner circle that he would have to be replaced and, to Engel's horror, Colonel Rudolf Schmundt, Hitler's Chief Adjutant and an avowed Nazi, wanted Hitler to take over as Commander-in-Chief. As November wore on, the German Army in Russia found the conditions increasingly difficult. Furthermore, there were growing indications that Russian resistance was stiffening. Indeed, Army Group South, which had become overextended, was force to withdraw from Rostov-on-Don in the face of a determined counter-attack. Hitler sacked von Rundstedt without even consulting OKH. Then, on 5 December, Army Group Centre eventually came to a halt just nineteen miles from Moscow. The following day von Brauchitsch confided to Engel that he had had enough and intended to request leave of absence. He recommended von Kluge or von Manstein to succeed him. Schmundt, apparently, was still convinced that Hitler should take over. On 19 December the blow finally fell, although Engel does not record it. Hitler took over as Commander-in-Chief and from now on OKH would be left with merely the day-to-day conduct of the war on the Eastern Front, while OKW took direct control of all other theatres.

Engel has few entries for the first half of 1942. No mention is made of the Soviet counter-offensive that lasted until the spring or Hitler's plans for renewing the assault which were enshrined in his Directive No. 41 of 5 April 1942. His main objective this time was the seizure of the industrial region lying between the Rivers Donetz and Volga and the Caucasian oilfields. Prior to this, the Crimea was to be secured and a salient created by the Russians south of Kharkov during their counter-offensive eradicated. While Army Group Centre remained on the defensive, Army Group North was to link up with the

Finns and secure Leningrad. It was the Russians who struck first, when they launched an attack south of Kharkov in May. The Germans counter-attacked into the flanks of the salient and, by the end of the June, the Soviet South-Western Theatre, which was to face the main German onslaught, was in tatters. The Crimea, too, had now been overrun.

The main German offensive opened on 28 June. Fedor von Bock's Army Group South had been divided into two – Army Groups A and B. Army Group B would attack first and establish a shoulder across the Don. Then Army Group A would drive south-east between the Donets and Don towards the Caucasus. Army Group B duly established a lodgement over the river in the area of Voronezh and Engel visited Second Army here on 9 July and reported the concerns of von Salmuth. However, as the relevant text note states, von Salmuth did not take over command of Second Army in the bridgehead until 14 July and so this entry was probably written some time after the event. It is possible that Engel was confusing this with a later visit he made to the bridgehead (27 November 1942), although, as the accompanying note details, he was again awry on his dates.

Subsequent entries show how optimism turned to frustration and pessimism as the advance into the Caucasus revealed destroyed oilfields at Maikop and terrain problems as Army Group A moved into the mountains. There was also the frustration that the Russians were withdrawing, rather than allowing themselves to be trapped as had happened earlier in the campaign, and concern that the German forces were becoming ever more spread out and stretched. As Engel shows, Hitler's own irritation revealed itself in threats to dismiss the faithful Keitel and Keitel's senior assistant Jodl and the actual sacking of Halder, the long suffering OKH Chief of Staff. But increasingly it was Stalingrad and not the Caucasus that was now the focus of Hitler's attention.

The ever grimmer fight for Stalingrad dominates the remainder of Engel's entries. Friedrich Paulus's Sixth Army had broken out of its bridgeheads over the Don on 25 July. Within three weeks it had reached the outskirts of the city, which Stalin determined was to be held. There now began the long bruising battle in the streets of Stalingrad. Engel reveals (2 October 1942) that Hitler believed that its capture was essential for world opinion and domestic morale. He therefore dismissed any suggestions that the assault be abandoned and the emphasis switched once more to Army Group A, which was now desperately short of air support and supplies. Engel also, and prophetically, shows the growing concern among the commanders in the field over the poor quality of Germany's allies – Hungarians, Italians, and Romanians – all of whom were now having to shoulder an ever heavier burden.

By early November, under the guidance of Georgi Zhukov, the Russians were preparing a counter-offensive designed to cut Paulus off in Stalingrad by attacking the Romanian armies protecting his flanks. Hitler, however, dismissed intelligence estimates to this effect, accusing the General Staff of consistently over-estimating enemy capabilities. When the blow did fall on 19 November, Engel portrays Hitler as being indecisive and issuing direct orders over the head of OHK in turn. Within four days Paulus was cut off. The OKH view was that he should fight his way out but Hitler insisted that Stalingrad could not be given up. On 23 November he telephoned Göring to ask whether the Luftwaffe could keep Sixth Army supplied by air. The answer was that it was possible, although Wolfram von Richthofen, commanding the Fourth Air Fleet supporting the Stalingrad operations, took a contrary view. Engel records a Führer conference two days later during which Göring confirmed that Paulus could be supplied at the required level and that many of those present were 'horrified at his optimism'. It sealed the fate of Sixth Army.

Hitler now pinned his hopes on a relief operation by von Manstein. It was mounted on 12 December and eventually reached a point some sixteen miles from Stalingrad, coming up against strong Soviet defences on the River Myshkova. But in the meantime the Russians had launched an attack further north. It fell largely on the Italians and soon began to threaten von Manstein's lines of communication. Unable to break through to Stalingrad, von Manstein asked Paulus to break out and link up, but the latter, conscious of Hitler's orders, refused. According to Engel, Jodl and others had hoped that Paulus would use his initiative. The upshot was that Hitler agreed that von Manstein could withdraw so as to preserve his lines of communication and by the end of the year he was 125 miles from Stalingrad, which aggravated the problem of air resupply still further.

When Paulus did finally surrender, Engel stated that Hitler looked for others to blame for the debacle rather than accept his own mistakes. In the aftermath there was anger among the field commanders. Engel records von Manstein, von Kleist, and von Kluge visiting Hitler to demand reforms in the high command, with von Manstein wanting a military Commander-in-Chief East. They also wanted Keitel removed. Apparently on his own initiative, Engel visited von Rundstedt in Paris to ask him, as the generally recognised figurehead of the Army, to represent the generals' discontent to Hitler. The Commander-in-Chief West refused, however, to get involved.

This was virtually Engel's last entry. Increasingly disillusioned, he had been trying for some time to be relieved of his appointment as adjutant. He vacated the post in early April 1943 and later proved himself to be an able combat commander, rising to the rank of lieutenant-general and being wounded during the December 1944 Ardennes counter-offensive.

While there are too many inconsistencies to make the Engel diary a truly definitive document, it is nonetheless a valuable contribution. It is particularly revealing on the workings of Hitler's mind and his constant antipathy towards the senior ranks of the officer corps, whom he believed lacked political will. Another important insight is Hitler's apparent indecision in times of crisis. Yet, often and increasingly, he meddled with the minutiae of operations, giving instructions to his commanders in the field via OKW and bypassing OKH. Indeed, largely thanks to von Brauchitsch's inability to stand up to Hitler, OKH's influence on operations became ever more reduced, especially once Hitler had taken over as C-in-C. One quality which Hitler did have, as indicated by Engel, was his prodigious ability to absorb and memorise detail. Too often he was able to display superior knowledge to his military staff, which put them at a severe disadvantage.

To sum up, this English edition of Engel's diary is very welcome in that it makes all this accessible to a considerably wider audience than before.

CHARLES MESSENGER

Introduction

The military *Adjutantur* to the Führer and Reich Chancellor was set up at a time when it was still common for his closest circle to address him as 'Herr Hitler'. The institution came into being immediately following the death of Reich President Hindenburg on 2 August 1934. Hitler had automatically become Head of State and supreme commander of the armed forces[1] upon Hindenburg's demise, and as such he exercised the power of command and the right to prescribe military regulations in the interim period before a new Reich President was appointed. In this interval all service business arising between the Head of State and the Reichswehr Ministry[2] had to be attended to by an intermediary officer.[3] The duty involved handling all business reserved to the Head of State[4] within the ambit of his power of command, and preparing the necessary directives in so far as that was not the responsibility of the Reich War Minister or a prescribed officer. Even the personal affairs of higher officers were to come under the microscope.[5] The burden of additional duties in the military sphere created the need for a Wehrmacht man at Hitler's side.

As Hitler himself had not expressed any guidelines of his own for his *Adjutantur*, his first military adjutant, Major i.G.[6] Hossbach, was able to put through his own ideas with the approval of the Reichswehr Minister von Blomberg.[7] As Hossbach saw it, the *Adjutantur* should under no circumstances develop along the lines of the model of the Prussian military cabinet, competing with the Reichswehr Ministry, and therefore from the beginning its personnel allocation was kept to the barest minimum. A few years later, the original sole proprietorship was enlarged by the addition of a naval adjutant (Lieutenant-Commander von Puttkamer) and a Luftwaffe adjutant (Captain Mantius).[8] It had been precisely defined at least orally how the *Adjutantur* should stand in relationship to Hitler: it was a liaison office of the Reichswehr Ministry *with* the Führer, not a Staff *of* the Führer with which Hitler might play power politics in the future, and as a further defensive measure in this respect, the dual function of the first adjutant is worthy of note.

In 1935 Hossbach was given an onerous additional responsibility as Departmental Head in the Army General Staff, but he proved equal to the challenge. Hitler adjusted quickly to the new arrangement after initial reservations and accepted unconditionally the 'Service Instructions for the Wehrmacht Adjutant to the Führer and Reich Chancellor',[9] thereby winning and retaining Hossbach's confidence until his departure in 1938.[10] The removal of Hossbach was part of the great Army command reshuffle following the dismissal of the Reich War Minister, Field Marshal von Blomberg, and the Army Commander-in-Chief (Oberbefehlshaber das Heer – ObdH), Colonel-General von Fritsch.

Blomberg's fall came about as the result of his marriage to a prostitute. The subsequent revelations greatly irritated the godfathers of the regime and Hitler was obliged to sacrifice a man in whom he had confidence, and who had advocated his political arguments to the conservative generals. To fill the vacuum, Hitler decided that he should take the reins of power directly and so thwart the reactionaries. Apart from his oft-expressed reproaches and disappointment at the lassitude with which Army commanders were pursuing rearmament, especially the motorisation of the armed forces, and their timidity in the face of his foreign adventures, Hitler nursed a distrust of the generals and disliked the watered-down spirit of the former 100,000-man army which had still not accepted National Socialism. That Army and Führer had failed to discover the basis for a firm relationship worried him constantly. Under the former commander-in-chief, Freiherr von Fritsch, no change had been possible, this he knew. To take full power of command over the entire Wehrmacht – insecure as he felt – Hitler had rid himself of Fritsch by means of a trick – as was later revealed, the old dossier which was used relied on mistaken identities, but it seemed to establish a relationship between the C-in-C and someone who might be termed 'a notorious young gay', and thus Fritsch's goose was cooked.[11]

The generals went along with the new situation, papering over the distrust and prepared to accept as C-in-C a man who had Hitler's confidence and would build, train and equip the Army with special emphasis on its motorisation. That Hitler should trust them was now an indispensable objective, for Blomberg's removal as Reich War Minister meant that Brauchitsch, the new C-in-C, stood directly subordinate to Hitler as his immediate adviser.

Colonel-General von Brauchitsch, Commander of Gruppen-kommando 4 (Leipzig), was chosen by the generals and approved by

Hitler after he agreed to certain future concessions. Thus, without any overtly recognisable effort, Hitler took into his own hands that 'centralised military completeness of power'[12] which Blomberg had exercised as Reich War Minister and Wehrmacht commander-in-chief. After the removal of Blomberg in 1938, Hitler combined in his own person the political offices of Head of State and Supreme Commander of the Wehrmacht. His immediate influence on the Wehrmacht was infinitely greater than Blomberg's had ever been. The new era of close contact had its effect on the future function of the military *Adjutantur*.

The replacement of Hossbach,[13] planned in the course of normal routine for 1 April 1938, was brought forward but did not go through as planned because General Keitel[14] as 'head of OKW' and Hitler's future military chief of staff, had taken steps to recruit for the *Adjutantur* a suitable successor who was also a committed National Socialist. Colonel i.G. Schmundt, latterly of the General Staff of 18th Division at Liegnitz,[15] was a friend and regimental associate of Colonel von Tresckow, a would-be Hitler assassin. (As with the later would-be Hitler assassin von Stauffenberg, von Tresckow was numbered initially amongst the supporters of the new regime but soon found himself allied in opposition to it with Stauffenberg, whose undesired victim Schmundt would later become on 20 July 1944.) Whether Schmundt's earlier work on Blomberg's staff at Königsberg influenced his nomination is uncertain, but undoubtedly his political loyalty, and many years service in department T2[16] of the Reichswehr Ministry, where he acquired a thorough grounding in Wehrmacht affairs, were significant in his appointment.

As Brauchitsch did not favour the embodiment of Wehrmacht (OKW) adjutant and Army (OKH) adjutant in one person, as had been the case since the setting up of the *Adjutantur* in 1934, he proposed that the Army[17] nominate the third man additional to the Kriegsmarine and Luftwaffe adjutants. It went without saying that the candidate put forward would not be expected to be a notorious reactionary likely to rock the boat.

Gerhard Engel was thirty-two years of age when he became Army adjutant to the Wehrmacht commander-in-chief, Adolf Hitler. To judge by Engel's autobiographical details it is apparent that his career until his appointment as Hitler's ADC had been mundane. He was born in 1906, the son of a jurist. The family came from Guben near Frankfurt/Oder in the province of Brandenburg. He was educated at Posen and Ostrow, obtaining his *Abitur* (school-leaving

certificate) at Prenzlau in 1925. He entered the Reichswehr the same
year and served with 5th Infantry Regiment at Greifswald. In 1929 he
passed through the Infantry Training College at Dresden, rejoining
5th Infantry Regiment in the rank of junior lieutenant in 1930. He
served with the 1st Battalion at Stettin until his transfer to Rostock
in 1933 where, with the 3rd Battalion, he commenced his career as
an adjutant. By 1935 he had advanced to become adjutant of 27th
Infantry Regiment commanded by Colonel Kurt von Tippelskirch.
Tippelskirch considered Engel the ideal ADC and he was a character
witness whose opinion – together with others of standing[18] –
presumably carried weight when a candidate for the newly created
post in Hitler's Wehrmacht *Adjutantur* was being sought.

After reporting to Hitler in his chambers at midday on 10 March
1938, Engel took up his duties and received instructions from
colleagues[19] on the technical requirements of his office. The
adjutants' work approximated the function of permanent liaison
officers for the affairs of the respective Wehrmacht branch of service
from which they had been detached. Senior adjutant Schmundt was
an exception in that he had been transferred from OKH to OKW on
his appointment and worked on matters affecting the Wehrmacht as
a whole. The *Adjutantur* staff were supported by a number of clerical,
telephone and telex NCOs.

Engel was responsible for the Army branch and acted as
intermediary between Hitler and Brauchitsch. In particular this
involved frequent – and often daily – communication with the C-in-C
himself or his 1a (No. 1 General Staff officer).[20] Engel had to fix a
schedule for Army leaders who needed to make reports to Hitler and
to obtain information for Hitler who, since taking the reins of
command over the whole Wehrmacht, now concerned himself more
than previously with Army requirements. In addition to this office
work, the adjutant attended to affairs of protocol, accompanying
Hitler on his trips both long and short and forming part of his
entourage when he received guests. Amongst these would be from
time to time royalty, statesmen and the military leaders of Germany's
allies: during the war the adjutant would escort such visitors to
individual HQs or to the special trains of the various heads of service
or the Foreign Ministry. Also in wartime the ADCs accompanied Hitler
on his trips to the front or on flights if the circumstances demanded.
Additionally each adjutant was given a Special Task or *Referat*.
Accordingly naval ADC von Puttkamer dealt with all questions of
protocol and Wehrmacht jurisdiction.[21] Von Below saw to Führer-

hauptquartier (FHQ – Führer Headquarters) requirements including service journeys. Amongst his secondary duties Engel handled all 'petitions for exemption' submitted by Wehrmacht personnel in difficulties by reason of their racial origins.[22]

These extensive connections and wide-reaching relationships created for the adjutant certain opportunities not available to an officer of equal rank in the mainstream. The ADC received invitations, played a role in the footlights, knew the channels. He was confronted along the way with all manner of pleas and supplications. A minister of state might write for help in securing the award of a decoration; a publisher might send thanks for assistance given to one of his authors; in wartime worried relatives might solicit support in their enquiry into the fate of a missing family member in the Wehrmacht; a former regimental colleague sent a positive report from within the encirclement at Stalingrad which was to be placed before the Führer; friends asked for a ladies' ski jacket size 44 to be got from France; there were parcels to be taken, love letters to be couriered . . . Necessarily the recompense was made in small coin: hard-to-get pocket calendars, ashtrays, books, occasionally the rarer trinket.

The reasons behind the great upheaval of 1 February 1938 which altered drastically the relationship of Hitler to the Army, and was incidentally instrumental in creating the vacancy which Engel filled, were at first explained to the newcomer with some circumspection by his colleagues. As Army ADC he was at the forefront of the affair and of necessity quickly developed a sensibility for the political climate in the Reich Chancellery – and kept the C-in-C informed of his impressions. Criticisms made by Hitler, or the stance he was adopting, especially with regard to foreign policy, had to be transmitted to the Tirpitzufer[23] with sufficient despatch to enable the Army to determine where it stood on the issue. Engel described himself as the 'ear of the C-in-C in the Reich Chancellery'. Such a task required diplomatic skill and tactical adroitness – if the OKH had undervalued the need it would have been an unforgiveable oversight.

That the promising beginning between Hitler and C-in-C Brauchitsch did not endure was not due only to their respective personalities, for there were more than enough points of discord elsewhere – the rehabilitation of Fritsch, and Beck, Chief of the General Staff, pressing for talks about a review of the command structure.[24] The new C-in-C, aware of his isolation from foreign policy decisions, and the encapsulation of all information respecting Hitler's intentions in matters of foreign policy, interpreted this as a reduction of his status to that of a pawn in the hands of the political leadership.[25]

More examples of this tense relationship are superfluous, for the author supplies plenty more in the text. If one goes by the notes, there was permanent friction between Hitler and the Army generals. Engel confirms it to have been the established tradition and this is probably reflected in the source material itself.

Engel's service as adjutant at FHQ was terminated at the end of March 1943 after Stalingrad, when he rejoined the fighting forces,[26] apparently at his own instigation.

* * *

The relationship between the retired Lieutenant-General Engel and the Institut für Zeitgeschichte (IfZ – German Historical Institute) began in 1953 at the suggestion of a former [IfZ] assistant, General Hermann Froetsch. Froetsch had identified the long-serving Army ADC at FHQ as an indispensable witness for Hitler research and on matters pertaining to the German leadership of the Second World War. From then on, General Engel advised historians both within the Institute and outside on numerous complex problems, referring frequently to his voluminous notes, and it was not long before the idea of publishing them was proposed. Engel eventually bowed to pressure and entrusted the edition to the IfZ – which was not the only competitor for the rights.

The Institute received from General Engel six volumes of notes spanning the period from the spring of 1938 to autumn 1943. The entries have the outward appearance of a diary such that it has become customary in professional circles to speak of 'the Engel Diaries'. In fact the volumes are contemporaneous material supplemented with additions set down by the author long after the event. Motivation for the latter was chiefly the repeated requests he received to help elucidate Hitler's military and political strategy, his attitude on the wider questions, and problems related to the German High Command in wartime.

In practice General Engel would note his answer in each case in a parallel volume linked to the chronological sequence. Apparently he was not relying solely on his above average memory, for he mentions a set of diary-style word-sketches, unfortunately not preserved, which he also used. This would explain the richness of detail of the later notes, and their diary form, which the author retained for style.

The result is a mixture of contemporary substance and memories. It is not possible today either for the editor or author to distinguish the respective elements. In many cases the contemporaneous nucleus is stronger, in others the product of memory is dominant. Because the chronological sequence may be arbitrary, errors due to memory lapses play a role, and the dating of individual notes is not infallible. Researchers are therefore cautioned against relying on dates which are not verified from other sources.

That being said, the notes are highly valued for historical research. General Engel belonged within Hitler's closest circle for six years and the fact that his notes are not contemporaneous in the strict sense of the term does not reduce the weight which should be accorded them or lessen the import of the text. Despite the passage of time between the experience or observation and when the finished entry was completed, General Engel's notes are listed amongst the important sources of Hitler research and knowledge to which the professional world as well as the general public have claim. On the other hand, it may be erroneous to place too much reliance on the memoir, as is evidenced from certain extracts published by academics.[27] The specific value of the material is above all atmospheric. Hitler, so often flanked by protocol chiefs and secretaries making a shorthand record, must have seized gratefully the opportunity to speak freely and off the record with his military adjutants. Alone with them he could make fleeting observations respecting 'history' and 'the future', and pass remarks of a political or military nature which were not only informal, but undeveloped. Whereas it may not be certain in these notes if it is Hitler who speaks, or Engel who speaks for him, nevertheless the gist of the transmission is a unique contribution to the Hitler scenario.

The IfZ received a total of 244 sheets of notes from General Engel: 166 of these are in longhand, and 68 shorthand, in all making up six volumes. The parts of the material in shorthand are shown by a cross (+) following the date. The remaining material consists of typed text indicated by an asterisk (*).

Reference in the notes to conversational partners and themes are made by the author. Round parentheses are carried forward from the original and indicate additions made by the author for the purpose of clarification. Square brackets have been introduced by the editor [and additionally, in the English translation, by the English translator and editors] to expand abbreviations and for other explanations. General abbreviations (usually of military terminology) and shortened names have been retained as in the original.

Names incorrectly spelled in the original have been corrected in the text and the error indicated by a note. The orthography has been corrected without comment. Details of military ranks or political offices of persons normally relate to the rank or office held at the time in question, but in some cases the editor has deemed it preferable to use details from other sources.

Since the dates employed by the author were used primarily for style, they are to be treated without exception as doubtful, unless confirmed by other sources. Verifiable dates have drawn comment in notes. As respects the dating problem, compare the notes of May 1938, 9 July and 27 August 1942 (with notes), and especially the commentary to the notes on the Battle of Stalingrad.

For their support I thank everybody who has assisted me in this work.

HILDEGARD VON KOTZE

Notes

Notes followed by ED are new to the English edition.

1. Per Reichsgesetzblatt: I/1934, p. 747.

2. From 1935 the War Ministry (*Kriegsministerium*). [Hitler obtained the people's consent to a fusion of the offices of Reich Chancellor and Reich President in himself as 'Führer and Reichskanzler' by plebiscite on 19 August 1934. ED]

3. Reich President Hindenburg's adjutant was his son, Colonel Oskar von Hindenburg.

4. And by virtue of Article 50 of the Reich Constitution required the counter-signature of the Reichswehr Minister. [The Reich War Minister wielded the power of command by virtue of the Wehrgesetz (Armed Forces Law) 1921, para 8. ED]

5. Hitler exercised no influence on personnel changes before February 1938.

6. i.G = *im Generalstab* – General Staff Officer.

7. For Hossbach's opinion on his own measures, these being the basis for this commentary, see his *Wehrmacht und Hitler*, pp. 9–16.

8. Mantius crashed during a training flight in 1937. His successor was Captain von Below. [He also wrote an account of his time as Hitler's Luftwaffe Adjutant. See Nicolaus von Below, *At Hitler's Side*, Greenhill, 2001. ED]

9. 'Dienstanweisung für den Adjutanten der Wehrmacht beim Führer und Reichskanzler'. This document is unknown at the Bundesarchiv-Militär Archiv.

10. For more on this subject see Hossbach: *Wehrmacht und Hitler*, pp. 115–18.

11. See Kielmannsegg: *Fritsch-Prozeß 1938*.

12. See also Hossbach: *Wehrmacht und Hitler*, page 68. [The plebiscite of 19 August 1934 legitimated the Enabling Act whereby the offices of Reich President and Reich Chancellor were fused. The term 'Reich President' was abolished in favour of the title 'Führer'. By Article 47 of the Weimar Constitution, the Reich President was Commander-in-Chief of the Reichswehr, but by virtue of para 8 of the 1921 Armed Forces Law (Wehrgesetz) the Reich War Minister had the power of command. Article 50 of the Constitution prescribed that all instructions issued to the military by the Reich President required the counter-signature of the Reich Chancellor or the Reich War Minister, and the latter then accepted the political responsibility. In 1934 all Reich Ministers were required to swear an oath of allegiance to Hitler personally. In the 1935 Wehrgesetz [Defence Bill] (never formally in force) Hitler elevated himself to Supreme Commander of the Wehrmacht, outranking the Reich War Minister, who was only Commander-in-Chief and had sworn an oath of personal loyalty to Hitler. ED]

13. Hossbach had recommended Major von Grolman from the command centre in the Army General Staff as his successor. Hitler would not accept the choice since he did not want an admitted confederate of Fritsch as his senior adjutant (observation made by former naval ADC Rear-Admiral von Puttkamer).

14. See Jodl: *Diary*, 27 January 1938, IMT XXVIII p. 359. Moreover Blomberg, then War Minister, had suggested Schmundt for Hitler's *Adjutantur*.

15. Schmundt's criticism of the Nazi Party there did not outweigh his positive attitude to National Socialism itself.

16. Army Organisational Section of Army Command, Manpower Office.

17. Additionally the military preparations in hand for the imminent annexation of Austria made urgent the need to fill the vacant chair for an Army ADC.

18. See 19 March 38 (second note) and report of (retired) Lieutenant-General C. Siewert filed IfZ 31 March 1974.

19. All four adjutants were on duty during the day: if necessary a night rota was drawn up.

20. Later, at FHQ, Engel had regular contact with OQIV (QM-General) General von Tippelskirch. See KTB OKW I, 1940–1, p. 188E. His relationship with Halder seems to have been less intense. If Halder's notes are accurate, Engel called on the Army Chief of the General Staff on only eight occasions in the years 1939–42. See Halder: *Diary*, I: pp. 33, 125, 165, 207; II: pp. 157, 163, 165 and 364.

21. Apart from petitions by Army officers, which were the preserve of OKW adjutant Schmundt.

22. See 15 August 1938; 2 May 1940; 28 and 30 May 1942.

23. The street in Berlin in which the Army HQ (OKH) and other headquarters were situated.

24. See entry 2 August 1938 and note.

25. See June 1939 (Military Attachés), also ZS 148, sheet 6.

26. See note 471.

27. In particular see Hillgruber: *Strategie und KTB/OKW* II, 1942; also Jacobsen: 'Dünkirchen 1940', in: *Entscheidungsschlachten*; Groscurth: *Tagebücher*; Broszat: *Polenpolitik*; Müller: *Heer*.

1938

13 March 1938[+]
Vienna – Guderian
At the Imperial[1] in Vienna I met General Guderian.[2] He was shocked at what had gone on.[3] I also kept hearing from him the word 'trust'. G. blamed everything on the Army High Command which had not been able to master itself in the . . .[4] spirit and so win the Führer's confidence. I was astonished at how frank he was to me as a young captain. Also spoke about our new OB [C-in-C],[5] of whom he had a poor opinion. I replied that the friction and this crisis of confidence were nothing new, I had experienced too much of it as regimental adjutant and company commander, and the attitude of the SS towards us was monstrous. General G replied this could best be overcome if the Reichsführer-SS or the present Field Marshal Göring[6] were appointed C-in-C. Then ways and means would be found to clear the path of complications. I was so astonished at this point of view that I made no comment, but I do not find it convincing.

14 March 1938[7]
By chance I witnessed the F[ührer]'s reception of Cardinal Innitzer [Archbishop of Vienna] in the Imperial. F. approached I., bowed low and kissed hands. The cardinal raised the chained cross from his chest and with it made the symbolic sign of the cross. In the evening the F. was much taken with the visit and believes he can get along well with the Church in Austria. Heaps praise in general on the Catholic Church in Austria in contrast to the Reich. Over there it had become ever more political because of the parity of the two confessions. Here it was the state church and had a quite different relationship towards the state. In the Reich Bismarck and Windthorst[8] had made the same mistakes. Churches should only be allowed to become political if they were in the greater scheme of things the pawn of politics, that is of the political power. He himself

had learned much from the Cath[olic] Church for his political struggle and would not talk of taking things to extremes. But whoever swam against the current and cloaked themselves with the Cross to oppose him would have to be eliminated. For this reason the declaration of loyalty by the cardinal seemed to him all the more precious. The cardinal had requested from him freedom of manoeuvre in the affairs of the Church, and had received from him an assurance.

19 March 1938
(Obersalzberg)

Himmler[9] came from Vienna and reported about his cleansing measures.[10] Presented a strident report in a previously unheard-of tone and sowed the first mines against the Church. Talks of 'regrettable' arrests. Continual shooting of Austrian officers of the Federal Army, who had to be got rid of. I was given a slip of paper with names to pass to OKH. Distinct impression that the thing is getting out of hand and old scores are being settled. In connection with the conversation, Reichsführer-SS asked F. for private talk. Doubtless the Fritsch[11] affair is to be discussed.

19 March 1938[+]

Amongst other things I reported to General Halder.[12] I was received with the same distrust as on most occasions with the other chiefs in the High Command, but the disrespect this time was the worst. I don't know what he thinks I am. Up until now I was an active officer chosen for this post by the highly respected former C-in-C.[13] In general I do not understand what is going on at OKH. The only thing certain is that everybody is talking of a crisis of confidence. Most blame it on the Party, the remainder are incensed about 4 February.[14] I fail to see clearly how it can have brought us to this. The only thing certain is that everything we experienced so far in Army life in terms of internal opposition to the Party has forced us into the current crisis, wherein the younger General Staff officers, colleagues of my year of entry, are quite forthright and lay the blame not least on the leadership at the War Ministry with all the subsequent consequences. Strange to record that there is a more positive attitude to the Party amongst the General Staff officers of the South German Gaue [NSDAP – Nazi Party – districts] than is the case with us. But, however one looks at it, it is not pleasant and as always since 1933 we in the Army are the lightning conductors.

19 March 1938*

Reported to General Halder. Distrustful reception as from most commanders-in-chief. Do not yet understand what is going on at OKH. One thing is sure: crisis of confidence of the first order. Most blame it on the Party, others on 4 February.[15] I do not yet know how it came to this. Everything is leading at the moment towards a crisis. The young staff officers blame much on the War Minister.[16] South German officers have a more positive attitude to the Party than is the case with us from North Germany. But, however one looks at it, it is not pleasant and the Army is once more the lightning conductor.

26 March 1938

A highly tense and unpleasant conversation with Schm(undt).[17] Schm. came from F. and, beaming with joy, related how he had suggested that the Hitler salute should be introduced generally within the Wehrmacht.[18] He had got the idea after witnessing the unprecedented wild jubilation shown to the Führer by troops he had met.[19] I was appalled and asked him if he could imagine a positive reaction particularly from officers and NCOs. At Liegnitz[20] he must have experienced at pretty close quarters the altercations with the Party, SA and SS as I did at Rostock.[21] Then the burden of the unexplained affair involving Fritsch. The officer corps would definitely see it as salt in the wound. Schm. gave me a long lecture about what we officers were lacking. We were primarily the guilty party in the crisis of confidence and were making it really difficult for the F. Fact was, he honoured his old teacher Beck and also the old C-in-C but neither had recognised the sign of the times. One should not always look to blame the Party bosses. He had the definite impression that F. was seeking the confidence of the Wehrmacht and correspondingly also the Army, but a number of generals were setting out to sabotage it. I did not agree and opposed what he said as far as I could, having regard to our respective rank and office. Today I recounted all this to Siewert[22] in confidence.

28 March 1938

Long talk with Siewert on how things ought to proceed. It is very difficult to get through to him because he is still completely preoccupied with how the C-in-C was treated and apparently cannot get along with Br. [Brauchitsch]. The latter is all tensed up and quite resigned. His reports to the F. are inhibited and hesitant, no relationship of confidence at all. However, he now has a good spy in the RK [Reichskanzlei – Reich Chancellery] for I keep my ears pricked and find out everything. Each day I pass information to S[iewert] and we both then try to give the C-in-C material to enable him to prepare the Army's rebuttal to accusations. F. does most of the talking and Br. does not dare interrupt or contradict him. Siewert hinted that Br. is very heavily weighed down with family problems and feels he cannot do what he sometimes wants to.[23]

19 April 1938
(SS-) Verfügungstruppe

Long conversation between F. and Sepp Dietrich[24] about expansion of the Verfügungstruppe [the military wing of the SS which became the Waffen-SS]. Motive was the setting up of 4. Standarte [4th Battalion] 'Der Führer' in Vienna.[25] F. says that this completes the expansion of the SS-Verfügungstruppe. He wants to keep this 'elite' small or it will not be an elite for long. It has to be a political force blindly loyal to state and Führer. In the event of disturbances, this force would put them down brutally. He sees it as a real Praetorian Guard[26] to snuff out all those, even within its own ranks, who swim against the current. Therefore [it has] to be equipped with the best and most up-to-date weapons, also with Panzers rather like a Panzer brigade. I am very concerned at this development and inform the C-in-C. It is high time that the Army did something similar or soon in Berlin we will all be evicted.

20 April 1938

I am on night duty and the solitude in the living quarters contrasts strongly to the hullabaloo experienced today throughout all Germany.[27] Shortly after midnight the Führer and I were alone, and I was very curious to see his attitude towards me for, although completely correct, he treats me with obvious distrust which is not surprising. We walked the length of the corridor without pause for over two hours. First he asked me personal questions about my regiment, activity as company commander and my General Staff training. Then he spoke about the parade which had visibly impressed him. Above all the Panzers in the new camouflage livery went down very well. Suddenly changing the subject he talked about the 100,000-man army, praising it highly. I waited my moment to mention the services of Colonel-General Fritsch and hoped for a favourable opportunity but the F. moved on at once to Field Marshal von Blomberg, beginning with the assertion that the necessary departure of both commanders had affected him deeply. The services of the War Minister in helping erect the National Socialist state were historic and would always remain so. He owed it to him that in 1933, knowing precisely the leanings of the generals, he transferred into the state structure an Army loyal and correct. Blomberg had also recognised the need to recruit modern officers who thought as National Socialists. He [Hitler] knew that the political reorganisation of the Army was only possible as a gradual process and he had often had to get the minister to apply the brakes. The majority of the generals had rejected him and that remained the case today. He embodied a different Prussian-ness to that of those generals. Before the seizure of power, only in Bavaria had he had close contacts with senior Reichswehr officers. Politically, as with all other officers, he had not trusted Blomberg a great deal. Blomberg had been opposed to his every bold decision, the worst when Germany left the League of Nations; on that occasion Blomberg protested like an hysterical virgin.[28] Yet that did not alter the fact that he was the first National Socialist-thinking commander-in-chief and in matters of rearmament he thought like him [Hitler], and not like Fritsch, who always worked at keeping things in check. The Fritsch affair would never have come into play if the War Minister had not made such an appalling choice. It was fatal only to get to know the bride's mother at the marriage ceremony. One could tell by her face the type of woman she was and her antecedents. Blomberg knew nothing and would not have believed it anyway if it had been explained to him. But most of all he [Hitler] had been shocked by the field marshal's attitude when they had had their last conversation. Blomberg had professed astonishment that he, Hitler, should be so reproachful and pointed out that he had been thinking as a National Socialist when he chose for his second wife a simple maiden from amongst the people. Whereas he [Hitler] and his Party colleagues might share a view of affairs different to, and freer than, the perverted morals of society, nevertheless he could hardly overlook a Party member in such a responsible position marrying a reformed prostitute. In the wake of this, he had taken no steps to intervene in the case of Fritsch because his confidence in the generals had been severely shaken.

I was absolutely shocked not to say flabbergasted that the Führer should speak so openly to me, a young officer. I was not in a position to respond, since Siewert and also the C-in-C had neglected to keep me informed. I had to labour at gathering the sum total of what I knew about both matters.

22/23 April 1938*

The birthday anniversary is gone and I have night duty again. In the vestibule I spent another ninety minutes walking up and down with F. We spoke a lot about the [birthday] parade. He asked a whole series of technical questions about weapons, amongst others the Panzer IV. Was very impressed by the military spectacle. So I dared to have another try about our former C-in-C.[29] I mentioned a lot about his life and the regard with which he was held within the Army. Told him about manouevres at Stettin in which he was senior artillery commander, and much of his activities as commander of AR2 [2nd Artillery Regiment] at Schwerin. The Führer, today looking pale, heard me out quietly and for a change did not interrupt. Finally I made a plea, also at the instigation of the C-in-C, that he should receive Fritsch, this being the latter's most cherished desire. He sought a personal reconciliation and clarification. This was more important to him than any reinstatement or employment elsewhere. Here the Führer became unsettled. In a long discourse he spoke once more of the disappointments he had known since 1934, all due to Fritsch. He had been the restraining element in rearmament. Quite apart from what happened, he would have had to let him go. I interrupted and recalled a conversation at Döberitz in 1935 which had made a particular impression on me as regimental adjutant at that time. To do nothing precipitate had been the byword and nature of Fritsch, since he wanted to avoid the Army being watered down. With that I rested my case. He departed and went to bed.

20 May 1938⁺
(Ideas for Uniforms)

F. made fun of the new Foreign Ministry uniforms.[30] Compared them with those of a circus master of ceremonies and suggested that the toilet ladies at the Foreign Office should have a nice uniform too. In all this palaver one saw the hollowness of diplomats and the 'need to do things properly' of protocol. He regretted very much that his foreign minister went along with this nonsense. Always people pointed out it was the same with other countries. But one should stop at idiocy. Moreover the cartel in other countries was always a small clique. His father had been a middle-ranking official in Austria entitled to a major's uniform but was only permitted to wear it on the birthday of Kaiser Franz-Joseph, at all other times it hung in the wardrobe.

Hewel[31] dared to contradict but made a bad impression. F. started to snap but despite it Hewel shifted the attack to Göring. The field marshal was also fond of fine fancy dress uniforms. The F. gave the surprising retort: 'That is a special case, and I let him have his fun. He happens to have an extravagant personality; these small weaknesses are redeemed by his services.'

22 May 1938
(Beck)[32]

Was with the Chief of the General Staff again to get him to attend the impending major conference of service heads with the F.[33] He was very friendly as usual. To my hint that he was the best person to advise the F. on how things looked in the Army and how necessary it was to tread warily in some areas, he clapped me on the shoulder and said: 'Dear E[ngel], it is pointless putting all that to the Führer. He thinks only along political lines and is deaf to military objections. Besides, I am not used to his demagogic way. Convey to him my warmest greetings and tell him I will send Gen(eral) Halder who can supply answers to questions in such a way that he receives clear advice.' I returned really saddened and informed Schm., who was likewise very disappointed.

22 May 1938*
Reich Chancellery – Rome Society

F. in a none-too-good mood the whole day. Talking about Italian Impressionists and let drop scathing condemnation of Rome society and Italian nobility. So much degeneracy, so many parrot figures and old frumps as he had never previously seen heaped together. Worst thing was, this society together with its hollowness and stupidity still exercised a fair degree of influence on politics because it was protected by the Quirinal [the royal palace] and, having the full support of the crown, made life difficult for the Duce. At the concert in the Villa Borghese ridiculous counts and countesses were seated in the first two rows and the deserving marshals of the empire in the fourth and fifth. At a gesture and at his request at least two of the marshals were brought forward. Worst of all was the queen,[34] that mutton-thief from Montenegro. She was at least still stable, but otherwise pig-stupid. He had the worst martyr's-road behind him, namely the polonaise [dance] through the rooms of the capitol. Women there had thrown themselves on him and almost poked his eyes out with their lorgnettes. Everything had to be done to support the Duce in his struggle against this corrupt society. But he didn't have it easy, all the more so because the officer corps was thoroughly infiltrated by this kind of nobility.

May 1938[+]
F. – Beck – Halder

The Führer has called a pioneering conference[35] of the responsible Army and Luftwaffe Staffs in order to discuss with them the political consequences arising from the return of Austria to the Reich fold.

In many strolls on which I accompanied him recently on the Berg [Obersalzberg] and in the Reich Chancellery garden, he undoubtedly has further intentions of a political nature. His next aim seems to be a solution of the relationship towards the CSR [Republic of Czechoslovakia]. The Sudeten-German question has really got to him deeply and he does not want to see these Germans continuing in a foreign union. In connection with this he rained down more well-aimed blows on the Army. Without a background of force political aims were not possible. In this Fritsch obstructed him and for this reason he had to go. He would not condemn the whole German General Staff for that. On the contrary, based on his observation of the Wehrmacht manouevres, he had grown to value General Halder for his modern ideas and he could picture working together with him rather than with General Beck. The latter was a senior officer still trapped in the concepts of the 100,000-man Army, to whom the [mortar] traversing plate was more important than the fire trench. He would not pass any detrimental remarks, for his personal reputation, for example from the Ulm trial, was an absolutely good one.[36] But nowadays he could not use people who did not share his beliefs, and therefore even Beck's days were numbered. Accordingly he wished that not only General Beck, but also General Halder, would put in an appearance at the major conference.

May 1938[+]
Attitude Schm. – Beck – F.

Schm. asked me personally to invite General Beck to attend the conference arranged by the F. for 28 May. This is a manoeuvre. However, Schmundt thinks a lot of Beck and wants him to experience the F.'s train of thought at first hand more than he has done previously. Schmundt is convinced that Blomberg, and especially also Fritsch, deliberately obstructed the rapprochement between Beck and the Führer. For this reason today I made the personal invitation to Beck and was really taken aback at his response. I made an effort to explain the current mood in the Reich Chancellery just as I had done shortly before for the C-in-C. He just smiled and replied: 'Convey my kind regards to the Führer, but I don't know whether I can come, for I have a lot to do and am working on a memorandum[37] which I will put before him in due course.' I did not think he would attend. But in the event he did appear for the conference. Unfortunately, like the C-in-C, he took no sort of active part in it but just listened.[38] Only Göring did any arguing, and what he said was not really to the point.

15 June[39] 1938[+]
(F. – Br.)

The conversation [between] Führer and C-in-C was not enjoyable. One cannot speak of trust and I am disconsolate that the very precise pointers which I gave in the last fourteen days to the C-in-C, and above all to Siewert, were totally useless. The C-in-C [was] inhibited and unable to speak for us; he leaves that to me, that is when it concerns something unpleasant. They went over the rearmaments plan for autumn, and eventualities for Case Green.[40] I had given the C-in-C a whole list of matters regarding which the Führer had been misinformed and which had to be remedied. Thus, for example, accusations against the Army Weapons Office regarding the 21-cm gun,[41] the short barrel on the Panzer IV,[42] to the reactionary goings-on in the officer corps, which an awful case at Stettin has made worse.[43] But he failed to take steps to investigate this for himself. The two got no closer at dinner. Rather rashly I told this to Siewert and he was very unhappy about it. Unfortunately he still clings to the former C-in-C with all his fibre and just accepts it. So much so that in my opinion he is unable to exert the right influence on the new C-in-C.

25 June 1938[+]
F. – Gö – Hi

Very distasteful table talk. Göring, in field marshal's uniform, went on and on criticising the Army, lashing out wildly at the General Staff, expressed himself very tactlessly about the Westwall Inspectorate (Speich).[44] Himmler held forth similarly, the first time he had really come out of his shell in conversation since I have known him. He wanted to get shot of Halder. Maintains he used to be called 'The Mother-of-God General' and had no front-line experience in the First World War.[45] The Führer was very reserved in his comments but one could see that these tactless criticisms did not find him an altogether unsympathetic listener. He said only that he wished the Wehrmacht had the same elan and willingness to fight as did all his political leaders, particularly the Gauleiters. He often heard reports of friction between his Gauleiters and commanding generals, and mostly the latter were responsible as they did not yet have a feeling for the new epoch.

14 July 1938[+]
(F. about Army Weapons)

While strolling with the Führer I gave him a statistical file concerning the modifications to the sFH18 [15-cm howitzer]. The result was the crudest outburst against the Army Weapons Office. General Becker[46] was a good technologist and an even better professor but understood nothing of the Army's needs and even less about why we had to press on with rearmament. That there were only four[47] prototypes of the 21-cm gun[48] was criminal and yet here they were turning out more prototypes while the weapon remained unavailable to the troops. To my objection that the Army was experiencing difficulties procuring steel, the Führer replied that that did not explain it. Göring got everything he requisitioned, the difference being that the Luftwaffe used the material while the Army hoarded it.

18 July [1938][+]
F. – H. – Förster

The Führer talked about progress being made on the construction of the Westwall and the fact that work had advanced as far as it had being due entirely to the Organisation Todt.[49] If he had given the German Army the job they would still have been building it ten years from now. The report which Engineer-General Förster[50] had given him very recently about bunker strength, and his knowledge of the effects of modern weapons, had come as a shock.[51] He would not be able to discuss the subject with the Chief of the General Staff of course. The gentleman was still possessed of the mentality of the 100,000-man Army of the epoch when the Reichswehr was being created, a time when peace and order was required to bring it about. He [Hitler] preferred not to think that in the next few years we could be involved in massive battles which might decide the fate of Europe. Europe would either be under German leadership or fall victim to Bolshevism. He would rather not have had to build the Westwall. But one could not simply put the job off, and the more pressing the questions as to our destiny in the East, the greater had to be the reinsurance in the West.

18 July 1938
(Beck Memorandum)

F. had Beck's memorandum[52] in front of him and [remarked] to Todt, Schm. and myself that it was a fraudulent piece of paper, but did not deceive him. Childish calculations of strength. While the French included the Mobile Guard, Police and Gendarmerie in their ratios of fighting strength, in the German listings no mention at all was made of the SA, SS and so on. Even the German police were omitted. B. should not think he was stupid. He would draw up a list in riposte and hold it up in front of the gentleman's nose. Schm seconded this very loudly and strengthened the F. in his resolve. I told Siewert about it this afternoon. He complained about the C-in-C, saying that he had no initiative or drive.

24 July 1938
(Beck Memorandum)

The Führer returned again to the Beck memorandum[53] and went over it with the C-in-C. The latter was fully on the defensive. The F. bombarded him with statistics which he had got from the Weapons Office. C-in-C was not in the picture at all. Increased intake White age-band[54] and stepping up of armaments production were discussed. First objection by Br. the F. said: 'Then you must also release the steel which now as then is still being kept back.' At that the F. got calmer and promised to discuss these matters with the field marshal[55] so as to obtain an increase in steel allocation for the Army.

August 1938⁺
Bayreuth[56]

Uneasy hours at home of Frau Wagner[57] with close circle. Major Claus of the Fortifications Inspectorate came with new bunker designs all of which were rejected out of hand by the F. Not strong enough, too complicated. Masterpieces of German architecture but of no practical use. Insults rained down on the Fortifications Inspectorate.[58] The Führer drew up his own bunker sketches and said that he wanted a big conference with Professor Becker and other technicians as soon as we got back. Führer was beside himself with anger about the 'stone-cutters' amongst the Army technical people. Officers should not concern themselves with things they did not understand. Large building firms were much better at it and had more experience. Schmundt and I countered that it was not simply a matter of structures. A building firm could not really judge what type of bunker was best for a particular terrain. That was a matter of military planning.[59] We went backwards and forwards over this subject and the F. was extremely worked up. There was nothing to be gained in discussing it further. He interrupted all the time.

2 August 1938
Command Structure

OKH submitted a study about the command structure. The central point of contention was the leading role of the Army General Staff in all questions of defence and operational planning.[60] Schm., K[eitel][61] and F. all highly indignant. The last turned it down out of hand. He wanted just the opposite. These were reactionary ideas bearing Beck's hallmark, aimed at sabotaging his political aims. If it had been up to the German Army, the Rhineland would still be occupied, not to mention no general conscription, no naval treaty and no Austria. Even Blomberg had shrieked like an hysterical virgin[62] about all these things. I informed C-in-C of this response. He will speak to Führer personally about it.

6 August 1938
Church (Question) – Mu(nich)

Very long and strikingly calm conversation with Führer about churches and religion. Bormann[63] had complained to the F. about church attendance as a duty in the Army and Navy.[64] Apparently complaints by Party bosses on short-term service with r(eserve) units. F. had surprisingly declined to intervene. Spoke about his attitude towards the churches. Now as before he was a Catholic and would remain so. The [Catholic] Church was far too astute to excommunicate him. How he had learned a tremendous amount from the tactics, organisation and doctrinal method of the Cath[olic] Church. During the period of struggle he had seen the thing in a quite different light. His goal then had been to create a unified German Reich Church. The concordat was the most liberal advance he had achieved so far. This Church could be a fairly loose community of the two confessions in the form of a council. But he had to insist on its unconditional subordination to the state and National Socialist politics. He was very disappointed by the Reich bishop[65] who so far had not even managed to unite the Protestants under one hat. France did it much better. There the Church was without political influence but on national holidays the tricolour decorated the altars and church towers, whereas in Germany he still had to remunerate his adversaries. Ritual, liturgy and other practices of the churches were neither here nor there as far as he was concerned. It was just that the churches had to be nationalistic as had always been the case in Poland. There the red and white flags and church banners had preceded their troops into battle. The time is still not ripe to get involved, but it will come. For the moment he had too many other problems and as leader of the people he did not underestimate the power of suggestion the churches wielded.

11 August 1938
Schm. – v. Tresckow

Schm. incensed. He had passed on a telex from Obersalzberg containing F.'s agreement to merge various reserve troop units and mobilise them in divisions. The telex went to Chief OKW, (was forwarded) from there to Chief of General Staff, then (to) Operations Division. That is where Schm.'s best friend Tresckow[66] is. Beck had written a note about Schm. in the margin: 'This officer has distanced himself from General Staff point of view and is to be removed from General Staff service as soon as possible.' Unfortunately Tresckow showed the note to Schm., which was oil on the fire. Schm. wants to report it to the F. I hope I have dissuaded him. I told Tresckow that this was not very clever.

13 August 1938[+]
Persons of Mixed Race

F. talked today to his close circle about the Nuremberg Laws[67] again, and the consequences arising therefrom. When he thought about it, these laws had actually been too humane. Jewish citizens had been deprived of certain rights and excluded from state positions; what remained, however, was activity and work in the free economy and that is precisely what the Jews are best at. Few Jews become civil servants, that is a contradiction of their character. Their instinct for business could not flourish there. Not for nothing in historical times and the Middle Ages had the Jews become the wheels of commerce and moneyed activity; they were in their element. He had travelled through Munich recently and had requested that the Jewish businesses, insofar as any remained, should be pointed out to him. Practically all of them were still there. He would now consider the introduction of supplementary laws to restrict Jewish life in Germany to such an extent that the mass of the Jewish populace in Germany simply would not want to remain. That would be the best way to get rid of them. As far as he was concerned, they should be allowed to take out their money quietly, main thing was that they emigrated. The question of the many mixed marriages and the racially tainted offspring was problematic. He did not yet know how he would handle it. He was sorry for many of them, say what you will, in the world war there had been many brave Jewish soldiers, even officers. One could always make an exception in these cases, for it was not the fault of the children. In all these mixed marriage cases he reserved the right to retain them in state service and the Wehrmacht. Decisive here was their perceived attitude to the state, but above all the racial appearance. He would only go as far as 50 per cent mixed blood, though;[68] any more was beyond the pale and no allowance could be made for them. I interceded with F. on behalf of the numerous officers with part-Jewish blood and could recount a whole series of cases in which really tragic circumstances were playing a part. I saw that he was reluctant to hear this but he promised to investigate every case. The most unpleasant contribution from this close circle, which included amongst others Dr Ley,[69] his head of staff whose name I do not know and Secretary of State Hanke,[70] came as usual from Bormann, who insisted in a very violent tone of voice that officers of part-Jewish blood were still serving. Anyway, in this respect I have a not altogether pleasant responsibility.[71] But one can also do a lot today.

14 August 1938
Reich Chancellery
Uproar about the Westwall. F. has looked over the plans and talks about delays by Army agencies. He had asked the field marshal to look into the rights of the matter.[72] They had either done nothing, or done things imperfectly. Sharply criticised Engineer-General Förster. Reichsleiter Bo. [Bormann] was standing near F. He clapped Bo. on shoulder and said: 'If I could do as I wanted, I know to whom I would transfer the work in place of the generals, Bormann. At least then I could rely on it.' F. did not see me as I was standing off to one side.

17 August 1938
(Schm. – Reichsführer-SS)
Apparently Schm. had had to put up with a long and bitter litany from F. about the lukewarm and sloppy approach of the Army generals.

One would soon not know what to do next. Now Himmler even thinks it necessary to monitor the construction of the Westwall and came to the Führer with the usual criticisms already uttered by Göring. He offered concentration-camp prisoners from the Emsland to speed up the work. F. was very keen on this suggestion. The C-in-C, whom I will inform, will definitely not be. The tragic thing is that Schm. is allowing himself to be influenced more and more, and tends to magnify the guilt in our own ranks. We had a violent argument, including about the personality of Himmler, whom he considers an idealist.

20 August 1938[+]
F. – Memorandum – B.
What I prophesied to Siewert has happened. I warned against submitting the memorandum.[73] The C-in-C had me present it, and that was very unfortunate. The harshest criticisms against the General Staff and Beck were the immediate consequence: his policies were being sabotaged. Instead of being glad to have the chance of working within his wealth of original ideas, the General Staff rejected out of hand any thought of a war. It was a disgrace in this memorandum to include in the numerical ratio of fighting strengths every English bobby and French Civil Guard, and in the German figures to leave out the SA, SS and Reichsarbeitsdienst [Labour Service]. He could see the intention, of course. It was now high time that the Chief of the General Staff disappeared. Up to now he had confidence in General Halder. As he saw it, he had a modern outlook and spelled out his ideas openly, as he had concluded generally, the Bavarian officer corps was apparently significantly more progressive, and more positive towards National Socialism than the so-called Prussian officer corps. It was a scandal, who was now occupying Moltke's chair. Moltke had had to be restrained by Bismarck, and now the thing was happening in reverse.

20 August 1938
Purchasing Works of Art
Yesterday I had night duty. Suddenly F. decided to drive to the Haberstock Gallery[74] to have a second look at some paintings with a view to purchase. As I was in civilian clothing I accompanied him. Additionally I was curious because there were some confiscated works of 'degenerate art' available for inspection. Haberstock had bought abroad a number of Rubens and Rembrandts and offered them to F. who bought them all. There were some Italian security

people present who had come from London. They were not there as
buyers but on behalf of a British gallery arranging an exhibition of
'degenerate works'. Along with some ugly examples were works by
Corinth, Liebermann, other Impressionists and moderate Express-
ionists which were really good and about which I could enthuse. Also
available were canvasses covered with ghastly splodges of colour and
in my opinion it was not a matter of regret they had been classified
degenerate. F. was invited to barter and he was as pleased as Punch
to be able to get old masters so cheaply.

After return to Reich Chancellery there followed a long
conversation about paintings to which I listened in silence. The
opinions of F. were not uninteresting, but his opinions about art in
general deplorable. He dismissed international art and even asserted
that art and politics could not be separated. Painting and sculpture
were the precipitate of political interest and a reflection of political
relationships. The Greeks and Romans were a proof of it. When they
were still a warrior race, their works reflected this; later, homo-
sexuality was read into works good in themselves. It was like that in
1918. Oddly enough Jews had always been the carriers of degenerate
art and he would not tolerate it any longer in Germany. For that
reason he had banned from public display in Germany all paintings
and works by Jewish artists irrespective of whether they had any
merit. The talk went on long into the night. I was really appalled, but
even more so by what the other partners to the conversation had to
say. Even a layman would realise that Hoffmann's[75] opinion was that
of an amateur. Worst of all was the post-mortem on the discussion
and many tried to out-trump the Führer.

25 August 1938[+]
Conference with Br. (Siewert)[76]

The conference with Br. was very unpleasant again. He spoke in an
extremely harsh vein about the Führer's reaction to the memorandum.[77] He ignored my suggestion that he should confer with him
personally. Siewert said I was 100 per cent right and stated candidly
that it was useless for the C-in-C to attend a conference and when he
was there say nothing. As it happened, Keitel had shown the
memorandum immediately to Göring, and for the latter the whole
thing was grist to the mill. I also told Siewert that, if we shrank from
seizing the initiative and did not energetically combat defamatory
remarks and false accusations by the Luftwaffe and Party, we had not
seen the last of 4 February.[78]

26 August 1938[+]
Conference with Halder

Naturally urged on by Himmler, the Führer is again planning to equip the so-called Totenkopf [Death's Head] Standarte[79] with heavy weapons. That means another enlargement of the SS. And I said to Siewert today that if we do not start looking to our own interests it will keep on growing. But the C-in-C will simply not discuss the question of the SS with the Führer.

Without Siewert's knowledge I went to Halder, who received me with extreme reservation, almost rudeness, told me candidly that he felt he was being followed and watched. As he said this he laid his service pistol on the desk with the remark that he would not allow himself to be knocked off, he would defend himself. I did not understand this at first and he gave me the impression of a very nervous and frightened man at the end of his tether. The OKW and Reich Chancellery were definitely not giving the OKH an easy ride. I supplied him with an insight into the goings-on in the Reich Chancellery both in the organisational respect with regard to the Army and also political. It was significant, and in my opinion is a very grave affair, when the Chief of the General Staff dismissed this with the sentiment: 'Don't bother me with this laughable garbage. I am interested in the thoughts of the German Reich Chancellor regarding the world political situation, but not his organisational ideas and military passion. I have my colleagues for that.'

5 September 1938[+]
Volkswagen Works

F. was visited by Dr Ley. The latter had test-driven a new car. I was not present at the test.

During a stroll F. spoke in great detail about the world's traffic problems and stated that the development of the automobile and increase in its production would lead to a situation in ten years at the latest when the highways were no longer adequate for the traffic. He had tied in special ideas to the creation of the Volkswagen works. It was not only to be a good source of foreign exchange for the Reich but would above all replace the worker's bicycle. He would not rest until the production over the years had reached such a level that, at a certain time, which he hoped to live to experience, every professional employee at least would have his own Volkswagen. The time was coming, passing on the way the motor cycle which, by the way, he did not think much of, when the baby's pram and bicycle would become obsolete. The latter would be ridden only by boys and small girls.

For him, construction work on the autobahns was not proceeding fast enough, but it was simply not possible to go any faster, for one had to bear in mind the steel and armaments industries. A nation which had tackled the traffic problem before he had was the United States. Some years ago they had begun to construct large highways which by-passed the cities. Above all they had created multi-lane highways while in Germany, bent on retaining the pre-Flood means of transport, namely the horse, whole companies of provincial councillors fought like madmen to keep the summer paths open. He wanted to do away with this ridiculous idea, and he had already given the necessary instructions to his Gauleiters. In fifty years at the most horses would be seen only at military parades or in zoos and circuses, where children would gaze at them with the same astonishment as they now view camels and elephants.

8 September 1938
Conference at Nuremberg Br. – Ha.

After the concluding ceremony in the Kongresshalle, C-in-C and Halder were summoned at midnight to a conference about the invasion plan.[80] There followed the dreadful showdown which Schmundt and I had prophesied. The Führer spoke of them dividing his forces, lack of decisive operational objectives, deliberate under-use of Reichenau's army and so on. It was very unpleasant. In conclusion he demanded in unmistakable terms a modification of the plan so that it corresponded to his own ideas. He even went so far as to dictate how his beloved SS-Leibstandarte[81] should be deployed. I was unhappy that the C-in-C and Chief did not stand up to him. They simply went along with it and put forward no convincing counter-arguments. And then came the worst part. Quite unprompted, Brauchitsch made a declaration of loyalty on behalf of the Army. He had not waited until the Navy and Luftwaffe adjutants had been asked to leave the hall, and naturally the occurrence was reported to their respective commanders-in-chief next day. The consequence was that even the Führer was baffled as to how he was supposed to respond and contented himself by delivering a long harangue detailing how the Army had always disappointed him in the past. Brauchitsch had nothing to offer in reply. The only person who found it good was Keitel, but that proves it is precisely the opposite.

10 September 1938
(Party Congress)

Bad situation for C-in-C and Chief of the General Staff at invasion plan conference in the Deutscher Hof at Nuremberg.[82] F. put the whole thing on its head, changed the motorised ratios, deprived Rundstedt[83] of the mass of Panzers and gave them to Reichenau.[84]

Lamentable that Brauchitsch simply makes no effort to oppose him and just goes along with it all. After these two had gone, K. [Keitel] played a laughable role, agreeing that the F. was right in every instance, then gave him the benefit of his own 'strategic' thinking in meticulous detail. This put the F.'s back up against the Army, and as he got more annoyed he even spoke of their fear and cowardice.

Actually he would like to see his armies led by the Gauleiters. His political leaders at the Zeppelinwiese[85] would all drop by parachute to attack if he ordered it. The difference was that they had belief in the cause while the Army generals did not.

An awful state of affairs and one simply does not know how it will all turn out.

11 September 1938

As Bodenschatz[86] was there yesterday,[87] the field marshal [Göring] was naturally told everything and, as he sees it, it is oil to the lamp as far as the Army is concerned. He holds long talks about the invasion plan and speaks of it as like the work of a bad cadet. I have the impression that even the F. finds this talk embarrassing. He is very reserved about G.'s views and makes little comment.

26 September 1938*

F. returned to Berlin[88] yesterday. Had there long conversation with Reichsführer-SS,[89] was drawn into it as duty military adjutant. F. informed me that in connection with Sudeten crisis an SS-Totenkopf Sturmbann [battalion] 'for special purposes' had been formed. It would march into the Ascher Zipfel.[90] He would use it to guard an autonomous Sudeten-German Government[91] if one were set up in Asch. This Sturmbann needed heavy weapons, and the OKH would transfer to the SS forthwith about four light infantry guns. Reichsführer-SS, who was present, asked for six guns, and these were agreed without further enquiry. My objection that a battalion rated only two guns was not accepted by F. and he brushed it aside with the observation: 'That does not apply here.' Informed Chief of General Staff about this order. He promised to comply.

28 September 1938*

F. enquired as to situation regarding the equipping of the 'Sudeten-German Freikorps',[92] as it is now called officially, with weapons. Apparently there was a dispute between SA and SS. SS was naturally the winner. Obtained the necessary information from Army General Office [Allgemeine Heeresamt – AHA] and learned that the guns had been supplied. Former Austrian weapons were in the pipeline. These weapons had been given to the SS, so it seems concentration camp people[93] were armed with them originally. Now they are in the hands of the Sudeten-German Freikorps.

Important, and bringing some calm to OKH is F.'s decision that the entire Sudeten-German Freikorps has been subordinated to the Reichsführer-SS for special police tasks.

28 September 1938

(With Siewert) at OKH. Updated ab(out) readiness of Mussolini and Daladier to come to Munich. I kept repeating: F. does not want war, had good things to say about Chamberlain. Long conversation concerning Freikorps.[94] Told him of harsh words directed at Army and C-in-C by F.: *everything*[95] was being sabotaged, even weapons for Sudeten-German volunteers (only delivered in dribs and drabs).[96] F. will now use Totenkopf units to do the fighting. So I suspect that new SS units will be formed. F. praised the Party; at his order they would all drop by parachute to attack (every Party member) – where was the Army's will to fight?

Also saw Chief of the General Staff. Seated at his desk in a state of collapse, crying, considers everything lost[97] does not believe in [Sudeten] unification. Harsh words about C-in-C for not arguing sufficiently forcibly the inadequacy of the Army and its fighting strength. I calmed him down and repeated what I had told Siewert, that F. above all does not want war with Britain. Ha. [Halder] is apparently being influenced very unfavourably and pessimistically by people from Foreign Ministry[98] and Wiedemann.[99]

End September 1938

Propaganda march [through] WK [Wehrkreis – Military District] III.[100] War of nerves continues. 'Brown papers'[101] about conversations doubting the total German mobilisation eavesdropped at Fr[ench] and Brit[ish] embassies presented to F. F. suggested convoys of motorised units through Berlin. Referred this to Siewert. All up in arms about it. I to Gallenkamp[102] (officer commanding III Corps) and Mellenthin[103]

(No. 3 Staff Officer, III Corps). Decided to improvise a march by Wünsdorf,[104] the artillery and infantry training schools and some flak units through Berlin to include the streets where embassies situated. Mellenthin with Schm. and me in Reich Chancellery.

Due to shortage of time no parade (possible). F. in a rage and only calmed down when embassies reported to Paris and London that it looks like he means business.

1 October 1938[+]
Chamberlain – Flat
Today there was an odd situation. The British Prime Minister arrived at Prinzregentenplatz 16 and used the lift to the F.'s flat. It stuck but was restarted successfully, thank God.

Afterwards F. spoke for a long time to Schm. and myself about the agreement.[105] My impression is that he genuinely likes the elderly gentleman and would enjoy further dealings with him. F. expresses the opinion that now for the time being it has all fallen quiet. The prime minister had said that he believed he was able to influence opinion in Britain and defuse anti-German feelings. The main thing was that we remained at peace. He had also assured him of this. He [Hitler] himself always bore in mind the primary requirement not to take any step which could be dangerous politically. First of all that which had been regained had to be digested. He would not lose sight, however, of the need for a solution to the points of dispute with Poland.[106] At the right time he would soften up the Poles and make them ripe for attack; to that end he would now apply the tried and tested method. Peace and quiet was something for the long term, when the Versailles Treaty was cancelled in its entirety.

16 October 1938
Reichenau – F. (in) Flat (on Prinzregentenplatz)
General von Reichenau is back and reported on China.[107] F. was annoyed and complained that gen[erals] knew nothing about politics. R. was in the act of ruining his whole Japan-concept. (Reichenau came home, as they all did, 'infused' with China).[108] F. discussed recent weeks with R., recounted how difficult it had been with Army High Command, impossible invasion plan (scattered decisive points). He had given to him, R., the job of striking the first decisive blow.[109] The Army was the most uncertain element of the state, worse than the Foreign Ministry and judiciary.

17 October 1938
(Schm. – Himmler)

Schm. had a long talk with Himmler, the former taken in as ever by the latter's respectable, benevolent and adept manner, behind which so much lies concealed. Schm. was definitely 'very impressed' and believes that Himmler wants only the best for everybody and also has nothing against the Army. The SS-Verfügungstruppe would develop into an elite body only; he had no plans for a broader expansion. Neither for that matter did the Führer. But in the OKH there was a certain clique working to sabotage even the Führer-directives. General Fromm[110] seemed to be at the forefront of it. Apparently H. was full of praise for Fritsch. He was very sorry about what had befallen him. Above all Fritsch had lent great support towards the setting up of the Leibstandarte.[111] He knew that the business involving [Fritsch] had only cropped up in the wake of the Blomberg affair, in which the trust placed in the High Command people had had to come under scrutiny.

This was all well and good, but the worst thing is that Schm. is frightfully gullible and believes anything too easily. In conversation Schm. even stated that theoretically one should slip the Reichsführer-SS into the Army structure in order to bring him closer to the heart of things. I merely said to Schm. that he could not be serious about this.

18 October 1938
F. – Bo. – Bouhler (Divorce)

(F. spoke about Colonel-General von Brauchitsch's divorce. Reichsleiter Bouhler[112] had visited shortly before, subject was divorce of the C-in-C. F. spoke quite openly about it.) F. was generous. Offered extensive support to satisfy material demands (of) Fr(au) von Brauchitsch and is anxious to avoid C-in-C being burdened psychologically in any way by the divorce. Everything else (will be arranged) immediately through RL Bouhler. He administers F.'s special accounts and (can make corresponding) disbursements.

Br. (was afterwards) with Bouhler on a number of occasions. Apparently affair (has been handled up to now very) discreetly and is known only to the smallest circle.[113]

18 October 1938

Put my oar in again about Fritsch. After midnight tried to engage F. in conversation about Fritsch. Opportunity was favourable since F.

had spoken out in praise of Army; re-occupation [of Sudetenland] had gone off marvellously and our troops made a tremendous impression. Said that these were the fruits of the work of the former C-in-C who was held in great esteem. F. listened attentively, at first said nothing, then pointed to the lack of enthusiasm for rearmament Fr. had shown. When I dared to interrupt, F. curtly broke off the conversation.

11 November 1938

The uproar and shame have dissipated somewhat. Early morning the day before yesterday I drove (to) (Waeger)[114] at the Weapons Office to fetch some files the F. wanted. On the drive back through Tauentzien, Kleiststr[asse]. Lützowplatz I saw many large shards of glass being swept up. When I asked my chauffeur Stegmeyer if he could explain, he told me that the previous night the SA had smashed all the Jewish shop windows. I have seldom been so incensed. In the Reich Chancellery I met Schmundt. He was also very angry and said quite rightly: 'This will cost us a lot abroad'. I did not stay for breakfast at the Chancellery but went home and discussed it with my wife. At midday Schmundt was a changed man. He told me that I had missed something at lunch. Goebbels had been there and explained convincingly the reason for the action. Now he was certain that the action was justified and it would demonstrate both to international Jewry and people abroad in general that they could not treat us just as they liked. There was no open season for Germans abroad. Every future attempted assassination[115] would accordingly attract a reprisal in some such manner.

12 November 1938

Below[116] came from the Reich Air Ministry where he had seen Göring. He told me confidentially that the latter was beside himself with rage about the anti-Jewish action and the crap Goebbels was coming out with to justify it. Göring had said: 'Economically and politically this will cost us damned much abroad and now I shall have to practise economies again.'

1939

17 January 1939
(Niemöller)

Himmler was with F. and had apparently visited Pastor Niemöller[117] in Oranienburg. Related that he was well and receiving special treatment.[118] Führer became extremely critical of this person. If during his lifetime there was somebody who would never be released from custody it was this clergyman. He had the typical mentality which constantly rejected [sic], and was an opponent on principle, not from conviction, not to mention from religious belief. He knew all about his pledges of loyalty.[119] And what had become of them? And all because he (Niemöller) had not become what he had hoped after the seizure of power. Now he was inciting people against the state using the cloak of God's word. He (the Führer) would not allow him to preach in the camp. Niemöller was the typical renegade with the fanaticism of a Jesuit. He was a definite danger for the younger generation. Raeder[120] might intercede on his behalf as much as he liked out of old naval loyalties, but he would remain hard as iron and never allow N. to go free. Himmler added that his followers amongst the pastors were well known and being watched.

19 January 1939
Marriage – Officers

I have just put behind me a farce for which the Personnel Office, but above all the C-in-C, bear the blame. A lieutenant from Weissenfels had business in the house of a provincial court jurist in Halle. The latter's 19-year-old daughter lived there. The 22-year-old lieutenant and the girl became very close and the affair had its consequences. The officer reported it at once as he was bound to and asked permission to wed the girl at once. The jurist was incidentally a reserve officer. The divisional commander acted on the lieutenant's behalf in the petition to marry, but his superior turned it down and so did C-in-C. Afterwards Little K.[121] rang and asked what he should do. C-in-C wanted me to advise F. of refusal. Word was that the lieutenant was going to lodge an appeal. I advised the Head of the Personnel Office to dispose of the matter with a consent to the marriage, admonition and disciplinary transfer because I know the F.'s viewpoint in these things. Everything was then down again to the 'reactionary' Army. K. sent me to Siewert and to the C-in-C where I found no change. So the affair ran its full course. I presented the appeal and the response was as I expected: a wild tirade against the Army, officer corps. They were all liars! The gentlemen could not see farther than their own noses. Outcome was consent to marriage with transfer to 1st Division. What is one to do when confronted with this sort of behaviour? And the worst of the bunch are in P2.[122]

18 February 1939

The talk suggested by Schm. for all Army colonels (and) ([Navy] captains) in command positions throughout the Wehrmacht was held in the Kroll Opera House.[123] F.'s veiled criticism of the Army's position with regard to pol[itical] matters humiliating and depressing. He did not mention actual names of units but everybody knew who was meant. What I found surprising was the F.'s openness regarding further pol[itical] aims and solutions ahead. Here the Wehrmacht was the indispensable guarantor of success. Long explanations of world view which had not yet become generally accepted in all Wehrmacht areas. Quite clear utterances ab[out] intentions, to negate the Versailles Treaty with regard to Poland, if necessary availing himself of other means than diplomacy, with which he was at odds in any case. Very positive towards Party in this respect. In the Nat[ional] Soc[ialist] State the Wehrmacht should not think of behaving like the Reichswehr.

Afterwards reception and banquet in the Reich Chancellery. Very mixed reception to the speech by commanders and generals, some enthusiastic, other highly sceptical. Once again Schm. gave the F. a false picture about its effect on commanders. Spoke of whole-hearted enthusiasm and approval.

8 April 1939

F. up in arms about the Italians and their invasion of Albania.[124] Possibly there was some envy in it. F. himself described the attack as aping his own recent political moves. In this Mussolini did not wish to be outdone. While he would never forget the Duce for his stance during recent events, particularly in March 1938, nevertheless he had the definite feeling that M. was not exactly overjoyed at his success. In all probability it came down to the fact that the Duce thought the F. understood military matters better than he did. Undoubtedly the Italian generals and nobility had played a sinister role and done everything in order to denigrate him, F. He regretted that Mussolini had not consulted him about the invasion of Albania but could understand why he had not, thank God, because he himself had refrained from seeking the Italians' advice. If one told the garrulous Italians absolutely anything, one could be sure the press would get it. In general, he considered the penetration of the Balkans at this time to be risky, and the Italians must surely be aware that it was a powder keg. The dual monarchy [of Austria-Hungary] had been feared, but the Italians were hated and not feared.

Present were Schmundt, Keitel, Brauchitsch, Siewert, also Goebbels, Kerrl, Hewel, Lorenz[125] and myself.

June 1939*

Conversation with Bormann, Hoffmann, Brandt in Munich

On the terrace of the HdK,[126] F. embarked on the subject of artists and their peculiarities. This came about after two plain-clothes officers made a heavy-handed attempt to prevent Weiss Ferdl[127] from sitting two tables away. F. intervened to let him have his way.

Unfortunately many Party members did not subscribe to the idea that artists could be anything other than normal earthlings. There was a certain something about the very word 'artist' which one had to respect. Such people were beyond good and evil and could not be just forced into the general run of things. They did things differently, and the crazier they appeared, the greater was their talent. He had not siphoned off Jewish artists because they were different to other people but on account of their racial predisposition to foster bad art. The race had the knack of transforming everything good into something to be despised, and they frequently did it with masterly satire. But there was more behind it: the tendency to impugn and demean authority. This meant a fight to the finish, at least as far as he was concerned. Actually he was not an enemy of humour and of people like Weiss Ferdl or even Schäffers[128] and Kläre Waldoff[129] could slate what they liked, provided it was kept within limits, but to mock and belittle oneself was unworthy of a National Socialist. On the other hand it was quite wrong to sniff an attack on the state every time a cabaret artiste started cracking a few jokes. The worst error was to lock up those artists who would not allow themselves to be forced into the scheme of things, because then they became martyrs and drew strength from that.

June 1939*

The question of appointing a military attaché for Kabul became acute today and was discussed by F., C-in-C and Keitel. F. said suddenly, 'Toussaint[130] must go there.' He thinks the world of him since learning of his activities in Prague. F. then talked in general about military attachés and their duties. For some time German attachés had had their shortcomings. Military attachés were nothing more than accredited spies whose diplomatic passport enabled them to find out more than the Abwehr [Military Counter-Intelligence] could. If they were rumbled it was just bad luck and they flew home. He knew his Pappenheimers[131] very well in this respect, and could draw a picture from the content and manner of presentation of their reports of which ones put breakfast with colleagues above all other duties, which ones went for an in-depth investigation of the host nation's army or were trying to establish the intentions and aims of the host nation's General Staff behind military-political dodges. Of the political reports he read with special pleasure those rendered by Bötticher[132] in Washington; he could see through the stage props, had a very good appreciation of the Americans and their intentions and was also a very good judge of what in practice was going on behind the scenes. The worst were those attachés – and their recall was something that [was] necessary forthwith – who had become imbued with the mentality of the host nation, found everything there to be wonderful, and when the opportunity presented itself abroad were quite happy to mouth off against their own people. Here was something impossible to eradicate amongst career diplomats. That was one of the reasons why, one after the other, he was filling consular and ambassadorial posts with competent and proven Party members who had, above all, the correct world view. The C-in-C might well say in closing that, with a few individual exceptions, he was well satisfied with the attachés. But it was also important that these should be instructed politically by their embassies, and that was not always the case.

4 June 1939

Up in arms about elementary school-teachers. F. had apparently got annoyed about Gauleiter Simon,[133] therefore the emotional outburst. Spoke about the great danger in half-educating.

Intelligence without education was a bad thing, discontent and complexes were the result. The King of Prussia [Frederick the Great] had done it the right way with the old NCOs. These had been modest people and taught the youth discipline and order. At that time nothing more had been necessary. But now the whole thing was much more difficult; political enlightenment and socialism had sharpened the critical faculties of the masses and the talented had become more ambitious. As the vehicles of social democracy, teachers had taken advantage of this development. In addition there came the stupidity of which the Army was guilty in the world war when it created hybrids which were neither fish nor fowl: the sergeant-lieutenants and commissioned warrant officers. These people often made up the soldiers' councils of 1918 and in many cases were teachers by profession. In due course he would abolish all that once and for all. Teacher-training institutions must become similar to the Party-run Ordensburgen and Napolas;[134] moreover teachers should be paid a respectable wage and be given a proper title. When rearmament began, there were still people in the Army who wanted hybrid grades as in 1914/18, and he had stopped that; and he did not want to see the French troupier[135] in the Army either. That had nothing to do with the idea of earmarking intelligent Hitler Youth boys for the NCO career-path.

14 June 1939[+]
Radke – SA – C-in-C
Had a long conversation today with Schmundt about the intentions of the C-in-C regarding the SA.[136] One gains from Sch. the distinct impression that he is unhappy about the politics of the C-in-C in this respect. He is a Keitel-man, and very often Himmler and others are at his ear, influencing him to face in a particular direction. Schm. is a victim of circumstance. He realises that he is only nominally a member of the General Staff and that they do not think of him as a full member following Beck's devastating marginal note.[137] From his own stand-point the C-in-C is right. Since its backbone was snapped in 1934 [as a result of the Night of the Long Knives], the SA is, for the moment, politically speaking the most harmless Party organ. A big role in the C-in-C's politics is being played by Radke, who is carrying out his special duty as the so-called 'Political Officer' in the C-in-C Staff very conscientiously and with zeal. He has undoubtedly been successful, for it was exclusively his doing that the SA has been intensively nursed in the pre-military respect, and he has no doubt been trying

to pour oil on Army–SA troubled waters. So far, however, he has had no luck with the Hitler Youth and Party, while the NSKK [National-sozialistisches Kraftfahrkorps] is pursuing the course laid down for it by Chief of Staff Lutze. One thing is quite clear, and Schm. almost swore to it: the SA is now powerless against Himmler and Heydrich. It was certainly also the will of the Führer to concentrate political power completely in the SS, probably goaded on by Bormann who, as one sees daily, exercises an ever-growing influence on F. He[138] has upset Reich Minister Hess to such an extent that Hess is almost never seen in the Reich Chancellery, and we have the impression, as does Schm, that he wants to kill off Hess politically and reduce him to insignificance.

Schm. spoke very critically about Radke himself, in reply I argued most forcibly. And the strange thing was that Schm. referred me to the opinion of his General Staff colleagues. A few days ago he had a talk with Groscurth[139] who had made a long complaint about Radke. Harsh criticism fell from his lips, for example Party hack, puppet of the C-in-C and similar. But really that does not seem right. Radke is undoubtedly very crafty and slippery as an eel, but from numerous conversations I have had with him I have the definite impression that his main objective is to consolidate the position of the C-in-C and with it that of the Army.

18 June 1939
Führer about Churches

Conversation with F. about Wehrmacht priests. Surprisingly, F. said that he had been thinking of cooperation with the churches quite differently. Contrary to his stated policy he had been hoping to be able to give the churches a national character. But churches had even refused to display national symbols, contrary to the practice in France and Italy. Politics had no place in church and he did not want God becoming a Party member. The churches (however) criticised the state instead of supporting it. Originally he had been thinking of a German Churches Federation composed of both confessions, but Rome and the likes of Niemöller had put paid to the idea.

18 June 1939
Naval Visits Abroad

After watching a film about calls made by German warships to foreign ports, F. talked about these voyages. They were a wonderful thing, and one saw in the naval officer's deportment and conduct the self-awareness of the worldly man. Horizons and degree of education would be greatly enhanced by them. Confidence would result from learning to judge what was better abroad, and more importantly, what was worse. An officer of the *Emden* had told him[140] that one returned home comforted by the knowledge that nothing could beat German sense of order, precision, incorruptibility and thoroughness. There were complaints, of course, unfortunately often justified, about the foreign representation handling such visits in too stiff or formal a manner. He would discuss it with Bohle.[141] He would have to involve the Party Foreign Organisation (AO) if a spineless ambassador was being stupid. In conclusion F. said he was considering whether it would be possible later to arrange for large parties of land officers to go on that kind of voyage.

28 June 1939[+]
Prince(-Regent) Paul

F. spoke at length about the Yugoslav visit.[142] He repeatedly expressed his anger and disappointment that the couple had practically pulled a fast one. He cannot get over the fact that the pair of them, without even so much as a peep beforehand, will be going on to England after visiting Germany.

He considers Prince Paul[143] a complete weakling who would be better employed running a section at the Haus der Kunst rather than as a Head of State. The lady was undoubtedly charming, but remains a typical ice-cold Englishwoman as we saw today.[144] It was interesting that Prince Paul asked him several times if he might settle in Munich once Crown Prince Peter had come of age. Politics were insufferable to him, and the Serbs, Croats and Slovenes were just a mish-mash with whom he had no desire to spend the rest of his life arguing. F. said, probably rightly, that she was behind this attitude. She wants to have an English life-style. But Prince Paul was slippery as an eel and he [Hitler] had not succeeded in getting his claws into him. Always when he thought he had got him, he dodged and hid behind his parliament.

All in all, I have the impression that, despite the big parade and other notable events, F. was not overly enthusiastic about this visit.

July 1939[+]
Haus der Kunst

F. spoke again about his appreciation of art and went over one of his favourite themes of recent times: Leda and the Swan. It had given him great satisfaction in this matter to have prevailed against the otherwise very progressive Frau Troost.[145] He had informed Director Kolb[146] that in his opinion somebody had deliberately tried to deceive the latter with regard to this work of art. If, while strolling to the gallery, he had not happened to notice that this painting was standing upside down, and had not observed from Kolb's confusion that something was amiss, this work by Padua[147] would either have been incinerated by now or reside in some boiler room. The painting was unusually beautiful in colour, unsurpassed in its arrangement and was technically a masterpiece which the Dutch would be overjoyed to get their hands on. If people had gone out of their way to hide the title of the painting from him, those who were responsible need not have been so fussy. There was no reason for it and they were mostly the worst hypocrites themselves. The whole picture breathed strength, and this was the strength of the male over the bending female, and that was the way it should be in life. A woman wants a man and not a puppet. That kind was mostly abandoned by their spouses who then sought out something stronger. Padua was not the first to use the title 'Leda and the Swan' but there were no earlier works quite like it. It was not the artist's role to be ashamed and prudish. One did not come into this world clothed, but in the glory of the body. What appeared to Jewish artists to be the right thing to do was cheap to his artists. On the stage too he allowed a great deal of licence and would not be perceived as ridiculous as the old Queen of England, Victoria, had been, when she censured her daughter for wearing a dress without stays: a female child of royal blood was not supposed to have any legs. He would have tried to get the old queen to see that no institution existed which forced her to think in that way. And in her case obviously, her children must have come directly from the heavens.[148]

Art ought to strike out at everyday life, to be a talking image of human strength, also human mistakes and weaknesses and frequently the expression of heroic opinion.

4 July 1939
Danzig – SS

Today I pulled a fast one on the SS. From the very talkative Wolff,[149] Chief of the Reichsführer-SS Staff, I heard that Himmler was proposing arming and reorganizing the *Totenkopf* units into a brigade at Danzig.[150] I went at once to Fromm and Koehler[151] and expressed my opinion that it was high time to mobilise and arm the Danzig police, thereby facilitating their transfer later into the Army. I then received from the Army General Office an organisational plan with dates. I presented this to the F. that evening, he approved it and signed it at my request. Tomorrow the AHA will advise the SS-Verfügungstruppe (Jüttner)[152] of the order, and that will dispose of the *Totenkopf* question [in Danzig], since from experience even there they tend to fight shy of things which bear the Führer's signature.

8 July 1939

Bormann's pathological agitation against church and religion simply has no bounds any longer. Today at table another violent outburst on account of Prof[essor] Schreiner[153] of Rostock, who is well known to me and is waging a brave struggle there against the Gau and Kreis leaderships. B. is demanding amongst other things that the Wehrmacht be made religion-free, and that the military-district and parish priests[154] be discharged. Schmundt – finally, thank God, in this case – and I spoke out against him saying the idea was very risky. At least 80–90 per cent of Wehrmacht conscripts had religious beliefs and wished to retain them. B. mouthed off loudly maintaining that the officers had ordered and forced them. He knew his young Party people and the SA better than we did. Nevertheless we didn't relax our hold.

F. was strangely quiet and asked only that B. obtain information from the Gau heads as to the percentage by which church attendance had fallen amongst the general population.

In the evening I succeeded in saying a few things about Prof[essor] Schreiner to F. and took up the cudgels for him. F. is fairly disinterested in the personality, but was not sparing with some angry remarks about Dohrmann.[155]

12 July 1939
Albrecht Case

We have put a quite bad spell behind us, but I am not yet done with the business. It concerned the conduct and future of a close colleague, and stirred up a whirlwind of dust. Albrecht[156] had married and took three weeks' marriage leave, from which he had not returned. In response to my enquiry to the OKM [Oberkommando der Marine – Navy High Command] Chief of Staff Schulte-Mönting,[157] I was supplied with an evasive answer and given some talk about supplementary leave, all frightfully secretive, and he continued to behave throughout the whole affair in the most stupid manner possible. Meanwhile something filtered through. It had to do with Albrecht's young wife, and I found out about it in the following way.

The Grossadmiral[158] appeared unannounced at [Obersalz]berg and spoke for over two hours with F. privately in the vestibule. Voices were raised occasionally and I heard F. speaking in a highly excited manner. The Grossadmiral left without a word to me, and afterwards I walked with F. At first completely silent, then it came out, words to the following effect. Apparently there was a typical officer-type intrigue going on again, but he refused to put up with any suspicions against his naval adjutant. It was always a bad thing if third parties alleged something and just left it at that. All the same, he had not let the matter drop and would have it investigated fully. In response to my question as to the nature of the occurrence, F. blurted it out. After the wedding it had been reported to the Grossadmiral that Frau Albrecht had previously been following an immoral life-style. There was talk of various relationships, the main one with a rich friend. Big parties had been thrown, a smoke screen being laid to disguise slightly what they were. One had to wonder how it came about that something like that was not general knowledge until after the marriage. In his view there was a large amount of bad judgment involved. This assumption appeared all the more justified as some of the accusations had apparently been made by officers' wives. As a first step he had recalled Albrecht from leave and arranged to be introduced to his wife so that he might obtain a personal impression of her. As a result I was given the job of collecting Frau Albrecht tomorrow from the Berchtesgadener Hof and bringing her to the Bechsteinhaus.[159] As the Führer was very worked up, I did not ask further. Spoke in the evening with Below in Berlin. Since the Navy had not kept us informed, we had no excuse to bring the matter up with them.

13 July 1939[+]
Albrecht Case

Today I had a mixed bag of experiences. I fetched Frau Albrecht from Berchtesgaden. He himself was not to be seen. Impression: a strikingly attractive woman, very self-confident and apparently also very self-assured. She gave me a very hostile reception and we drove to the Bechsteinhaus in silence. F. was already there and conversation lasted an hour and a half. Afterwards I drove her back to Berchtesgaden. This time she was more communicative. She said in very emotional tones that she had met a person who had complete understanding for her as a woman, and steps would be taken to ensure that those who had denounced her would not go unpunished. I cannot say that she is nice. Despite her good looks, there is something hard about her face. It is obvious to me that there is a great deal behind the exterior. We parted formally and she said only that she was taking the night train to Berlin with her husband. I returned to the Bechsteinhaus where F. was standing on the doorstep and went with me to the Tea-House.[160]

The whole affair was to be kept strictly secret. Apart from his valet, nobody was around. Now he let loose: the liars in the officer corps, the hypocritical morals, the staff doing what they could to break people and meddling in things which had nothing to do with appearance, conduct, achievement and opinions. The only thing new to come out of it was the fact that the Navy was more jesuitical than the Army. Albrecht had been within his rights to marry this good-looking woman and to overlook her past. The wife had simply had friends, which was a woman's right if she looked good. The Grossadmiral had brought up the Blomberg case. The Blomberg case was something quite different. There was no way of telling how many officers' wives who were now playing the moral guardian had had affairs in the past. Those were domestic matters for man and wife and were no business of third parties provided they did not become public property. The Blomberg case was quite different, he had knowingly married a street-girl who offered her body to all-comers for money. That was obviously not acceptable. But he understood enough about women to know that this was not the case with Frau Albrecht. He would not brush the matter aside. If the Grossadmiral wanted him [Albrecht] out, he could have it. But one could not speak of great Fatherland-conviction and responsibility in doing so. It went on and on in the same vein and I was glad when the time came to drive F. to the Berghof. On account of the secrecy I did something that had not happened before and chauffeured the Führer and Reich Chancellor home in my own car.

17 July 1939[+]
Albrecht Case

F. spoke to me again about the Albrecht affair which is now probably drawing to its conclusion. We had not seen him again. Below and I agreed not to inform Schmundt, who was on leave, about it so that he can continue to relax for a few days free from the cares of office. Apparently he had been going backwards and forwards for some days. F. pledged me to silence about the affair. Continued to heap abuse on the lying generals in the officer corps. F. said he had remained hard towards the Grossadmiral. At his suggestion Albrecht would leave naval service and enter the personal *Adjutantur* as No. 4 Adjutant. He would award him a high Party rank and that way the Grossadmiral would also get what he wanted. He had spoken in laughable terms about the burden of the officer corps. His preoccupation was cowards and defeatists, these were worse than officers' involvements with women. This standpoint did not originate with him, but the great king [Frederick the Great] had a similar outlook and therefore also [did not want] rotten eggs.

18 July 1939
Was witness to a long talk between F. and Bormann who has apparently submitted another church-paper. Speaks bluntly about the 'handservants' of the churches ensconced in the Wehrmacht. Long legal arguments about whether and how one can incorporate the churches into the state structure or otherwise bring them under state control. Borm. is fire and flame for this project. F. more reserved. Even casts doubt on the figures produced by Bormann about reduction in church attendance generally. Complete lack of influence of the German Christians asserted by F. and admitted by Borm. With state help he wants to set up a 'Church of God' or something similar using pastors who have left the ministry, and thus set up a rival body to the Bekennenden Kirche [Confessional Church]. Suggested that all Party members should be forced to leave the church, which F. waved aside and distanced himself from any coercion or pressure in this respect. Then they noticed me and went out to the Winter Garden terrace.

20 July 1939[+]
Albrecht Case
Schmundt had an in-depth discussion with Schulte-Mönting and put Below and myself in the picture at once. The affair is significantly more serious than it appears to the Führer. We learned for the first time what accusations lie against Frau Albrecht. The thing in itself combines the most tawdry gossip with a corresponding salvo aimed at indecency. The fact is that the lady was not exactly unknown to naval circles at Kiel and had a year-long, very close relationship with a mill-owner – but also with others. The gentleman in question threw a series of rousing parties in which both sexes were scantily clad, and

all this could be seen and confirmed from officers' quarters opposite.

All well and good, but in any case the Führer is right; nothing was said about it until after the wedding and then apparently it was brought to the attention of the ObdM in a very back-handed manner. In general it is customary that wives whose husbands are adjutants at the highest level are vetted as thoroughly as a company commander has to do with regard to all marriage petitions submitted by his NCOs.[161] I see in the whole affair an indictment of the Navy. It is regrettable that once again things fell into the Führer's lap, leading to sharp criticism of the officer corps with respect to its conduct and outlook. It has been clear to us younger officers for some time that the so-called marriage regulations require a thorough overhaul, and most importantly should not employ two differing yardsticks.

28 July 1939[+]

Today an interesting table group at the home of Frau Wagner. Present were the ubiquitous Lady Mitford[162] and her sister Frau Mosley.[163] The conversation ranged at length over the possibilities for Fascism in Britain. Frau Mosley presented a very optimistic picture. Emphasised that anti-semitism in Britain was increasing steadily. More interesting were the assertions of Lady Mitford, as is known a niece of Churchill.[164] She showed herself to be an expert on the British armaments situation. That was music for the ears of F. If what she said was correct, then the files of the German military attaché were wrong. She stated firmly that Britain could not fight a war. At the moment there were only eight anti-aircraft batteries available for the whole of London. The Army was equipped only with obsolete weapons and had armoured vehicles for only two divisions. And so it went on and on. Only the Navy got any praise. This was strong and could be mobilised swiftly.

To us soldiers it is not clear what Lady M.'s role actually is. Is she a spy, an informer or just the fanatical Führer-supporter she makes herself out to be? One thing is clear – she has access to an excellent information network. She always knows where F. is.

8 August 1939
Film 'Worthless Life'

Today we watched something really vile. Bouhler and Bormann showed F. a film called *Unwertes Leben*. It was about the life of incurable mental patients in a variety of institutions. It is really shocking to see it and one does not understand how the poor nursing staff can spend every working day with these unfortunate people. It must require all kinds of idealism and Christian commitment to devote oneself to it. Apparently the Reichsärzteführer[165] had the film shot and edited. Finally came the maddest idea of the lot: Bormann suggested to F. to put it on general release as a trailer in all cinemas. Brandt[166] objected at once on the grounds of causing public disquiet, and he would not exaggerate to those present the effect of having such a thing seen. He asked B. sharply what he would say if it was one of his own children there. Thank God F. agreed and forbade it.[167]

The subject attracted a long discussion. F. had very strong opinion about duties and responsibility of doctors respecting maintaining or not maintaining such lives. If he had such a child, he would always request that its life be extinguished, not least for the sake of one's fellow man. The peoples of the Orient did things better and in a more practical manner by placing the newly-born child in cold water or in the snow to establish if the creature was capable of life. Finally we came round again to the racial theme and selection in the SS. As the circle was a fairly big one, it was only a general discussion.

15 August 1939
(Flags)

F. up in arms against Army again on account of the colours trooped before him at a march-past. He could get really annoyed because he had given the nod to tradition in these things and approved the flags in the old style. The emblem of the Third Reich had been included in a modest way, but so craftily that a short-sighted standard bearer wouldn't be able to see it. Unfortunately Blomberg had let him down there. He himself had really wanted to introduce all flags at once with the national colours. The unit identification could have been sewn into a corner or on a strip of material. One could see how other countries did it in a quite reasonable way. The French had done so since the time of their Revolution. Unfortunately the German Army was anything but a revolutionary army. Tradition here, tradition there, he did not want the past to be forgotten, but the design and content was determined by the future, otherwise it might come about that flags would be paraded whose original bearers had fallen at Jena and Auerstedt. It was a very unpleasant conversation. The Führer was undoubtedly angered by other matters of which we learned nothing but his excitement was such that there was no point in interrupting him to ask. Here again Bormann seconded his

Führer and master vociferously and even went so far as to say that everything could still be changed. At the next Party rally, new military standards, in reality no different to Party banners, would be lent to the Army and if necessary theirs would be put in some drill hall.

22 August 1939*

This evening F. spoke calmly and was impressed by his talk to the generals. Gave Schmundt the job of finding out what the reaction to it was. It was particularly important with the generals, he thought, to be a really good popular psychologist and at his gatherings, irrespective of whether they involved the people in general or Party colleagues, he always knew what effect his words had had. It was different with the older officers, they adopted a staring, mask-like expression which betrayed nothing. That was how it had been today.[168]

Politically, he reiterated, he was convinced that Poland would remain isolated, Britain and France were only bluffing, and he was not intending to negotiate with the latter in the near future. If the British left him alone, he would also leave them in peace. It was different with France. There was an account to be settled over Alsace-Lorraine. That was a worry for later; but it would certainly be sorted out. F. recalled his visit to Kehl. From up on the water tower, looking at Strasbourg Cathedral, he had embraced an unshakeable resolve, and he would keep it in mind.

F. repeated, that he now saw the developments ahead more calmly than for months. The front lines were drawn up and the other side could choose. His only fear, that at the last moment a 'stupid acrobat of emotion' could spoil his determination 'with soft suggestions', and he would be forced to give ground once more.

24 August 1939

Sp(eech to the) generals (Obersalzberg).[169] Am outraged at optimism of Schm. He reported that the generals were very impressed by the speech the day before yesterday and would tackle what lay ahead with confidence. They were also convinced of the necessity for the impending moves.

Nothing could be farther from the truth. F. was very calm and objective, but the mood amongst the generals is grave.[170] Not just over Poland, but what will follow. They are expecting definite consequences with France and Britain. The fear amongst many is that F. will resort to the use of arms to settle the Polish question.

25 August 1939[+]
Reich Chancellery

The C-in-C had his big day today. Before noon the Duce's answer was received to the effect that that he was not in a position to go to war.[171] F. was totally downcast. He seemed not to know what to do next. Doubtless influenced by Göring, at midday he summoned Ribbentrop, Brauchitsch and Göring. Finally I had to fetch Halder.[172] Outcome was that the attack scheduled for tomorrow will be called off and Brauchitsch guaranteed that he would be able to blow the whistle and get everybody back in time.[173] F. was pleased and will set up new negotiations. Göring announced talks with middle-men.[174] This evening the opinion is that an attempt will be made to avoid war provided that the Poles are reasonable.

26 August 1939[+]
OKH

Have been with C-in-C, who talked at length about yesterday's conference and is not wrong in ascribing to it the successful postponement of the outbreak of war. He remarked to F. that he could push forward the mobilisation more intensively and said that this yesterday had only been a feint. He knew that many peace feelers had been put out[175] and in this question for the first time Göring had been his best confederate. Through tight lips he added: 'He knows very well that he does not want war, for it wouldn't get any better than this in wartime.'

27 August 1939[+]
OKH

Have been with C-in-C again and brought him up to date with events in the Reich Chancellery. The place is a complete shambles. Yesterday there was the collision with Hewel, with whom F. wanted to bet that even if war broke out with Poland, the British would not get themselves involved. Hewel challenged this very forcibly and replied: 'Mein Führer, do not underestimate the British. Once they see that there is no other way, then they get stubborn and do what they have to. I think I am a better judge of that than my Minister.' F. was very annoyed and broke off the conversation.

The C-in-C sees it the same way and puts the situation in such a way that F. is lost for a solution. The expected[176] step back by the Italians[177] had been a grievous disappointment for F. Now the important thing was to convince him that Britain and France would stand behind their guarantees if we attacked. He sets great store by Göring, who apparently has good contacts in England to arrange something, not only through Sweden. Dahlerus[178] is definitely one of his leading horses. Unfortunately his influence only reaches to certain English politicians and does not extend to the Cabinet or the Crown.

29 August 1939
Reich Chancellery

Another day of utter chaos and nobody can see the way clear. Certain circles are again doing what they can to abort new peace efforts, and also I now believe that these forces – they come primarily from within the Party – are stronger than those who really want to remain at peace.

F. is as never before on edge, irritable, sharp with everybody. Thus Schmundt and I had to receive a heap of abuse against the Army after it had been all quiet on that front for some time. F. emphasised that he now knew how the General Staff were thinking. Certain things had come to his knowledge about which he preferred not to speak at present. One thing was clear: he would not allow the military to give him counsel on whether there should be peace or war. He was simply unable to understand those German soldiers who feared battle. Frederick the Great would turn in his grave if he saw today's generals. All he wanted was an end to unjust behaviour by the Poles vis-à-vis the German state.[179] He did not want war at all with the others. If they were stupid enough to get involved, the blood would be on their hands, and they would have to be destroyed. He did not want another 'First Silesian War';[180] even the flags authorised by him to the Wehrmacht needed to have secular strips recording their battle honours, otherwise a glorious army would lose its identity. We left thoroughly depressed.

10 September 1939+

It keeps on revolving, i.e. around me as Army adjutant, the Fritsch affair. The Führer knows that he is with his regiment[181] and apparently it annoys him but he cannot do anything about it. Meanwhile a letter has arrived from Blomberg in which he offers his services and requests a position. Schmundt is playing an unfortunate role in this and in a conversation today with the Führer explained that Blomberg would be content to be given a corps. Undoubtedly he is seeking rehabilitation. Keitel had his doubts about showing this letter to the Führer. After discussing it with Siewert I brought up the subject with the Führer today and requested that if possible he decide

against offering Blomberg an appointment;[182] it would not be understood in Army circles, especially since Fritsch is with his regiment.
Fortunately the Führer was more clear-headed and resolute in this
matter than his senior ADC. He emphasised in candid terms that an
appointment would only be considered once Blomberg had left his
wife. Despite everything, however, he would never forget his service to
the cause that is when he gave him the 100,000-man Army for safe-
keeping, and above all his attitude towards National Socialism,[183] for
the 100,000-man Army had been a state within the state. That might
have been the right thing during the Weimar Republic but he had not
been prepared to put up with it in the Third Reich. With Blomberg's
help a large number of reactionaries amongst the Army generals had
been put out to grass and the others muzzled and shown the path of
discipline and subordination. Despite its great abilities and high
standards of training it had become a necessity to slot the
Reichswehr Army into the state, for the state was now powered by a
soldierly Party and not by portfolio-wielding parliamentarians. A truly
politically unified Army would not come into being until the next
generation, by when the spirit of the 100,000-man Army would have
been banished and that of the Hitler Youth would permeate the officer
corps. But that was a long way ahead. I put the C-in-C and Siewert
in the picture about this conversation first thing this evening.

19 September 1939
Excursion to the front with AOK 8 [Eighth Army Command].[184]
General Blaskowitz[185] escorted F. through Lodz. Visited several
divisions, also parts of the LAH [*Leibstandarte Adolf Hitler*]. Sch. and
I were horrified when Bl. suggested to the Führer forming the
numerous available Green-Police[186] and SS-*Totenkopf* units into a
division. That evening F., who had seized upon suggestion with great
enthusiasm, ordered the Reichsführer-SS to form a police division,[187]
and at the same time the majority of the *Totenkopf* units into an SS
division.[188] I told C-in-C and Gen. Fromm. Both were raging. On
political grounds F. turned down my suggestion that these units
should be given to the Army.

26 September 1939+
(Racial matters – Poland)
F. gave long and involved talk about annexation of former eastern
provinces of Posen and West Prussia currently in hand. In this
connection he explained the future of Poland, its resettlement by

Germans and how the Poles generally are to be treated. Those stratas of the Polish population considered racially valuable can be Germanised. Racial appearance and heredity are the important factors here. Originally, several centuries ago, after being settled by the German military orders, these racial groups were made up of Slav and German blood in roughly equal parts. German peasant settlers who had emigrated from the Magdeburg Erbrecht[189] to the east sought wives there. As German women were not available they had settled for Slav females, and these hot-blooded women had very quickly imposed a powerful influence on their upright husbands. In accordance with local tradition, the female was the dominant partner and accordingly much Germanness was lost and the thing had now to be overturned. A special racial group was going to be created in which the language was the most important thing. Children had to forget Polish and learn only German, although the parents could more or less carry on as they were. The benefits of the transformation process would be felt by the next generation. The important thing was, above all, that the peasant stock was maintained. He placed no value on the Polish intelligentsia. There was no place for them in the overall picture. They were dangerous, being the vehicle of Polish nationalism. Incidentally one should not overlook the church. From time immemorial Poland had always had the most radical national church; in itself that was not a bad thing but it could not be allowed in Poland. How often had he said that he wanted for Germany a radical church of that kind, whose processions were led not by modest church banners but by the national flag, and he wanted this same flag dressing the altars and flying from church towers.

28 September 1939[+]

F. is very pleased about his talks with Gauleiter Greiser.[190] The latter had the right politics for the Warthegau. As a child of the east he knew Poland and the Westmarkenverein.[191] He would liquidate the Polish intellectuals wherever he thought it justified. They had killed us earlier, one should not now shrink from the task if it was about getting rid of trouble-makers. He would have another talk with Greiser and Forster[192] regarding the direction to be taken. The two of them did not see eye to eye on this. Forster was probably a soft-liner, even towards the Polish intellectuals, and that was not promising. It was hardly surprising, though, because he was from Franconia and even in Danzig had not had many dealings with Poles, but he would soon have that straightened out. Under no circumstances did he want the smallest fragment of Polish influence to survive in the Reich provinces. In thirty years' time he wanted people to be able to drive across the country and have nothing to remind them that once upon a time these regions had been the subject of disputes between German and Pole. He would let the Reichsführer-SS know, for example, that a heavy-handed police chief[193] was coming to Danzig, a person to whom all maudlin sentimentality was anathema, who would suppress with all means at his disposal any cultural activity of the Polish people.

1 October 1939[+]

F. was outspoken in his anger at Forster, who differs from Greiser[194] in his ideas on how to handle the Polish people. As was to be expected, the Army received a few more side-swipes. F. said to Schmundt and myself that von Heitz's[195] influence was undoubtedly making itself felt with Forster. He had heard from other sources that Forster was in favour of the mild route. But that was typical of those officers who were sometimes like children in political matters and as a result of their upbringing and work simply did not understand historical connections and political requirements. In a short while he would announce that no Polish lawyer was practising in Posen and West Prussia, and Polish doctors were only there under German control and if necessary. It is now clear even to the simple-minded that no Pole has a place in any remaining offices and positions. The best thing would be if large sections of the Polish people could be resettled in an area where they could be reabsorbed. A good example was the Ruhr, where virtually all Poles there have been Germanised.

4 October 1939

Very serious and interesting conversation with Brandt.[196] Br. had spoken to Bishop Gr(af) Galen[197] in Münster and [had] discussed Church and other problems with him. It appears that the bishop had been very forthright and told him a great deal about morale generally, war morale and how the people felt. Apparently the bishop also held nothing back even when speaking about the Jewish question and detainees. Br. was very impressed by the personality and very reflective over many things. To my question if (he) would be making a full report to the Führer he was evasive and replied: 'If I repeated to the Führer everything that Gr(af) Galen told me, he would have us both locked up.' They got on so well together that Graf Galen asked Brandt to visit again.

On the same day I was able to inform C-in-C and Siewert about this matter.

8 October 1939[+]
Ghettos

Within a small circle F. spoke comprehensively about the Jewish problem which had come to his attention so visibly during his visits to Poland and had to be resolved not only in Germany but also in other countries within the German sphere of influence. It was not a religious but a racial problem. He continued to ponder why he had been so humane and liberal with the Nuremberg Laws. At that time the idea had occurred to him to rid himself of the 600,000 German Jews in a kind of business deal, and his 1937 plan to offer this half million or so Jews to Britain as a workforce for Palestine had been perfectly serious.[198] But it had not gone down well with the British and other nations. Britain had told him in no uncertain terms in a diplomatic note that they had quite enough of this problem in Palestine already and preferred not to invite further unrest.

Even if the political influence of the Jews in Poland had been slight, the whole affair would still have had to be dealt with rigorously. The setting up of large ghettos, such as those at Lublin and Lodz, had already begun. But these would be insufficient, and there would have to be several more. Former army camps and fortresses would be ideal. Within them, Jews could have autonomy, even their own police, and could then resolve their differences amongst themselves; that they would have to work was obvious. Such a solution had been neglected in Germany. It could not be achieved by distinctive badges and so forth. Together with Himmler and Heydrich he would decide, once Poland had fallen, to what extent the main Jewish population could be shifted around locally, or into the Protectorate.

F. laughed as he recounted the episode in which the Foreign Minister had been in Moscow with Stalin working out the respective limits of the mutual occupation zones. When Ribbentrop demanded the Suwalki height, arguing that it formed part of the border with East Prussia, Stalin attempted to talk him out of it with the following advice: 'Don't take this area, if the Reich Chancellor knew how many Jews live there, he would certainly reject it.' F. then embarked upon a monologue, and none of his Party friends butted in. I sat in the background near the fireplace, the only officer present. Also there amongst others Dr Dietrich,[199] Schirach,[200] Esser,[201] the Munich Gauleiter Wagner[202] and Murr.[203]

I was very depressed and will report the matter to the C-in-C tomorrow, for the whole affair will greatly involve the occupation forces.

15 October 1939[+]
Heitz's Report

F. was very excited and rained reproaches on the Army. Reason was that Heitz had presented a report from local centres which mentioned the arbitrary executions of Jews and Polish intellectuals[204] including at Mewe, Graudenz and Thorn. This document had been forwarded to SS- and police chief von Alvensleben;[205] from him it went to Heydrich, who sent it on its short journey to the Reich Chancellery. The point was, officers had to keep all maudlin sentimentality to themselves. What was necessary to be done to bring peace to the old Reich territories was no business of the Wehrmacht, and it should keep its nose out of what did not concern it. Earlier, the Poles themselves had not been fussy when their turn had come to deal with the German minority. He had already given instructions that the process should be made known to all heads of the Westmarkenverein. I saw the C-in-C again today to keep him informed. He cursed and is asking personally for a report from Danzig.

7 November 1939
Reich Chancellery

Br. requested a private talk with F.[206] Siewert told me that Br. wanted to make some decisive points to F. Asked F., and to my surprise he agreed. C-in-C left F. at 1350 hrs; said to me in passing only: 'Now it's all up, he doesn't believe me.' S. told me that C-in-C had presented a memorandum from Gen.Qu.[207]

1700 hrs with Schm. to F. The latter very irate, spoke of sabotage by Army. The memo was a pack of lies and asked for the alleged mutinous groups to be identified. [Engel's addition: Only third-rank divisions were involved which by their nature did not have the same outlook as active units.] Ordered me to ascertain the facts by going there myself to clarify the situation. Now he wants to distance himself from C-in-C and dictated a record of the conversation to Frl. Schröder. F. placed this in his safe.

F. is significantly calmer today. He had a long talk with Keitel. Latter told Schm., he had advised F. against dismissing C-in-C as there was no obvious successor. In the evening spoke at length with Schm. [F.] told him the whole crisis of confidence was the fault of the

Army and change would eventually have to come about. F. stated that he could not accept Reichenau or anyone else.

10 November 1939

F. received C-in-C in private.[208] Was there briefly to deliver various reports. Impression was awful; without advice or having been put in picture by ourselves, C-in-C had submitted a memo about the state and preparedness of the Army. Files came from General Wagner. Contents according to F.: Army (was) unreliable; amongst reserve-units (cases) of signs of disintegration in Poland; (Army) not in the position to carry out further aggressive war. F. was beside himself, sent for Christa Schröder for dictation regarding dismissal of C-in-C. We endured some bitter hours. Siewert told me in the evening it had only been done in order to make F. think in terms of peace.

18 November 1939
Reich Chancellery

Siewert sent for me and handed me a memorandum[209] from Gen. Blaskowitz about the situation in Poland; serious concern about illegal shootings, arrests and seizures. Worries about Army discipline amongst those who see these things going on; local discussions with SD [Sicherheitsdienst – Security Service] and Gestapo unsuccessful, they refer back to orders from Reichsführer-SS. Please, restore rule of law, above all only carry out executions which result from proper judicial proceedings.

Submitted the memo, which is precisely factual, to F. the same afternoon. He read through it calmly then lashed out furiously against 'infantile attitude' in Army High Command. The war couldn't be run with Salvation Army methods. A long-held aversion came to light. He had never trusted Gen. Bl. He had been opposed to giving him command of an army, and considered it right to relieve him of it since he was unsuitable. Informed C-in-C and Siewert, also OQu.IV.[210]

22 November 1939
Reich Chancellery

Telephone call from Guderian. Wanted to speak alone with F. Came at once. In with him an hour.[211] Told me afterwards he had retrieved Gen.Qu. memorandum.[212] Considers relationship between C-in-C and F. intolerable. Had assured F. that troops were not as portrayed. Did not have a name in mind for successor. (I) was present at the tail-end as I had to fetch some Panzer files. Conversation was warm and friendly and then turned technical. Agreement on need to upgrade weapons Pz. II and IV. Also all Pz. division artillery [to be put] on mobile chassis.

23 November 1939
C-in-C – Talks
Decisive conf(erence) with F.[213] All possibilities of an end to the war and a separate treaty with a Polish government, of which F. has spoken several times, have been destroyed. F. informed C-in-C, Keitel and Jodl of his firm resolve to attack in the W(est) as soon as possible, and moreover in the winter, in any case before Christmas. In his opinion the Army is ready. Long waiting periods were a curse, cold and frost less a danger than people always said. F. spoke of offensive which would begin if possible at the beginning of December.[214] He was making that dependent on what the meteorologists promised, however. This was decisive because the Luftwaffe was essential. In the midst of political and operational ideas he switched to trivialities, considering the possibilities of surprise raids and landings near anti-tank obstructions. He hit out at the Army repeatedly. In conclusion all three C-in-Cs asked for more armaments, Field Marshal Göring the most strident. The attitude of the ObdM [Raeder] was rather peculiar, welcoming the invasion of Belgium and Holland from a naval point of view because he would then have better forward bases for his U-boats.[215] I accompanied C-in-C, who was very serious and thoughtful.

6 December 1939
Dramatic argument about the decisive point of attack.[216] F. dismissed the 'old Schlieffen ham'. Other ideas were floated, primarily to split the French and British. He saw no problem in sending Panzers through the mountains. Ordered a new plan to be worked out but offered no concrete suggestions himself based on how he saw it. In this connection very critical of Br. and Ha. His ideas were being deliberately sabotaged, but he would prevail even if he didn't happen to be a learned General Staff officer.

10 December 1939
Succession C-in-C. The disaster is still rumbling.[217] F. had a long talk with Schmundt and me about his decision to make the final break with C-in-C.[218] He needed optimists, not the opposite. He had

nothing personal against the colonel-general, but he had no use for political worriers. Actually the best thing to do would be to smoke the General Staff out into the Bendlerstrasse and start again with young people. Frederick the Great had said that generals understood nothing about politics, but the fact they were frightened to go to war was knowledge that had been kept from him. If only he knew a possible successor. He had had to turn down Reichenau since he considered him unreliable. He was not demanding a National Socialist, only somebody who would be faithful to, and blindly follow, his political aims. Schobert[219] was very passionate here, but in his opinion not sufficiently mature, and even Guderian was out of the question for various reasons; and he had a lot of enemies amongst the generals. Schmundt pleaded for Reichenau, but failed to convince F.

14 December 1939

F. and the visiting Himmler greatly irate about the allocation of divisional priests to the SS-Polizeidivision.[220] Scathing remarks about military spiritual care. The pastors were viruses and agitators, closet reactionaries misusing religious belief in order to fish in dark waters. One had to consider how to abolish spiritual care altogether. Better to employ the clergy as drivers instead of pastors.[221] Hard words about Bishop Dohrmann; one knew only too well what circles he frequented and how closely he was tied up with the 'Bekennenden Kirche'. These were Himmler's words, and he went on to say that nobody was being accepted into the SS if he had not demonstrably abandoned the church.[222] F. would not go as far as that, but was not sparing with biting remarks directed primarily against the evan[gelical] Church, which was currently a threat to the state.

26 December 1939
Hymns and Carols

Back from our Christmas visits.[223] We went to [Infantry Regiment] *Großdeutschland*[224] at Montabaur, to the *Leibstandarte* and Spicherer Höhen near Saarbrücken along the Westwall. The festivities of *GD* at Kloster Montabaur and also 75th Infantry Division at Saarbrücken were particularly impressive. Grim and anything but Christmassy were the *Leibstandarte* celebrations. Schmundt and I were surprised that even the F. talked about it for some time and for a change shared our opinion. In this connection he mentioned hymns and said there was nothing more uplifting than certain German hymns he knew. Bormann had tried to get him to issue a directive

that Christmas carols should not be played or sung in F's presence.
He was very much opposed to this. 'Silent Night' was one of the finest
carols ever, and irrespective of his views about the church he would
never miss hearing this carol sung at Christmas Eve. Church
leadership and cultural heritage was something else. He was at
present at odds with the church leadership since they insisted upon
remaining outside the state–political sphere. He would need to be
stupid and ill-informed, especially in view of the spiritual values of
the Catholic Church, if he failed to recognise what lay behind it. But
even Luther and his movement had made enormous strides. As head
of state, however, he was not going to let the church have a final say
nor, what was worse, that church authorities prescribed what he had
to do or permit within the state in which they enjoyed the rights of
hospitality.

1940

20 January 1940[225]

Relationship to the Church

F. spoke at length again about religious belief and his attitude to the churches. Undoubtedly under sniper fire from B(ormann) and H(immler) a less conciliatory attitude is developing. Whereas in the past he wanted to live and let live, he is now determined to fight the churches. F. literally: 'The war, here as in many other areas, presents a favourable opportunity to dispose of it (the church question) root and branch.' In days gone by, whole peoples had been liquidated. Tribes had settled nearby, the Soviet Union had recently provided plenty of examples how that could be done. One thing that the Germans had not been bettered in was their thoroughness and inclination to tradition, even to mysticism. If he continued to take no action against the rebellious clergy, then that was not least for the sake of the Wehrmacht. There the men ran to religious services in the field, and he preferred to have a soldier who was brave because he believed in God rather than a soldier who was cowardly because he did not. But here education in the SS, which was proving in wartime that a man schooled in the world view of affairs could also be brave without God, was showing the necessary way forward.

22 January 1940

F. – Schm.

F. spoke out in highly excited tones to criticise the Wehrmacht marriage regulations, describing them as 'reactionary, aimed at encouraging celibacy and narrow-minded'. A youth suddenly thrust into manhood with the responsibility of bearing arms had to be allowed to consort with a woman to satisfy his sexual predisposition. This was obviously the healthiest way to prevent him sinking into degeneracy. At the latest by age 22 the soldier must have the right to marry, and so he would amend these stupid marriage rules; the SS was much more up-to-date and closer to the people in this respect than the Army. How would one go about increasing the population if the foundation of a family was put back another five years? In wartime such regulations were sheer stupidity, since they postponed the next generation. I argued intensively to the contrary. F. allowed me to make my point in full. Schm. seconded me but not unreservedly, although he found the age of 27 too high.

My argument was that in barracks young officers and NCOs were responsible for the personnel subordinated to them even once the daily duty was terminated: financial provisions for married ensigns were completely absent. The conscript was being trained not only while on duty but also off duty. It was undesirable that young officers and NCOs should have the additional responsibility of a family. Commitment and supervision would suffer together with inner morale. Absolutely clear that once again the Reichsführer is agitating behind the scenes. When I informed C-in-C and Siewert, the former said he would not be changing anything.

February 1940[+]
Sumner Welles

The visit of the American Secretary of State S.W.[226] has whipped up a lot of dust. I fetched him once for a conference. S.W. was dazzling, ice-cold, dry, and converses, so far as we the escort can ascertain, with a very careworn expression. To judge by the talks with the F., latter is not in the least delighted by this visit. He is raging about the attempt by the US President[227] to pre-empt him. There was no doubt but that this individual was sent to Europe to spy and sound out the situation. It was truly infantile that this man had addressed him regarding the status quo in the Polish question. He would show him what such a status meant. Here he was, just starting to introduce a New Order in Europe when along comes this person suggesting he should put everything back just as it was. He had made it clear to him in no uncertain terms that it was quite out of the question and had also explained that, as much as it pained him to be at war with Britain, he must pursue a new direction in Europe. It was now too late for anything else. He knew well that this emissary had left him in a dissatisfied mood, but could be sure that he could expect nothing from him. It would appear that S.W. had made the allegation that the Wehrmacht High Command had a more moderate political outlook. He had also discovered that the man had attempted to conduct talks within Wehrmacht circles, which he had forbidden at once.[228] He would not permit this clever personality to be alone with Göring[229] for he was dangerous, that could not be mistaken. But there was one good thing about this visit. Roosevelt would definitely learn through his emissary that it would be a very costly step for America to enter the war.

4 February 1940[+]

Schmundt was at Koblenz[230] where he spoke to the C-in-C,[231] Manstein[232] and Blumentritt.[233] He returned very impressed by a long conversation with Manstein who had expressed great reservations with regard to the proposed OKH operational plan.[234] Schmundt was very excited and told me that, whilst with Manstein, he had ascertained that M.'s plan contained the same opinion regarding the best concentration of forces, albeit in a significantly more precise form, as that continually advocated by the Führer. He had also spoken to Blumentritt whose ideas coincided with those of Manstein, except that B. was more cautious although very critical of Halder.

5 February 1940[+]

Schmundt reported to F. about his Koblenz impressions. He spoke frankly about what Manstein had said and the Führer became more and more interested despite his personal aversion to Manstein which he is unable to hide. Schmundt suggested summoning Manstein to hear his ideas.[235] F. agreed at once but ordered both Schmundt and myself not to mention this proposed conference to the C-in-C or Halder. This made me feel very bad, because I have instructions from OKH to the contrary and I also happen to see it as my duty to report there everything that goes on at the Reich Chancellery.

10 February 1940

Diplomatic protocol has hit F. hard again. He complained of it in terms which were not nice. It was a reservoir of blockheads who had been unable to make the grade as hoteliers or the chief wine-waiter at a trattoria. In one thing these protocol officials led the world: they took themselves extremely seriously and the late arrival of a head of state at breakfast was worse than his declaring war on the Emperor of China. In due course he would make revolutionary changes and deprive these imposters of their power, at least insofar as it affected himself or Party and state receptions. He sometimes felt like a pointer being led round the showring by the tall Dörnberg.[236] It went on like this for some time. Ribbentrop, who was probably the real target, tried to argue, but made little headway.

13 February 1940
Reich Chancellery
Present: Reich Minister Frank,[237] F., some of the time v. Below and I, Bormann. R(eich) Minister Fr. reported about situation in General-Government Poland. Reported about resettlements, rounding-up of Jews.[238] Vile stirrings against the military commander, field commanders etc. (These) disturbing the 'peace'. Commanders had no instinct, obstructed him and his offices frequently in the execution of their appointed tasks.[239] He requested the greatest possible exclusion of the military, above all in political matters, since they had a pronounced anti-Party attitude. F. broke into a rage which persisted into the situation conference. I advised C-in-C and Siewert.

19 February 1940[+]
(F. – Manstein)
The F. – Manstein discussion has taken place. The Führer is overjoyed at Manstein's ideas and observed: 'The man is not to my liking, but he knows something about how to get things done.' F. used disparaging comments to describe Halder and C-in-C. Remarks like 'Army-cadet ideas' were typical. There are going to be some new, earth-shaking revelations, because F. will now definitely do what he had always insisted, and change the operational plan.

Schmundt and I escorted Manstein on his way out. He complained about the OKH and said that his ideas were nothing new there. In gratitude he had been given an infantry corps, and this to a man who had begged for a Panzer corps. Halder would not now be able to oppose it. With Beck this had been rather different.

28 February 1940[+]
Today something really crazy which Hewel told me in the strictest confidence. I was talking about the visit to Munich. H. and I were of the same opinion that these trips are heavy going for those members of the entourage who have no personal affiliation to Munich. There is nothing to do there and one is practically homeless, spending half the time in front of the telex machine at the Prinzregentenplatz [flat] and cannot wait to leave. I said that the only things of interest were the visits to the Haus der Kunst and F.'s art purchases. At this H. asked me if I knew that the curator at the Führer building, a Frau Aase or something similar, was a full Jewess. I could simply not believe this. Whether F. knew or not he could not say. Bormann certainly knew and without a shadow of a doubt Hoffmann, who worked closely with

this woman and never got a raw deal with her. She had first-class contacts abroad, especially in France, and obtained valuable works of art which were collected for the Linz Gallery[240] by Bormann and Hoffmann. The whole thing seems incredible as far as I am concerned, but is probably true because H. went into it very thoroughly.

4 March 1940
(Schm., F., Nat. Soc. Schooling)

F. complained to Schm. and myself about numerous clashes between Party members and Wehrmacht, mainly in the Rhineland, and placed the blame squarely on the officers. There were still far too many reactionary elements there who provoked trouble. Both Schm. and I disputed this quoting unequivocal proof from reports we had received that the Gauleiters were responsible. F. expressed some completely new ideas about political training in the Wehrmacht which had now become necessary.[241] He did not want unpolitical soldiers any longer. It meant that they had no world view and therefore now no war aims. The way they did it in Russia was not such a bad thing. There the troops had political officers who taught world politics and also cared for the men. He wanted something similar if in a somewhat different form. He would speak with Bormann and Keitel about it. Suitable officers were definitely more widely available now than previously; they might come from the officer reserve, the SA, the SS and the political leadership. The non-political attitude of the Reichswehr had been understandable of course, but in principle a bad thing. On the one hand strong, on the other for the political reason weak. Many officers of the former Reichswehr were undermining this so-called strength today. The principal danger had now been averted, since there were no longer Party disputes, but only the will of the Party. I was horrified and Schmundt inspired. He wants to start the business straight away and put it into writing for Keitel. Not sure how I am going to put this to my C-in-C, who will certainly gnash his teeth when he hears.

Saw Siewert who, as I expected, was anything other than edified. Took it soberly and will discuss with C-in-C and Halder how these ideas can best be opposed when the time comes.

14 March 1940
Princes

Today occurred an embarrassing and almost inexplicable uproar about princes on one of the regular occasions when the subject crops up. The Army Personnel Office had submitted through Schmundt personnel changes in which Prince Oskar[242] was recommended for promotion to general. At the moment the prince is commanding a regiment at the Westwall near Trier. F. took it absolutely personally and vented his feelings in the most extravagant manner, calling them drones, good-for-nothing etc., only interested in the upkeep of their own households and their own advancement. He knew very well the stance of these people towards his person and did not intend honouring this disguised sabotage. If it were up to him, he would not have any prince serving in the Wehrmacht. In this regard unfortunately Göring had a peculiar romantic streak. A short while ago he had given him to understand that the continual meetings with the crown princes were completely wrong, irrespective of the individual case. The families were international and, especially in wartime, ideal sources of information for the enemy because of their internationalist taint.[243] Indicative here were marriages between individual princely houses, where belief [in dangers of inbreeding] was also not taken seriously. Degeneration then followed and one could see what the result was. It would have been far better for the princes to have taken robust farmgirls as wives to improve the stock. The tirade was turbulent as never before and not pleasant. To Schmundt's credit it has to be stated that he made the case once the anger had subsided, and praised Prince Oskar as a soldier. As so often, F. broke off the discussion, left us standing and shut the door behind him on leaving. Schmundt said that no matter what he would bring the subject up again.

15 March 1940
Paragraph 175
I presented to F. several petitions for sentences to be mitigated to front-arrest in respect of officers and NCOs sentenced for homosexual offences. All cases were so-called borderline breaches, mostly the consequence of alcohol. OKH had approved the petitions. I made my report accordingly but came off badly. F. dismissed all the applications in harsh terms. In explanation he said that in sexual matters his attitude was neither puritanical nor jesuitic. If it concerned normal congress between the sexes and involved neither violence nor intimidation of dependents one would be open-minded. Hypocrisy lay here with the churches and old maids. In this respect the Lord God had created animals and humans similarly. History

taught that sexual relations between members of the same sex were the beginning of the end of a nation's existence. Sparta and Rome, where the cult of the gods had been extensively misused, had proved it. It was high level decadence which he was going to destroy root and branch. He knew the dangers in colleges very well, and he would see to it that the sexes found each other in early youth, for example through dancing and sport, and if there happened to be offspring, the only thing that needed to be ensured was that they came within Nat(ional) Soc(ialist) guidelines racially. Bringing them up would be the responsibility of the state. In this regard the SS had embarked upon a very sensible path. My heart was heavy, for I had wanted to help two colleagues.

4 April 1940
The Clergy
During a related discussion Bormann surprised F. with files he had received about the anti-state attitude of Cath(olic) clergymen in Bavaria. He presented so-called pulpit-letters[244] whose authenticity we doubt. Presently it became obvious to Schmundt and myself that these files were simply a means to an end and served the exclusive purpose of attacking spiritual care in the Wehrmacht. Amongst these clergymen was allegedly a divisional priest, currently on leave, who had preached a sermon in Wasserburg, I believe, about the 'unspirituality' of the Party. B. was up in arms and this time recommended F. to abolish religion in the Wehrmacht. Said that according to his information the troops did not want priests and found them a nuisance. The SS did not have them, and they were no worse for it. Schmundt and I disputed this violently and said frankly that priests engaged in care work, above all with sick and wounded, were indispensable and frequently a support for the commanders. To Bormann's objection that it was all done under duress, I challenged him to support his allegations with names and units. F. stopped the discussion. These things were premature and, despite his known aversion to the clergy, he did not want to change anything at the moment.

16 April 1940
Reich Chancellery
Am back from my Norway flight with Deyhle.[245] Explored situation in Oslo, Andalsnes. Situation southern Norway not in least desperate. Army magnificent. C-in-C certain of victory. Worry about whether

Luftwaffe can keep skies clear. Attitude of Norwegian population varies.[246] Call for more Panzers. Pz. Abt [Panzer Abteilung – Battalion] 40 (Volckheim) not enough. F. very sceptical about Army mentality (Falkenhorst).[247] They are too weak and do not understand the political necessities. Will advise C-in-C tomorrow morning.

2 May 1940
Gypsies

Once again great excitement and hullabaloo. F. received files, either from Bormann or the Reichsführer, about German gypsies enjoying their military service and the Army generally. These would be the so-called 'sedentary' gypsies from the Nuremberg area. In this connection F. explained to Schm. and myself in very excited tones that gypsies are aliens and must be treated in the same way as Jews in accordance with the Nuremberg Laws. The Reichsführer-SS had quite definite instructions on how this racial group[248] was to be handled, and they would be taken out from there. Here again he expected there would be another of the usual efforts – similar to that experienced with many persons of part-Jewish extraction – to have them disappear into the Army beneath the mantle of Christian neighbourly love. This outlet for mixed race persons and similar was too much for him, and he would talk to Keitel about it. Schm. gave me the job of getting the matter clarified as soon as possible with OKH and above all with the BdE [Befehlshaber des Ersatzheer – Commander Reserve Army].

3 May 1940
Gypsies

Have clarified the gypsy situation with the Army General Office and OKH.[249] Once again we have been ambushed by the Prinz Albrecht Palace.[250] The facts are correct, but not the circumstances. These are people of so-called gypsy descent with bona fide identity passes, therefore they are in the system and the WBKs [Military Districts] were correct in conscripting them. The thing was set in motion following reports by informers to Party centres. Apparently, as always, there is an economic interest, since these former gypsy families are rich and have prosperous businesses. This evening in the presence of Schm. I reported this clearly and candidly. The Führer did not like it; however, he made no comment except that he would have further investigations made. Whatever the case I have told him the truth.

23 May 1940

Telephone conversation F. with Göring. Field marshal of the opinion that the great mission of the Luftwaffe is imminent: wipe out the British in northern France.[251] All the Army has to do is occupy. We were furious, F. happy. Jodl said: 'He's bitten off more than he can chew.'

25 May 1940

Field marshal paid a visit to F. lasting an hour or so. During stroll G. reported on his assessment regarding elimination of enemy by Luftwaffe. Impression: G. successfully stirred it up against Army. F. emphasised repeatedly the political reliability of the Luftwaffe in contrast to the Army.

26 May 1940

Jeschonnek[252] delivered a report at situation conference. Confirmed that Luftwaffe would wipe out British; however, would need support of Army Group B units.

27 May 1940

Field marshal landed in Fieseler Storch. Discussion with F. in conference barrack. Göring reported success at Dunkirk, said: 'Only fishing boats are coming over [sic]; I hope the Tommies are good swimmers.'

27 May 1940
Charleroi [Army Group B HQ]

Detailed discussion F. with Ru(ndstedt).[253] Sodenstern[254] and Blumentritt delivered reports. Diverse assessments, no real clarity. Surprise that F. broadly leaving decision to R. On return to Felsennest[255] will ring R. and put him in the picture.

28 May 1940
Kaiser Wilhelm II

Today a short, interesting discussion between F. and Keitel to which I was witness. Keitel had apparently received a communication from the royal household at Doorn, that the Kaiser had expressed the wish to be allowed to return to Germany. F. curtly dismissed the idea with the observation: 'That would suit reactionary circles.' There would be sharp reaction abroad, too, and the idea of the restoration of the monarchy would receive fresh impetus. Keitel blew the same trumpet and asked only, by way of an answer, that the final decision should not be taken until the termination of hostilities.[256]

10 June 1940[+]

F. is horrified by letter from Duce.[257] What upset him most was the 'official announcement' of a declaration of war on France. Phrases like: 'This is the last declaration of war in the world I wanted' dropped from his lips: 'I had never thought the Duce could be so primitive': 'I have often been amazed recently at his naivety. For me the whole letter is the proof that in future in political matters I will have to be much more cautious with the Italians.' F. also did not understand the general sense of the letter. Apparently Mussolini has the idea that this 'campaign for booty' will be just like a stroll in the 'Passo romano'. He is going to get a surprise! The French have less respect for the Italians than they have for us. It is not going to be a stroll. In itself if is embarrassingly opportunistic: first of all they are too cowardly to fight with us and now they cannot join us fast enough to get their share of the swag. Declarations of war are just a symbol of a hypocritical political stance which wants to portray itself as chivalrous. Ethics did not arrive until the growth of civilisation. There were no declarations of war in ancient times. One simply marched in, surprised them! That is of itself the proper, healthy method. I will never in my lifetime sign a declaration of war, only act.

Once again it was pathetic how Keitel seconded what was said and egged F. on with ridiculous interjections of support.

14 June 1940
F. – Schmundt – Hewel – Engel – and Others
Long discussion and dialogue by F. about Oswald Mosley after dinner. Does not think much of him as a personality; on other hand said he is only Englishman to understand the German–European idea, [and] was taken more seriously in Britain than in Germany. Even Churchill and Bernard Shaw were frightened of him, but respected the man. When a vain personality like de Gaulle,[258] who in general does no more than roll up his sleeves, pays him respect, there must be something behind it. Pity that he was no statesman, but more a member of the intelligentsia. Labour [Party] had committed the worst stupidity in letting him go. Perhaps he might have been able to prevent this war. In Bayreuth he had often talked about M. with Lady Mitford and her sister. But these had typical English reserve and were distrustful. Mosley could never have become a leader of the people

like himself, but at least the spiritual leader of a real Anglo-German accord. He was convinced that Mosley's role was not yet over and done with. He was in any case a rank opponent of the cronyism.

20 June 1940
Chimay (Bruly de Pesche)[259]

C-in-C with F., had his big hour. Described winding down of operations and preparations for armistice.[260] Advised F. absolutely necessary either [to negotiate] peace with Britain immediately or prepare to invade and do so as quickly as possible. F. was sceptical and considers Britain to be so weak that major operations on land not necessary after aerial bombing campaign. Army would move in and perform mission as occupation force. F. made observation: 'so that in one way or another they back down'.

20 June 1940
Chimay

F. wants Breker[261] and other artists and architects[262] to visit FHQ. Even if the gentlemen understood nothing of war and politics, they were indispensable for the development of German art. Schm. asked: What should they wear? F. answered: Whatever they like, fancy dress is best, in uniform [they are] only comical figures.

26 June 1940
Bruly de P.

F. talked again about trip to Paris[263] which had impressed him deeply; praised Napoleon and French kings, who had really thought and planned on the grand scale. Lucky for him that he had artists who knew Paris and for whom it was an example. Lacking knowledge of the beauties of Paris, Speer and Breker would never have developed in the way they had. F. had a laugh about the fantasy uniforms worn by Giesler and Breker;[264] it just went to show, that truly great artistic men could never be soldiers, only unmilitary figures, but he did not mind. Artistic men could also never be politicians. He did not remember ever having exchanged a word on politics with Breker, and the latter had never addressed him on anything political. After his visit to Paris, however, he understood his love of France. Artists saw only the beauty in things and transmitted it to others. Since politics was anything other than beautiful, true artists saw in politics only something of disinterest, something which at most could disturb their social circles. It was rather different with the Jews. These needed art as the expression of their character and saw in nature and humanity something to be distorted, with much irony and frivolity. Otherwise it was not possible to understand such de-beautified art. Here the best example in painting and sculpture was above all the depiction of the female body. There one could only speak of a mockery of the being modelled by God.

4 July 1940
Kaiser's Postcard
Today there was a droll thing. F. was shown a gold-edged postcard from the Kaiser bearing the former monarch's picture. On the reverse was the text of a letter from Wilhelm II to F., in which he had sent his best wishes for military success and expressed the hope that the change in fortunes which had crowned the glorious German Army with new laurels might enable him to re-visit the homeland at the earliest opportunity.[265] The text was respectful throughout, typical of what we have heard said of the Kaiser of old. For him, time has simply stood still. F. laughed about the postcard but all the same asked if it was being distributed through the Wehrmacht as a leaflet. He was reassured on this point by Keitel. It was merely a postcard which the Kaiser autographed and handed to officers and soldiers who came to visit Doorn Castle.[266]

15 July 1940
Canaris[267] was with F. Main point of conversation, as always in recent weeks, Britain.[268] F. mourned not having brought the Duke[269] aboard when the opportunity existed. Even he had been at fault there and taken things into consideration which he now regretted; but the former king's hands had been tied from the start too, and who knew how decisive had been not only the court advisers but also the connection between his wife and Amer[ican] high finance. One thing was clear, the Duke was through and through a socialist and in his train of thought more Labour than Conservative.

The case of Mosley was another matter. If and when one could get hold of him. Here F. regretted fate of Lady Mitford. She had lost her nerve just at the moment when for the first time she could really have been of use to him.[270] Previously she had often been a nuisance, and he had heard loud mutterings from his circle, now her relationship [to Mosley] could be useful.

My impression is that F. is now more irresolute than ever and does not know what to do next. If he will make the Reichstag speech?[271]

22 July 1940[+]
Awards

F. spoke about promotions following the French campaign and mentioned especially those he had approved in the case of the highest Wehrmacht generals.[272] He had done it intentionally and deliberately, having learnt from history. In bygone ages kings and Roman emperors had bestowed great awards upon those responsible for great achievements, and even the Prussian kings had been very generous in this respect. It had been a quite clever thing to do, for the more one honoured bravery and military success, the more indebted and duty-bound did the recipients become, quite independent of their personal beliefs, to their oath and to the figure they had to thank for the honour. In this way he was linking a tax-free gratuity to the promotions to field marshal and colonel-general which – he would discuss this with Reichsminister Lammers – would amount to RM 4,000 monthly for the former and RM 2,000 monthly for the latter.[273] When the war was finally won, he would not be miserly in the distribution of land. Many inherited properties of the nobility had come into being in this manner and even Frederick the Great had been very open-handed in this regard. He did not require of a general that he be a National Socialist, but what he did expect of a general and an officer was that he subordinate himself in politics utterly to the political leadership and execute blindly whatever the political leadership demanded of him. That would be easier to accomplish, even against one's inner conviction, as the recipient of honours awarded by the head of state, and by this means of itself and also towards the state he would feel duty-bound to so act.

10 August 1940
Only F., Hewel, Lorenz, Schaub,[274] *A(lbert Bormann),*[275] *(Engel)*

Flew to the Berg (Obersalzberg). F. had received detailed reports (from) Guderian about impressions and experiences with Red Army September/October 1939 at Brest-Litovsk etc.[276] Reported very unfavourably about Soviet armaments and morale. Especially tanks, old and obsolete. Signals system also very backward. In the evening F. spoke at length about the observations and said: 'If we get to grips with this colossus the right way first time, then it will collapse far quicker than the world expects.[277] If only we can destroy it.' Advised C-in-C next day about this conversation.

17 August 1940

In today's situation conference uproar and powerful outburst by F. against Luftwaffe. The occurrence was basically a personnel matter. In response to a question by F., the Chief of the General Staff reported that two General Staff officers had been shot down over England and were now PoWs,[278] Schlichting and Bremer, both close colleagues from Stettin. F. is provided every day with foreign newspaper reports, had read about this claim in the British press and took it for a hoax. Now he was up in arms, all the more so because the British were gleefully announcing that Schlichting had been a long-serving General Staff officer to Secretary of State Milch.[279] F. wants to speak to Reichsmarschall [Göring] about it: he could not be reached (or got somebody to say so). Poor J. [Jeschonnek] had to take the brunt. F. ordered that General Staff officers were no longer to fly on operational missions. This fooling around over England had to stop; it was sheer stupidity and now look what the result was. F. wanted to be informed if these officers had had the consent of their superiors to fly with a bomber squadron, and if not there would be courts-martial. It went on in this vein for hours.

Once the situation conference finished we had a long discussion about it and decided it was not so tragic. It was almost beneficial that this time for a change it was the Luftwaffe fat in the fire and not the Army.

19 August 1940

Situation Conference (Göring, C-in-C, Jeschonnek)

Reichsmarschall reported on air war: strengthening of ground defences, neglect of aerial defences. F. broke out in rage when G. reported on Bremer and Schlichting being shot down. G. denied any culpability and shifted blame on immediate subordinates who had given permission for these General Staff officers to accompany raids. It had now been most strictly forbidden by him. Jesch[onnek] tried to argue on the basis that even General Staff officers had to obtain impressions of the front and the enemy. This was rejected harshly by F.; they could take over units and leave aerial excursions to others. Long discussion about Schlichting, Milch's No. 1 General Staff officer. F. afraid they would be especially pleased to get their hands on him. J. made good character references for Schl. and also Bremer and rejected his concerns.

In the evening F. brought up the subject again and was still very annoyed. Nevertheless we argued the point. I compared it to opportunities in the Army, there too General Staff officers had to go to the front to gain their personal impressions.

15 September 1940
Berg(hof) (F.-Gö)
Long discussion about the situation. After Britain turned down offer,[280] Gö. still of the opinion that Britain can be defeated in the air. Condemned Raeder and Navy, since they were frightened of invading. Demanded increase in armaments for Luftwaffe. Detailed discussion about Russia. *Both* [italics in original] evaluate Russian forces as scanty. Guderian report about impression of Brest-Litovsk.[281] Intention, eventually also attack on Russia in order to deprive Britain of any future pact possibility.[282]

24 October 1940
Montoire
Was with Dörnberg in the train. He asked about the discussion at Hendaye, in which I participated in part as 'air raid siren.'[283] F. very upset, if not actually wild, since Caudillo [Franco] very reserved and made the Gibraltar operation conditional on fulfillment of comprehensive demands: fuel, coal, weapons. F remarked: 'He is a waverer just like many of ours.' Doubtless an allusion to C-in-C and Chief General Staff. We expected a lot from today's meeting. Dörnberg appalled by his chief,[284] who continually stirred up F.

28 October 1940
F. in a rage when he learnt about the Italian attack on Greece.[285] Denigrated German liaison staffs and attachés who only 'breakfasted' and were useless as spies. Observed that this occurrence had spoiled many plans he had in mind. Judged the position to be that Duce was doubtful of his own, that is German, economic influence in the Balkans[286] and doubted if the Italians would be able to defeat Greece, since the latter were by no means bad soldiers. F. expressed it thus: 'This is the revenge for Norway and France.' He, F., had not been able to handle affairs other than in secrecy because every other Italian was either a traitor or a spy. Harsh words about Rintelen,[287] who had let himself be taken in. The only advantage was that the British would now also be forced to entrench themselves there. F. has asked to speak at once to Ambassador v. M(ackensen)[288] and also wants a word with Mussolini. He is extremely worried that Italy's action will bring the

entire Balkans together in sympathy and provide the British with, to them, a welcome excuse to set up an air base in the Balkans.

4 November 1940
Reich Chancellery

Unpleasant discussion at FHQ; present were Göring, v. Br(auchitsch), Keitel.[289] For the first time F. doubted Luftwaffe successes and statistics of enemy losses on the basis of Brit(ish) and other press reports. For the first time, too, Jodl supported the Reichsmarschall and said he believes that the British are putting up their last fighters flown by trainee pilots and base commanders since they have nobody else left. F. was visibly depressed. Impression is that at the moment he does not know how it will turn out. At the most inopportune moment possible the C-in-C started talking about the postponed Operation 'Sealion', and attacked the Navy and Luftwaffe, completely against accepted custom. Göring flew into a rage, nearly got personal, and accused the Army of wavering in indecision at Dunkirk. Nobody mentioned the real reason.[290] Even Keitel had to leave the C-in-C in the lurch, since he did not understand the discussion. In the end everybody agreed to blame the Navy because they had admitted not being equipped properly to defend the landing beaches wanted by the Army. Nobody from the Navy was there!

11 November 1940
F. – Schm. – Keitel – Jodl – v. Below – Lorenz

After the situation conference interesting observations by F. about the role and duties of a minister for war. Throughout the world the role varied very much; frequently he was the real wielder of power, but also, as in Britain and the United States, a puppet of democracy and servant of the parliament. German-Prussia had taken the best path: here there were the greatest number of personalities who preferred to be political advisers rather than politicians. An exception was Schleicher;[291] he had considered him to be one of the most intelligent and intriguing of politicians and military figures, but also totally dishonest, a characteristic of the true politician. He had never underestimated Schleicher, remained in his debt with regard to many things and would even have had him as minister of war if he had not recognised in good time what an absolute rotter he was. As it happened, the Old Gentleman[292] had been one of those who had found Schl. repugnant. More proof that it was wrong to consider him addled then.

15 November 1940

F. spoke at length about Molotov visit.[293] Said that he had not expected much to come from it. Talks had shown the direction the Russian plans were taking. M. had let the cat out of the bag. He (F.) was really relieved; this would not even remain a marriage of convenience. To let Russia into Europe would be the end of Central Europe; even the Balkans and Finland were dangerous flanks. In this connection Schmundt and I to F. In whatever case field headquarters were to be constructed with all haste, and primarily South, Centre and North.[294] F. wants a permanent headquarters in East Prussia; he left it at that and will explore everything else with Minister Todt.

11 December 1940
F. – Ribbentrop – Schm. – Hewel – Dr. Dietrich

After a long discussion about the situation in the French colonies F. spoke about colonial politics. Over the course of the years he had changed his point of view in this regard, something which previously he had seldom found it necessary to do. Earlier he had been a great enthusiast for German colonial policy since we had proved that we were able to handle the black and yellow races, and above all that we could educate them. Now he saw it as a blessing, the only blessing of the Versailles Treaty, that we had been deprived permanently of our overseas territories. The colonial period was past. The black portion of the Earth was awakening. In the age of progressive technology one could not persevere for centuries with policies to keep them ignorant. The Japanese were the pacemakers of this development, and the time was not far off when Britain and France would have to relinquish their colonies. It was principally Britain which would receive the bill for arrogant educational methods and to maintain so-c[alled] lordship. France, however, would also not avoid the spectre which came in the shape of black officers and high-ranking officials. In this connection, without F., the sober Hewel said that for his part the Führer used two different yardsticks in Europe, as for example in Poland.

18 December 1940
C-in-C

The Barbarossa directive has been issued.[295] C-in-C has asked me to find out if F. really intends war or is only bluffing. I am convinced that F. himself still does not know what will happen. Distrustful of his own military leaders, uncertainty about Russ(ian) strength, disappointment over British stubbornness continue to preoccupy him. In my opinion he believes, and in this he is fortified by Köstring's[296] reports and dissertation, that Soviets are weak. Hopes Eng(lish) will relent; does not believe USA will enter war. Big concerns about Africa and the Italians. Astonishing faith in capabilities of the Luftwaffe. Keeps repeating that he is holding all decisions in reserve. Molotov visit had shown that Russia intended to put its hands on Europe. He could not let the Balkans go its own way, Finland's independence was already sufficiently dangerous. The pact had never been really necessary, for the political abyss was deep enough. – I informed C-in-C and Siewert, also OQu.IV [Head of OKH Intelligence Branch] for Chief of the General Staff accordingly.

19 December 1940

Schm(undt), Min(ister) Todt and I have returned from Rastenburg.[297] Explored FHQ. F. asked specially to look at it from point of view of camouflage and also defence against enemy paratroop attack. On pretext of wanting a change of scenery we went over the satellite HQs for Ribb(entrop) and Reichsführer-SS. F. is insisting on completion by April. Everything comes under the pseudonym 'bomb-proof armaments plant'. Locations for other FHQs are to be sought in Poland and Galicia; these will have a more temporary character, however.

1941

17 January 1941
Reich Chancellery

Report on Barbarossa. Pleasant accord between C-in-C, Chief of the General Staff and F. regarding moving up troops and decisive points of attack. F. adamant on North and South. Economic arguments cropped up continually, also political: below, oil and cereals; above, the destruction of the Red political fortress, Leningrad. F. and also Chief of the General Staff very optimistic with regard to fighting strength of Red Army, which had obsolete equipment and above all few aircraft and old tanks.[298]

30 January 1941[+]
(F. – Schmundt – Puttkamer – Jodl)

Chief of the Finn[ish] General Staff, General Heinrichs[299] was at OKH where initiated into projected plan Barbarossa. Everybody astonished at the determination this officer has towards all plans. F. is very impressed by him and believes we have found a good brother-in-arms: made general observations about Finland and its politics. It would be a difficult partnership because the Finns did not want a pact or to break with United States under any circumstances, nor with Britain if possible. This did not worry him. They were a brave people and would at least provide him with a secure protection on his flank, quite apart from that it was always good to have brothers-in-arms bent on revenge, and that had been noted. Politically one had to exercise caution. The people were sensitive and could not be patronised as had been the case with the Slovaks. General Heinrichs's big worry was probably the question of imports and keeping the harbours open. Here we could give extensive guarantees. Finnish nickel was as important for us as oil and cereals were for the Finns. F. gave OKW free hand for talks with the Finns, but no longer than three months.

1 February 1941[+]
Keitel – Jodl – Halder – Gercke[300] *– Schmundt – Puttkamer and Myself*[301]

General von Funck[302] has returned from Libya and reported clearly and soberly about the situation there. F. was shocked and unsettled. Was realistic regarding condition of Italian divisions. Funck was brutally frank about fighting spirit, particularly amongst Italian military leaders, which was so poor as to verge on sabotage. It was crazy, F. said, that on the one hand the Italians were crying for help and could not complain enough about their substandard armaments and equipment while on the other [were] so jealous and childish that they wanted neither German soldiers nor German help. He expected Mussolini would be content if German troops wore Italian uniform and German aircraft wore the Italian tricolour on their wings [*sic*]. F. had the gravest doubts that the situation in Africa could be kept within bounds: he could not plug all the gaps everywhere, and if something was withdrawn from a spot, those involved screamed like a stuck pig.

C-in-C was inspired by Funck's report and surprisingly threw in frequent favourable observations, alluding to what he and the OKH had been saying all along, and not least with references to his visits to Italy and Africa. F. gave instructions that cooperation with the Italian General Staff was to be strengthened if possible and the study group reinforced, above all the liaison officer was to be advised to keep a sharp watch in order to gauge and monitor the loyalty of the Italian military commanders.

2 February 1941[+]
(Keitel – Bormann – Hewel – Ley – Speer)

The Jewish question was brought up by Ley and discussed in detail. In a long discourse, F. described how he thought about the whole thing. In the first place the war would accelerate the solution of the question; on the other hand many additional difficulties would also present themselves. Originally it had only been in his power to break Jewish power in Germany, now it had to be the objective to remove Jewish influence in the entire Axis commonwealth. In other countries, such as Poland or Slovakia, it could be done with state organs. In France it had become significantly more difficult after the armistice, and precisely there it was crucial. If he only knew where the couple of million Jews could be sent; with so many it was difficult to know. He would approach the French and ask them to make space available for a settlement on Madagascar.[303] In response to Bormann's question how they were to be shipped there in wartime, he (F.) replied that would have to be considered. His preference was to use the whole KdF [Kraft durch Freude] passenger fleet, but that would be difficult while there was a war on, one did not want German crews lost to the torpedoes of an enemy submarine. He had pondered on many other ideas which were not quite so nice. He had actually once thought it possible to ship the half million German Jews to Palestine or Egypt with the help of the British. When he tried that through diplomatic channels in 1937, the cousins over there had turned him down. They explained they had quite enough to do with their own and did not want additional unrest.

2 February 1941[+]

Another big discussion today about jurisprudence. Reason was petitions for pardons presented and advocated by Keitel. These involved front-arrest and demotions, in themselves harmless enough. It was really too stupid to put before F. There followed a long monologue in presence of Keitel, Puttkamer, Schmundt and myself. F. covering the whole crass concept of deterrent and custodial penalties, especially for military offences. Reform was suitable for youths, but only very rarely for adults. Amongst the troops bad examples spoiled morale. The French knew how to deal with it better in 1914–18. After the first executions calm was restored in the army. In general that sort of thing was necessary for the maintenance of good order and discipline. He, F., had been toying for years with the idea of justice reform,[304] but now the war had intervened. He had never been completely satisfied with Gürtner[305] although he would never forget his help in 1923. Schlegelberger[306] wanted to be a good National Socialist but remained an old-fashioned lawyer and as for Freisler[307] he did not trust him an inch. Any jurist who had once been a Communist he would believe capable of anything. Good lawyers were mostly bad on jurisprudence and Freisler was a brilliant talker, but trust him, watch out. We listened to all this in astonishment.

9 February 1941

F. was completely open with C-in-C and Chief of OKW on how he judges developments with Soviet Union. Everybody still had plenty of time since he wanted to see first how the Russians reacted to the German troop movements to the border, about which they had undoubtedly not remained in the dark. One thing was clear: German victories in Poland, France and Norway had hit the Russians hard. Without doubt, Stalin was not going to allow a German-dominated Europe.[308]

2 March 1941
F. – Schmundt – v. B. (Bulg. – Turkey)

F. relieved that Bulgaria has finally come into the Tripartite Pact.[309] Attributed it all to his personal relationship with the king, who had had to overcome enormous opposition in the country, primarily in the Orthodox Church where his adversaries were very pro-Russian; but even the peasants saw Russia as the Motherland. His main difficulty was now with Turkey, which he needed more than Bulgaria.[310] Turkey had now become the gateway for launching invasions and the bridgehead for operations in Britain's rear, also the weather vane in the Near East. He was keen on enticing the Turks with commercial contracts and weapons, but it would rouse the Bulgarians' suspicions, since they presumably knew of the Turks' hate for Russia. The only thing the two of them had in common was their grudge against the Greeks, and in this respect he would also attempt to lure the Turks into the Axis.

16 March 1941
C-in-C, QM-Gen., Chief OKW

Unpleasant discussion between C-in-C, QM-Gen. and F. Draft of administrative regulations for Barbarossa presented.[311] Experience in France and Belgium talked about. F. rejected draft in very strong terms. Military administrations served no useful purpose. From case to case he was going to transfer administration into political hands, since the Army understood nothing of politics. C-in-C attempted to raise objections but was harshly shouted down and gave up. F.'s decision is that Wehrmacht will only have control as far back as the operational rear areas.

18 March 1941[+]

Today I finally admitted defeat! That is, on the repeated requests I have made to Himmler since the turn of the year to allow me to visit a concentration camp. On at least a dozen occasions this always outwardly amiable person has confirmed that I could make a visit to one very soon. But my numerous enquiries to his staff have always been met by the same assurance: 'The Reichsführer wants to escort you himself', or a similar excuse. As it happens, that is precisely what I do not want. I have been anxious for some time to visit Oranienburg where an old regimental colleague (v. S.) and a former officer from Stettin (v. B.) are [incarcerated], presumably on account of being too unguarded in their utterances. After Wolff[312] told me today that I should not pin my hopes on going because in most cases the Reichsführer did not even take his Waffen-SS adjutants with him, but SD officials, I accepted defeat.

20 March 1941
Streicher, Nuremberg

Bodenschatz with F. carrying a thick file. It looked very important, and we soon found out his reason for visiting the Führer with the 'weighty' paperwork. It was the Streicher[313] business again. On the basis of documents from the very active Martin,[314] Göring had assembled a huge amount of material against Streicher. B. presented this. As B. related, the Reichsmarschall wanted to initiate proceedings against Str. for corruption and prejudicing the defence of the Reich. There had been the most extraordinary goings-on. A stock of gold put aside to make reproductions of the Reich insignia had disappeared. A bad affair involving members of the Nuremberg Opera ballet. Dispossessing people of land and farms for his own use and similar. But the most shocking thing of all was the reaction of F. He does not want the courts to handle it under any circumstances, but is going to make it a Party internal matter. Reason: Streicher's services to the movement and his fight against Jewry are so great that they must be taken into account when deciding the consequences of his perhaps criminal errors and deeds. There was no way he would want to give world Jewry the pleasure of having a public criminal case. We are confronted by an enigma.

24 March 1941[+]

F. is very unhappy and worried about the situation in the Balkans.[315] Our imminent intervention has made him throw his entire conception out of the window; the great objectives have all had to be put back, and it is now impossible to launch the attack on the Soviet Union in the second half of May. By themselves a couple of weeks earlier or later are not necessarily so bad, but we do not want to be surprised by the Russian winter. The earliest date is now the end of June, and one never knows when the summer will come to an end. For this entire crap we have unfortunately to thank the Italians, who in politics do not always recognise the main goal, only small geographic targets enabling them to shout their victory from the rooftops. What these victories were really worth the Albanians proved to their pleasure. In the upshot he has been shafted by the stupidity of a third party. In this connection he spoke harsh words against the Duce, actually openly for the first time. He might be a genial popular leader and organiser, but he understood nothing about military matters. During the parade in Rome he had been inspired by the Passo romano but not seen the pre-Deluge artillery. Talking with Mussolini about military affairs had been a revelation. Since he had no military knowledge or ability, he was completely in the hands of his generals. This was not the case with himself, thank God; he had taken the time to appropriate the necessary knowledge and wherewithal; and, particularly in the technical respect, no general could succeed in deceiving him or getting him to accept false information.

24 March 1941[+]
Lend–Lease Pact
F. spoke at length and in ample terms about the Lend–Lease Pact[316] with frequent tirades against the Americans, particularly Roosevelt. The Americans had finally let the cat out of the bag; if one wanted, one could see a justification for war in it. Without anything further he could let it lead to war. At the moment he did not want to talk about the matter. Eventually there would be war with the USA. Roosevelt, and behind him Jewish high finance, wanted war and had to want war, for a German victory in Europe would bring with it enormous losses of capital for American Jews in Europe. The unfortunate thing was that we had no aircraft capable of bombing American cities. He would very much like to bring the lesson home in this way to American Jews. This Lend–Lease legislation brought him additionally major problems. He was in no doubt that success would only be hindered by a merciless war on sea traffic. In any case with regard to the U-boat war he would not make the same mistakes as had been made in World War I.[317]

Respecting the possibility of the war spreading further, especially the expansion of the conflict eastwards, he did not look on the dark side. The Americans could not do everything and the capacity of their armaments industry was still limited. The important factor was that the tonnage sunk by U-boats had not only to be maintained, but increased further. He was not altogether convinced by successes against convoys achieved by aircraft. How often had he read in the overseas press of ships reported sunk by the Luftwaffe which had arrived amidst great hullaballoo to discharge their cargoes at the ports of destination merely damaged or even undamaged. All in all, F. said that the useful thing about this of itself unpleasant Lend–Lease law was that it gave him a cause for war. Present were Speer, Pfleiderer,[318] Keitel, Bormann and Jodl.

28 March 1941
Vienna

Have come from the command posts at Litzmannstadt and Krosno.[319] Reported to F. at Imperial. F. very pleased about Balkans developments.[320] Now the last stone of the mosaic had been laid. At last he was free to address the wider decisive questions. Spoke harshly against the Italians whom he considers totally unreliable. In this sense big worry about Africa. Strange how little F., who mentioned the subject himself, seems affected by the fate of the *Bismarck*.[321]

7 April 1941
F. – Himmler – Heydrich[322] – Keitel – Schm. – Wolff

Himmler held the stage. F. raging. H. spoke out against Army and military administration in Poland, Holland and Norway. His 'pacifying actions' were being sabotaged by old generals. Demanded replacement of subordinate field and senior field command officers by SS leaders. Population was rebellious as they had the support of Army offices – in Poland military surgeons were even being made available to the general public. In Radom, a surgeon of the reserve had taken on additionally the management of a hospital run by Polish nuns. H. then moved on to plans for the penetration of Polish regions with German immigrants of good racial stock. The Poles would be gradually concentrated in five to six large enclaves. Cracow would be one of them. In Holland[323] and Norway he was setting up Reich schools to conserve German offspring amongst the population.[324] In Flanders he had come up against the resistance of the military government and church, people were even sabotaging his propaganda for the Waffen-SS.

Another successful salvo against Army and military administration. F. completely taken in by assertions presented with a respectable and regretful demeanour. Keitel and I are in a difficult situation, since first the allegations have to be investigated. But the manner of H. and also of Heydrich was simultaneously cunning and vile. Informed Siewert and C-in-C this evening.

20 April 1941
FHQ – Special Train (at Wiener Neustadt)[325]

Very harmonious birthday. Von Papen[326] brought very good news from Ankara. Reported on situation in Iraq and expressed regret that diplomatic relationship with Iraq still so loose. Something would be done there. Said to F.: 'If all goes well I will bring you the Turks.' These were only in fear of the Soviet Union. In any case they wanted to be involved in the rearrangement of the Balkans and spoke about ambassador to Cyprus. With C-in-C complete agreement regarding operations. C-in-C energetically opposed to Italian administration in Greece. Said that army and population would not go along with it.

24 April 1941

F. spoke once again about developments in Iraq.[327] It occupies him a lot, and one has the impression that he thinks he has made mistakes, or at least omissions. Criticised German diplomats: they were good breakfasters and armchair warriors, but not spies. Then he used harsh words against Papen, regretted the death of Bonzo Blomberg[328] and ordered that the elder son (Henning) and son-in-law should be recalled. Apart from the Mufti,[329] Gailani[330] was the only man of significance in the Arab world. Unfortunately the Arabs were unreliable and could be bought, something the British and French had understood. F. was sorry and apologised, but one could not be everywhere to render assistance. In itself the Orient was no problem if the other plan, here he meant Barbarossa, did not go awry. If it succeeded from there one could open the gate to the Orient.

9 May 1941[+]

F. was very concerned about possible British landings in Spain or Portugal. Abwehr has received a whole host of reports that they are busying themselves with it on the island over there. Talked about how it could be countered. In any case to take preparatory measures for occupation of Portugal which would be more difficult than marching into Spain. He was convinced that the Portuguese wanted to remain neutral but it was not always possible to do as one wished when a stronger force was present. He had himself already practised such a thing successfully with neutrals. Keitel's question about transferring SS units to Spain for political reasons was initially not properly understood [sic] by F. and then brusquely dismissed. The political circumstances between Germany and Spain did not warrant it. He would not like to see the long faces of the Falangists if his SS came without priests and omitted to demand Mass as soon as they got there. The strategic situation of the country bound him and Germany to Spain, along with his opposition to Communism and his glowing hatred of Britain. What a good thing it had been that Britain and France had adopted the stance they had towards Franco in the civil war; that was now worth its weight in gold. But one had to realise that Franco was not a leader like Mussolini and himself, for he was subject to a much more powerful dictator than was the case with the Duce and himself, namely the Pope and the Church. It was different there and Franco's struggle would have been much more dour if the brutal hatred of the Church on the part of the Communists had not existed.

10 May 1941[+]
(Commissar Order)

I have been in Poland. Salmuth[331] and Tresckow had a long talk with me about the Commissar Order.[332] They consider it to be a very bad thing and fear it will be counter-productive amongst the troops. We were in total agreement on this. Salmuth and also Tresckow told me in confidence that they had ways and means orally to influence the divisional commanders above all to side-step this order. Tresckow made the typical observation: 'If international law is to be broken, rather the Russians do it than ourselves!'

11 May 1941[+]
(Hess)

These are such turbulent hours that one does not know what is up; and I am myself not yet clear. Everything is unsettling. F. in total confusion and the others who have arrived meanwhile, such as Göring and Ribbentrop, no less so. We started out as the smallest circle at the Berghof. F. wanted fourteen days to switch off and rest to clear his mind for Barbarossa. Then the following happened. As the only military adjutant at [Obersalz]berg I presented the morning conference reports. There was not much going on. F. came down at about 11 o'clock. I was speaking when Albert Bormann came in and reported that Pintsch, adjutant to Herr Hess, had arrived and wanted to speak to the Führer about a most urgent matter. F., annoyed, threw B. out with the words: 'Can't you see that I am in the middle of a military conference and do not wish to be disturbed?' After one minute B. was back, rather pale, and said, P. would not go, it was very urgent and there was danger. P. came in with a letter in his hand which he passed to F. with the words: 'I am duty-bound by Herr Hess to give you this letter, mein Führer.' F. accepted it with bad grace. I managed to read on the envelope only: 'To be given to the Führer only if . . .' As he read it, I saw the Führer's knuckles go white. White as chalk he ordered me in excited tones: 'Get me the Reichsmarschall at once.' P. was dismissed but ordered to keep himself available at the command post. I managed to get hold of Göring when he arrived near Nuremberg. He was going to his retreat there. F. spoke to him only briefly and said: 'Göring, come here at once. Something terrible has happened.' Albert Bormann was ordered to fetch his brother. F. was pacing up and down in the hall with furious strides. Albert Bormann would only tell me that he had had to send for Ribbentrop from Fuschl and asked me what was up. I was ordered to compile in closest detail information about the flights of German aircraft the previous day and night. Dr Todt, who was present to make a report, was rescheduled for the afternoon. But the visit of Admiral Darlan[333] will go ahead. – It is now 20.00 hrs, endless talk involving those mentioned. We adjutants keep being sent out although we are very curious. Jeschonnek is there too. But he knows nothing. Darlan's visit was very formal and short.[334] Everybody under the impression that F. could not concentrate on matter in hand. We are of the opinion that either Herr Hess himself or a high-ranking Party member has flown over to the enemy. That is the only thing we know for sure.

11 May 1941
(Benoist-Méchin)

22.00 hrs. I was given the job of looking after State Secretary Benoist-Méchin[335] during the talks. He is escorting Darlan on Pétain's orders. B.M. speaks fluent German. We had a very enjoyable conversation and took a stroll. He is very pro-German, loved the Reichswehr and pleaded for us to give the French a free hand. Germany had to be generous, especially the Führer, then the French would come and be good allies. The tryst with England was a marriage of convenience without love. He begged me to tell the F. not to make the same mistakes as France had done after 1918. We should not punish the French for the injustice they had perpetrated against us after the First World War. If that were not the case, the Marshal [Pétain] would take an adverse stand and French possessions would pass to the enemy. Alsace-Lorraine had been written off, but nothing else. We should trust the French and treat them generously, then they would reciprocate in kind. The French people had really not wanted this war. In France, the sentiment was anything other than anti-German. But the French were very sensitive, and their present attitude could turn into one of hatred if their honour were impugned.

12 May 1941[+]
Hess

So now it is out of the bag. Hess has flown to England and F. simply devastated now it is certain. All night the talk was of whether he would make it or not. In theory, yes, the experts said; but the probability was 50:50. F. decided to compose a statement and put the flight down to mental aberration. He said: 'Hess always had crazy ideas. They got worse the longer he was under the influence of the Haushofers.'[336] Greatest worry of F. is that the Italians may now begin to doubt the strength of the alliance. Even if Hess were dead, he would have to make a statement, for who would guarantee that the flight could be kept quiet? It remained to be seen if the British would let the cat out of the bag. The Duke of Hamilton[337] had always been Hess's idol. Meanwhile Ribbentrop had been told to fly to Rome. P.[338] was arrested yesterday. It is typical that the only one circulating happy and carefree in the beehive is Bormann; we are all agreed that he thinks his hour has arrived. Otherwise the outlook here is anything but pretty for the present.

13 May 1941[+]
Hess

The Gestapo and Abwehr are apparently going all out. They probably know by now a whole host of details about the cover story Hess erected to conceal his clandestine activity at Augsburg. F. is furious; the Haushofer family came in for the worst of it. This Jewish-tainted professor had Hess on his conscience. F. blamed himself for not having acted earlier to break up and silence this whole Munich brood. As it was, he had accepted from the beginning that Hess would make it to England, for he was an outstanding pilot and also understood a great deal about aviation technology; but all his ideas were on the borderline between reality and madness. It would be best if the thing blew over quickly. Basically he would wait to see how the British received and treated him and if they – and most of all Churchill – took him seriously. Then propaganda could make what it would of the circumstances, namely to prove to the rest of the world that the assurances by the British of their will for peace are all hypocrisy.

20 May 1941⁺
(After Situation Conference with Schmundt, Below, Hewel, [Heinz] Lorenz and Finally Also Bormann)

F. spoke about the church. The Catholic Church had requested being integrated into the Winter Relief Work and offered its assistance. F. was most strongly opposed to having the church involved in Party and state relief work. Kerrl would write to the church asking that it set up its own organisation, thereby proving its positive stance to the state. There was no way he would now allow bishops or other princes of the church to inveigle propaganda of its own kind under the cloak of brotherly love in order to revive its dwindling influence on the people. One would have to keep a close watch on the Red Cross, because the church would definitely set course in the direction of this neutral organisation. Then the attitude of the church would have to undergo a basic change. State and Party could criticise the church with one hand, and accept its help with the other. Things were different in France. Napoleon had understood why it was necessary to separate church and state and why up to the present day the French authorities had seen no reason to change this. Nevertheless it was impressive to see the tricolour flying on a church tower and the altars were decorated with banners in the national colours.[339]

The German churches were just getting used to the idea. According to his information, no other state contributed so much in subsidies to the church as did the German Reich. He did not have the exact figure but it was probably close to a billion. (Bormann agreed.) Now we were at war it was not his intention to change anything, but after the war he would have a much closer look at these state subsidies and certainly investigate the actual uses to which they were put. In any case he would not agree to the state paying subsidies to the church which were then used to curry favour with blacks and Chinese. First of all came spiritual care for Germans and a long way after that for the rest of the world.

23 May 1941

Visited Field Marshal v Kluge.[340] Kluge more or less confirmed scenario. Russians were marching up and massing near border. Numerous grass airstrips in immediate proximity to frontier. Kl(uge) pleaded with me to get F. to change the dangerous Commissar Order,[341] and especially to put the SD Kommandos[342] more under military control. There had been some very bad goings-on in Poland, and he had had to intervene personally on several occasions, for

example in Modlin and Lublin. Considered political tactics in Poland
as very unfortunate. The worst was the uncertainty about police and
SS measures. In the evening I reported this in same terms to F.

31 May 1941
F. – Schm. – Keitel – Hewel – Lorenz – v. Puttk.

F. brought up subject of Battle of Jutland. Said it was one of the
greatest naval battles in history; unfortunately not with the outcome
it might have brought. Then spoke about sense of responsibility,
courage to admit error and pol[itical] horizons of top ranking military
commanders. Here there was not much he could say about Army
commanders that was favourable. Political knowledge, an overall
world-political view, was unknown to such officers, for that was
something greater than Fatherland or 'with God for Kaiser and Reich'.
In the past milit[ary] leaders had always provided him with false
information, their lack of instinct was appalling, even modern types
like Reichenau mostly adopted the impressions of the moment. He
was aghast when he heard R's suggestion to have China in the Axis
instead of Japan.[343] It was for this reason that he had not advocated
having Reichenau take over as C-in-C. Quite apart from that, despite
all his qualities and his stance towards National Socialism, he did not
trust him 100 per cent. R. was so flexible that he considered it
possible he would dabble in pol[itical] sidelines; accordingly he could
not consider him a reliable, loyal follower. Although he was an enemy,
a man like Hammerstein[344] was a very cool thinker politically. He was
dangerous and had to go, but for all his hatred for Hitler's person and
political views, his course had at least a basis of some consequence.
He also knew that H. was still playing cat and mouse and made no
secret of his aversion to the Third Reich.

28 July 1941
F. about Operations

During a short stroll after the situation conference, F. spoke with
Schm. and myself about further developments in the east. It was on
account of these that he was not sleeping at night, since he was
uncertain about many things. Within his breast two souls wrestled:
the political-strategic, and the economic.[345] Politically he would say
that the two principal suppurating boils had to be got rid of:
Leningrad and Moscow. That would be the heaviest blow for the
Russian people and the Communist Party. Göring had assured him
that it could be done by the Luftwaffe alone, but since Dunkirk he

[Hitler] had become a little sceptical. Economically speaking there were quite different objectives. Whereas Moscow was a big industrial centre, the south was more important, where oil, wheat, more or less everything was located necessary to keep the country going. A land where milk and honey flowed. One thing at least was absolutely required, and that was a proper concentration of forces. To use Panzers in fighting to demolish cities, that was a sin against the spirit. They had to operate in the open areas of the south. He had already started to hear the cries of those from whom they had been stripped; but that was neither here nor there.

6 August 1941
HQ Sixteenth Army

Was at HQ Sixteenth Army and also my old division,[346] with Col-Gen. Busch[347] and Boeckh-Behrens.[348] A long discussion about what had to be done and what the Führer was planning. I could hardly say: 'He does not know that himself' and so avoided it. I did say, however, that at the moment Leningrad was still at the head of his operational objectives. Both shook their heads and could not understand the point of having so many units on hand for the danger that the Russians would spread out into open terrain and attack there. It was interesting that both of them, army commander and chief [of staff] considered it very possible to have debilitated the Russians to such an extent by the end of October that they would not be capable of offensive measures.[349]

That evening I reported to F. about my flight. F. was impassive, said only that Leningrad was necessary prior to the link-up with the Finns. Also Marshal Mannerheim[350] [Finnish head of state] had informed him that Leningrad was also his goal and that later the city must be put to the plough.

8 August 1941
Wolfsschanze[351]

One sees clearly how indecisive F. is regarding the continuation of the operation. Ideas and objectives keep on changing. One emerges from the situation conferences as nonplussed as one went in. In the train of the situation conference this evening it seems that the following is the course of future events: Leningrad, come what may: this must be political and strategic, all the more so since Field Marshal von Leeb[352] has declared that he can do it with artillery and the Luftwaffe. In the Centre: shift to the defensive. Everything mobile to head south:

Ukraine, Donetz Basin and Rostov. At the moment F. sees the economic defeat of the Russians as the more important goal, all the more so since he is being advised from the front and by the OKH that the enemy has taken such a beating that the prospect of his being able to mount an offensive in the forseeable future, particularly this year, need no longer be taken into consideration.

9 August 1941
(Mauerwald)

Visited C-in-C at Mauerwald[353] where I found a dark mood. People are – rightly – up in arms about the meddling of OKW in details and trifles, furthermore at the laughably jittery reactions to insignificant enemy moves, almost losing their nerve, and are unhappy about leaving Moscow for later.[354] C-in-C said that at the moment from an operational point of view it was a complete mess and one could hardly wonder that each army group was striking out in all directions. F. was giving no clear instructions. As in France, we were back to group tactics. One needed instructions, with definite objectives. He would tell that to F. tomorrow.

20 August 1941[+]
Draft Marriage Regulations (Brauchitsch)

There has been another unpleasant episode. Because of various occurrences OKH drafted proposed new marriage regulations and passed them to OKW. I received the files and immediately warned the Chief of the Personnel Office, against presenting them for the time being. The Führer was not disposed to go into the matter at the moment and would not give it his attention.[355] Keitel had nothing more urgent on hand and so placed the files before F., which provoked a wild outburst. Some expressions were passed; people should concern themselves with operational affairs and the well-being of the men rather than go into the question of whether an officer should marry under given circumstances. In wartime that was something fairly irrelevant. Achievement and bravery were the decisive factors and not the question of whether the bride was of this or that civil status. In these matters he was very touchy towards the Army. The Navy had also disappointed him. He knew much more about the private lives of officers than perhaps he was given credit for. With marriage one should not be so jesuitic. Unfortunately he had had many harsh words with the C-in-C. As he saw it, a lieutenant whose bride or girlfriend was pregnant and who had asked her father's permission to marry was an honourable man, not the one who left her in the lurch.[356] He was still appalled when he recalled how somebody had had the effrontery to cashier an officer for doing the honourable thing. The officer had appealed to him, thank God, and of course got justice. The C-in-C had every reason to be cautious in these things and keep his own counsel. He [Hitler] had kept quiet about the whole thing, for these were private matters. But when it worked to the detriment of others, and third parties were prejudiced on the basis of rank and by completely revised so-called Marriage Regulations and suffered heartache and pain thereby, that he would not allow. The princes were the worst in this respect. His own Prinz Auwi[357] had come before him, probably on the advice of certain third parties, to plead for his refusal to the marriage of his son to a divorcée. That had been the last straw, and to top it all a private detective had been hired to ferret out information about the so-called past life of the lady. He, F., had thereupon made his decision and told Keitel that there was time for such things after the war.

I spoke to the C-in-C about the matter immediately and had a violent argument with Schmundt. I take the standpoint that in many things the Führer is right. But what is worst, and what we are continually discovering, is that along the way Bormann and Heydrich are setting up a political and personal monitoring system for the officer corps similar to that we saw during the time of the old C-in-C. The one observation is F. definitely let his excitement show too much, and I noticed that he later regretted it.

21 August 1941

Most serious conflict between C-in-C, Chief of the General Staff and F. The former two restate their objectives: capture Moscow and its industry. They are convinced that Soviets will have to plan for decisive battle before capital. F. of exactly contrary view: to capture the capital will not decide the war. Alluded to Napoleon. He needed Russian vital arteries: oil, cereals, coal. With his Panzers will, as previously, wipe out forces in south Russian region. Sensed disagreement amongst army commanders and chiefs of staff, which Jodl confirmed. C-in-C and Chief (of the General Staff) resigned to it and gave in. Operations based on a decisive thrust towards Kiev ordered. A black day for the Army. Outspoken personal attacks on Brauchitsch and Halder by F.[358] Mood similar to November 1939. Schmundt and I see the C-in-C's days as numbered. But what then?

Keitel plays a sometimes ridiculous, sometimes unknowingly malevolent role towards the Army.

23 August 1941
Mauerwald

Was summoned by C-in-C to meeting at Mauerwald. Grim situation. Führer Directive[359] received and considered totally unsatisfactory. Chief of the General Staff resigned to it, dismissed the possibilities from F. as unrealisable,[360] 'one cannot do everything', deploy forces which are not available was utopian etc., etc. In my unimportant opinion Chief of the General Staff is absolutely right.

I said that in this confused situation, F. himself did not know yet what he wanted. He kept vacillating between economic-political goals, strategic and unfortunately also racial and part-political goals for the pacification of European Russia, in which he is being most vehemently supported by our enemies, namely *his*[361] friends.

2 October 1941
Wolfsschanze

Present were F., Chief OKW, Jodl, Reichsführer-SS, Heydrich,[362] Schmundt, Engel, later Warlimont (in connection with situation conference.)

Himmler reported about putting foreign races (Jews) in camps, spoke about situation in Baltic States and Ruthenia. Main points Riga, Reval and Minsk. Mentioned question of Jewish population of Salonika, asserted Salonika was a city with one of the largest Jewish communities: danger of integration between Jews and Levantines.[363] F. accepted his opinion and told him to remove Jewish element from S. Himmler asked for and received plenipotentiary powers for the purpose. SD-Kommando with reinforcements would be sent in. Keitel asked if military commander should be involved. F. replied: Only if absolutely necessary. Keitel asked permission to inform mil. cdr. that Reichsführer-SS had received plenipotentiary powers and was not to be interfered with. Schm. and I glad that Wehrmacht and troops will not be involved.

4 October 1941[+]
Army

Unpleasant business. After the situation conference various officers of the Weapons Office were introduced. In the presence of Fromm a whole range of technical armaments and military-economic matters were discussed. F. had just previously sent for the red Weapons Office armaments book with the production figures for September. I had given it to him personally last evening and knew that he would stay up all night studying it. Together with numerous adverse observations of various statistics his major criticism was aimed at Panzer production and production of the sFH 18 field howitzer. Fromm committed the error of referring him to the figures calculated by himself. That was a big mistake. The Army General Office had quite different data to the Weapons Office. This led to F. making the most cutting remarks about the muddle in Army armaments.[364] Now he no longer knew upon whom he should rely. How was he supposed to fight a war, counting on 1,000 additional Panzers, and then somebody told him that really he only had 500. He had assumed at the very least that people in the Weapons Office could count, but that was not the case. The independent designs and developments of that office had the character of children's toys and in no way took account of the seriousness of the situation and the struggle for survival in which we found ourselves. Checks made by telephone calls to Berlin confirmed that the Weapons Office figures were correct and those of the Chief of Army Armaments false. Fromm inveigled himself extremely skilfully back into the course of the discussion and explained to F. that in this regard he was not master in his own house. We still had the Four-Year Plan, from which Göring, for example, extracted whatever met his fancy for the Luftwaffe. It was not greatly different with the Navy, and the Army had to content itself with the left-overs: 'And that will just not do, mein Führer', were his words. F. listened to this explanation with odd passivity, let Fromm talk, but finished with the cutting remark: 'I will investigate your allegations, Herr Colonel-General.' In the evening he spoke at length on this subject with Schmundt and myself. We both had to agree that Fromm was right, which we did. Something that appeared unimaginable to both Schmundt and me was that the Führer could quote and write down all statistics to be found in this ghastly numbers book, knew the whole thing by heart and saw it all in his mind's eye – right down to the production of pistol ammunition.

9 October 1941

F. praised especially highly Mannerheim, of whom he had been suspicious for some time on account of his pro-American attitude and his affinity for theatre boxes. But he was an aggressive soldier, and it was amazing how he kept his socialists toeing the line. His hatred for the Russians was not only a consequence of their communist leadership,[365] but had its origins in the long suppression of the Finnish people by Tsarist Russia. His recent observation – after its capture the city of Leningrad had to be razed to the ground and ploughed in, since it had only ever brought his people misfortune – was indicative of his hatred. It was unfortunate that this brave race was so small, and could not absorb much bloodletting. As it was, politically he would let the Finns do whatever they wanted. Main thing was that they remained true to the brotherhood-in-arms.

18 October 1941
At HQ Sixteenth Army.[366] Long discussion with Col-Gen. Busch and Boeckh-Behrens about future course. Surprisingly, amongst them the opinion is that Russians at their last gasp and will basically be forced under before the onset of winter. This is their unanimous opinion; if Moscow and Leningrad fall, Soviets will be deprived of their backbone, and only in a position to carry out partisan attacks, if large scale ones. Advised Siewert and C-in-C and also F., who praises Busch very highly and shares his outlook.

12 November 1941
Situation Conference
I could break down and cry! When one sees this 'Bosemüller Group'[367] coming and has informed the head of the class,[368] then the same picture always shows itself. Gyldenfeldt,[369] who escorted the group, said to me accurately: 'They are like a group of schoolboys waiting to get their boots polished.' That is exactly right and (it is) embarrassing. The situation is now to go for Moscow and the south.[370] Camouflage attack tag means partial attack.[371] What does it all mean? In the first place the devastating knowledge that F. does not express and explain clearly what it is that he wants. Result is that C-in-C and Chief of the General Staff give up and do what they think fit based on their interpretation of the uncertain intentions of F. Meanwhile . . .[372] Keitel continues to butt in at every inconvenient opportunity.

16 November 1941
Wolfsschanze
Unpleasant situation conference. Supply and railways reported on. Wild tirade by F. against Wagner (laughable theorist); Gercke comes off well. F. entertains more and more doubts that new full-scale attacks

(towards Gomel)[373] are right. F. was never convinced to view Moscow as decisive for the war. OB [Brauchitsch] is furious with B. [Bock], for v. Bock[374] is rabid for this idea (obsessed), case which he also makes to F. C-in-C said: 'He wants to move in there just like he did in Paris.' But as before, remains of the opinion that Moscow would be decisive for the war.

20 November 1941[+]
(Tiso)
F. sang the high praises of Minister-President Tiso.[375] This was a priest whom he could accept: hard, ready to fight, a son of the people who knew his Slovaks very well, certainly the weakness of his church as well, but cleverly avoided any mention. That kind of man had been the secret of success for the Catholic Church in the Middle Ages.[376] F. was very sympathetic to him because it meant that the Slovaks had a priest to lead them; they were a peasant people known to be very pious.

22 November 1941
This evening F. spoke within a small circle about the things which have motivated him these last months. Everything points to the fact that he remains uncertain what he intends. The whole situation is bringing him to make decisions which – unfortunately – are divorced from the influences to which he is subjected: Party, the old guard, state and, last of all, Wehrmacht.

It appears from all this that the objectives of the campaign have not been achieved, on the other hand in the eyes of the world's politicians, German successes would not be without effect. All wars were at first not popular but were economic in structure, without brokers no war could be decided. The weapons dealers determined the production of cannons, Panzers and ammunition. He *had to*[377] introduce a potential for German armaments which would take the breath away. The war in the east to be fought just so. To seize the initiative for oneself, that was the precondition for final victory.

22 November 1941[+]
Schmundt referred again to the imminent change of Army Commander-in-Chief.[378] I am in despair. He cannot be talked out of his idea to have F. take over as C-in-C Army himself. He sees in it a great opportunity for the restoration of trust. He does not understand my objections, that it would be merely symbolic and leave the Army leaderless. Also incomprehensible is his recurrent positive opinion of

Keitel; this fluctuates according to whether or not latter has upset him. At least he has turned away from the idea he had several years ago of advocating Himmler [for C-in-C]; he now probably knows about this one. But the situation is depressing, and our open discussions are often violent.

After the late situation conference I asked F. for some signatures and in conversation mentioned the C-in-C. F. spoke very calmly about Br. Considers him a very ill man at the end of his strength. I posed the question if he was proposing to replace him with Manstein or Kesselring.[379] F. clammed up and left.

24 November 1941

Another unsatisfactory, confusing situation conference. Also F. gave no orders, just delivered long dialogue [*sic*] ending up with C-in-C and Chief of the General Staff going home with the impression that they could do what they saw fit – meanwhile F. changed his thinking, everything which was is now not true and – the OKH is responsible. It is not the case, but the field marshal is not the man who can ward it off.

25 November 1941
Moscow

In the evening more long dissertations about future prosecution of operations. F. hit out. Major concerns about Russian winter and climate; we began a month too late. Ideal solution would be the capture of Leningrad, occupy the southern region and then eventually pincer movement from N and S towards Moscow with frontal assault. Then there would be opportunity to make the general front line into an Ostwall with military bases, similar to in the double monarchy in the Balkans;[380] but timing was his worst nightmare.

28 November 1941[+]
Antonescu

F. spoke about Antonescu.[381] It came as a surprise to us all that he rates him higher than Mussolini in intelligence, in character and also in calibre. On the other hand he was missing the motivation and energy and unscrupulousness which is necessary for a popular leader. Above all, however, as a trained general staff officer (on military matters) and of leadership he understood far more than the Duce. Also in racial questions he was much clearer and more objective. He had not spoken much with Mussolini on the Jewish question. Antonescu had once left a court ball and returned with his wife when he discovered from the guest list that Madame Lupescu[382] would also be there. It was a great pity that A. did not speak German, only French, otherwise he would understand him a lot better.

30 November 1941
Reich Chancellery

F. still much under influence of Ciano visit;[383] was hoping to have got both him – and with him the Duce – involved as ally. Italians always need a prod; the war with Russia is something enormous for them in any case. Had a long talk with Schm. about the conference, at which we were in attendance for greater part of the time. Were both somewhat appalled at the heavy emphasis on, and exaggeratedly optimistic portrayal of, the war situation by F.: Russia was on the brink of liquidation and at the last gasp industrially, and by inference on the armaments front, too, since the most valuable essential raw materials [are] in German hands. Astonished as well about unsparing exposure of his war aims. Told Ciano that his main objectives were Caucasus, Pers[ian] Gulf and with it the Near East. If he succeeded, Churchill would not know what to do next. F. appealed to the Italians to become active in North Africa with all forces at their command in order to 'open up things from ahead'; he would help where he could. Very distrustful of France, even Vichy. Even there they were outwardly loyal because it served their purposes, not out of conviction. We were appalled that F. in praising conduct of Ger. people mentioned intellectual saboteurs making his life difficult, but God be thanked they were only a small minority; he did not need to fear this circle.

Attitude of Ciano was inscrutable and very reserved. His objections as before [were] how hard it was for the Duce to sell the war to the Italian people, presenting it as an absolute necessity.

6 December 1941
Wolfsschanze

Trust between F. and C-in-C can no longer be patched up. Every situation conference is unpleasant. C-in-C can no longer cope with F.'s attacks and general approach to him. Told me this evening at Mauerwald he cannot handle it, also for health reasons. Is now going finally to request leave of absence. If F. decides he wants a replacement, then his suggestions (are) v. Kluge or v. Manstein, definitely not Kesselring, since (he) is merely an organ of the Reichsmarschall. Reported everything to Schmundt during the night, he will speak to F. tomorrow.

7 December 1941

Schmundt summoned me shortly before the situation conference. Said that he discussed with F. everything about C-in-C. As F. had no idea as to a successor, he, Schmundt, had confided to F. his long deliberated conception that [F.] should assume post of C-in-C. Chief of the General Staff could be made his immediate subordinate. F. asked for time to think it over and will discuss it with Reichs-marschall and Keitel. I was shocked and told Schmundt so. He just cannot understand me and enamoured with his suggestion, which will restore trust.

8 December 1941⁺
Jasnaya – Polyana

F. has been given Propaganda Company reports and also a memorandum from Guderian, who has installed a command centre on Tolstoy's property. F. very interested in this and wants above all that this national treasure remain undamaged; is in full agreement about protecting the sepulchre and farmhouse, less so with the reports he is receiving from [Commander] Panzers. Perplexity is self-evident; scapegoats are being sought for grinding to a halt in the thrust on Moscow.[384] Spoke about the OKH prattle to which he had given in. Concern about the Russian winter is now obvious but he is thinking along the lines of restarting operations towards Tula. Jodl spoke out very gravely, warned about partial operations and said that one had to make an overall decision about north and south of Moscow; doubted that it would be possible for the Panzer spearhead to hold on to the advanced positions they now occupied. Either one had to break through using a small pincer movement or be forced to accept an extensive pulling back of the front. F. disagreed and embarked – as so often – on an endless monologue. He did not believe in fresh Russian forces, considered it all a bluff, assumed it likely that these were the last reserves from Moscow. The OKH enemy reports were exaggerated and deliberately highly coloured. It would not be the first time that Germans had lost their nerve at the fateful hour. He did not want to hear the expression 'pull back' again. On and on it went in this tone, but from it all one sees how unsettled and uncertain he is. Unfortunately Keitel did not second Jodl, but as usual supported the views of F.

18 December 1941
Wolfsschanze

Guderian was with F.,[385] his psychological state was ghastly, and this was not lost on F. Quite out of character he spoke of the impossibility of holding the front. Withdraw possibly to the demarcation line.[386] Painted an appalling picture of the condition of the men.[387] Condemned OKH sharply on supply and winter uniforms. Clear to F. that Guderian not able to lead. Harsh words against OKH by F., to some extent unjustified since everybody, including himself, believed in the 'Bunzelwitz winter camp'.[388]

1942-43

27 January 1942
Wolfsschanze

Every day the 'Bosemüller Group', led by Halder, came to the situation (conference). Contrary to expectations all went well. Chief of the General Staff visibly at pains for good atmosphere. He was lucky, since situation apparently under control. Von Gyldenfeldt[389] and I were furious that he seized every opportunity cleverly to denigrate absent former C-in-C and attribute to him all previous decisions and recommendations which were opposed to F's thinking. Today he said: 'Mein Führer, if the field marshal had listened to you and me occasionally, today we would be in this position or that position.'

15 March 1942
Reich Chancellery[390]

Reichsführer-SS and Kaltenbrunner[391] with the F. Nasty atmosphere. I was there initially until requested by F. to leave the room: until then subject had been 'Reports on morale'.[392] Himmler loomed large; came out strongly for the first time against the Army. He had established that anti-Party and anti-state movements were in progress. Also officers were openly defeatist, particularly in the Home Army, it being worst in Bavaria. Himmler suggested replacing those commanders at the head of it by good, younger front-experienced officers.

26 March 1942
(F. – Hewel) (Bulgaria)

I brought King Boris from Sofia.[393] Nice time there; strange feeling when passing the brightly-lit Russ[ian] embassy. The king splendid, natural and open. Looked forward to his visit to the F., in the plane above Wiener Neustadt, pointed to Theres[ien] Akad[emie], where he had been a cadet. After he left, F. spoke at length about the situation in the Balkans. Highest praise for King B., the only monarch who understood the New Order in Europe; unfortunately he had many problems of his own. Was dour and remorseless with regard to the Russians. B. told F. that he would have a revolt on his hands if he broke with the Soviets. Less pleasant it had been for him, F., [to hear] hate and revulsion for the Turks, that was of no use at all. The spirit behind the Balkan Wars lived on. It was bad for us that on account of the tension between Bulgaria and Turkey he saw no possibility of drawing the Turks into our camp. Nevertheless for the time being as a neutral flank they were more important than the Bulgarians. He could make good use of both of them, the Anatolians and the 'Prussians of the Balkans', as they both produced outstanding soldiers.

21 April 1942[+]
(Bormann – Schaub – Schmundt – Puttkamer)
(Big Talk about Judges)

Bormann or Schaub had placed before Hitler some court judgments containing defeatist observations. It is astonishing how great his hate is for the judges. He spoke at length on justice reform after the war. All of German jurisprudence had to be turned inside out. The law gave judges more power in the state than Gauleiters and hereditary princes. The impossibility of removing judges was an unacceptable thing; he was currently considering whether the US system of electing and dismissing judges was not the right one. But above everything he had to have jurists who had passed through a particularly testing Party school. Only a man who understood ideology and the political mission of his own people could pronounce what was law in the name of the people. Most judges had no appreciation of the National Socialist state and being above politics used that as a shield to hide behind. Their being above politics was utterly illogical, for a judge, charged with delivering a verdict, had to find for or against an accused. It was utter nonsense, the lay judges, juries and jurors provided for by a very dubious system. They were like bulls in a china shop, and the damage they caused was irreparable, making it very difficult for even an experienced and renowned professional judge to deliver a proper verdict. Here again a guarantee would have to be vouchsafed, by means of a settled system still to be worked out within the Party, that if there had to be lay judges, then these would only be tested Party member stalwarts with an unequivocal political attitude. To my objection that in order to avoid such a state of affairs leading to difficulties, in that Party Members formed only a small percentage of the population, and he was opposed to the Party swelling its numbers, the F. replied that enough lay judges would be available from amongst properly trained Party members. In conclusion he made a few pithy observations about lawyers. Frederick the Great had hated them for their ability to turn black into white and vice-versa. With an undoubted dig at Frank and Freisler, the F. asserted that even his Party lawyers were a problem and set him many conundrums. It was often impossible to distinguish them from pastors with jesuitical training; they were for the most part impossible to understand and less convinced about justice than 'Whose bread I eat, His song I sing'. But these were all problems for which there would be plenty of time after the war.

5 May 1942
Speer, Rockets

Speer spent a long time with the F., and I sat with him alone at dinner, since everybody else was in the cinema. Sp. was not altogether happy with the conversation. After long talks with Dornberger[394] and W. von Braun,[395] he had tried to win F. over for Peenemünde and pressing ahead with rocket development, with negative results so far. As we know, for the time being F. is against the whole thing and a short while ago turned down out of hand all efforts by the C-in-C to obtain more cash for the project.[396] Speer is very impressed by Peenemünde and sees a great opportunity for us in rocket development. He told me confidentially that with the agreement of OKH he had managed secretly to obtain funds from the household budget in order to push ahead with development and testing. Moreover he had quite different projects, and had proceeded with acoustical tests, using supersonic effects from so-called sound machines, the purpose of which was to paralyse an enemy and making him unable to fight. In this respect he had the fullest support of the Minister for Posts, Ohnesorge, who was also very interested in rocket development. Sp. has at least obtained F.'s approval to arrange a conference at the earliest opportunity with W. v. Braun.

28 May 1942
Persons of Mixed Race

I take note again of Bormann's sniping. Schm. sent for me and let me know in advance that the F. is thinking of introducing in the future other means for making decisions with regard to applications by persons of mixed race to remain in the armed forces.[397] The subject had been referred to my field of jurisdiction from the beginning and I am able to produce a fine list of successes to show for it. Hundreds of 50, 25 and even the odd few 75-per-centers[398] were able to save themselves and remain in the Army with a 'Special Approval'. That had now been spotted by a number of Gau and Kreis leaders when they were card-indexed for registration purposes. I talked about it to Frey[399] of the OKW, who was as unhappy about it as I was. We made a lot of 'mistakes' with photographs and tried to help where we could.

30 May 1942
Persons of Mixed Race

I have presented fresh applications for exemptions and wait for the F.'s response.[400] F. was very annoyed, talked about attempts to pull the wool over his eyes. He had apparently been talking with Bormann and Keitel. In future such applications would be checked over by the Party Chancellery and would have to be counter-signed by the Head of OKW before being presented. This we do not want. I attempted to make a plea for First World War veterans and those with front experience in this war. But it appeared injudicious to go any further with Hitler in his current mood. Am at my wits' end and have no idea what I should do next. I spare a thought for the Reichsmarschall, who in this business has always been very liberal.

9 July 1942

Visit to Second Army HQ. Voronezh bridgehead, ugly situation, under heavy pressure from the Russians and ceaseless barrage. With Colonel-General v. Salmuth[401] very grave prognosis. Poor opinion of the Hungarians, who were now to be found more often looking back than forward. Von S. considers situation so serious that preparations must be taken in hand to evacuate the bridgehead if strong reinforcements not brought up. Flew back in the evening to inform Führer. Loud outburst against v. S. This latter also belonged to the old clique and had neither the will nor the political predisposition to master serious situations.

29 July 1942

Was with Paulus[402] and Freiherr v. Weichs.[403] Everywhere quiet optimism. Field commanders presented me with files about munitions supply and fighting strengths for the chief. Always the same concerns about whether Russians have exhausted their reserves or are bringing up fresh forces. All field commanders share the same opinion that manpower in ratio to tasks demanded is too weak and substantial requirements, such as counter-attacks, are no longer possible with available forces. P(aulus), Freiherr v. Weichs, most of all Winter[404] (Weichs' Chief of Staff) are asking that I report my impressions bluntly to F. since, in the opinion of the front, Chief of the General Staff does not do this.

15 August 1942

Visit to Army Group A, First Panzer Army and 13th SS Panzer Division *Wiking*.[405] Long discussion with List[406] and v. Gyldenfeldt. Optimism that goals will be reached although with proviso that Soviet counter-pressure cannot be calculated. Quite different at v. Kleist[407] and Faeckenstedt.[408] Troops more or less at the end of their tether; air and ground reconnaissance had shown that Caucasus south of Krasnodar and Maikop only negotiable along four skirting paths by mountain troops with mules. No possibility of setting up a decisive attack. Disappointment about so-called oilfields at Maikop, only the main administration confirmed there; operations off roads and paths totally out of question because of primaeval-type jungle and thicket, difficult for orientation. A Panzer division is totally out of place there. Tough Russian resistance in the mountains, heavy casualties, *Wiking* worst hit. Opinion at First Panzer Army is that opening up the mountains is only possible in the south from Kuban. 13th Panzer Division and *Wiking* think the same. AA [Aufklärungs Abteilung – Reconnaissance Battalion] convinced me *Wiking* in unfavourable terrain. Received (from First Panzer Army) comprehensive maps and appreciation of the situation. On return flight was with v. Gyldenfeldt again.

16 August 1942
Situation Wolfsschlucht[409]

Presented files and reported on my flight to the front.[410] Made an unfavourable impression on everybody, on F. and also Chief of the General Staff, who afterwards asked me in conversation why I had not reported to him first. Chief does not believe my despatches. Everybody is surprised. After situation conference, F. remarked to Schmundt: 'Our friend Engel has let himself be taken in by tittle-tattle.' F. expressed the desire that he, Schmundt, should check my information. In the evening it was decided that Chief of WFSt [Jodl] would fly to the front to clarify the situation.

27 August 1942 1400 [hrs] & 27 August 1942 2200 [hrs][411]

31 August or 1 September 1942[412]

Field Marshal List presented his report at Wolfsschlucht,[413] also there von Gyldenfeldt and Chief of Transport, General Gercke.[414] List's description of situation coincided with the reported assessment of the Chief of the General Staff over the last few days. At first very unpleasant atmosphere. F. interrupted continually, accused the army group of spreading its forces too thinly and thereby allowing the whole front to be whittled down. Noticeable that he is now recognising that taking the mountains is not possible. There was then agreement that, with significantly stronger forces than hitherto, an advance could be made from Crimea over Kuban and along the coast. He is irrevocably determined to reach Astrakhan and the Caspian Sea, in the Caucasus now he just wants to ensure loose contact without requiring the mountain troops to make decisive gains. After the conference there was a general impression of a considerable release of tension. For some time F. has even been exchanging friendly words with Chief of the General Staff.

4 September 1942

Trust in Chief of the General Staff is lost. For first time latter launched a major appraisal of the condition of the fighting force. Chief interrupted and [Hitler] scolded him: 'Who are you to say this, Herr Halder, you who even in the First World War occupied the same revolving stool, and now lecture me on the fighting man, you who have never been awarded the black Wound Badge?' Embarrassing. (I) told Gen(eral) Heusinger),[415] Chief of the General Staff should report sick, this damage was beyond repair.[416] In the evening F. attempted to make light of this outburst by being especially friendly to Halder.

7 September 1942[417]

Jodl is back from Army Group A. Brought a clear appreciation of the situation confirming that it is no longer possible to force the Russians over the mountain chain and into the sea. Only flexible tactics possible in area of opportunity and in it last attempt will be made to reach Grozny and Cas(pian) Sea with concentrated forces; not Astrakhan, no forces available for it. F. got more worked up minute by minute, sensing the failure of the offensive, had harsh words for supply service, deficiency of initiative on the part of the higher field commanders, placed all blame on OKH, Chief of the General Staff and Jodl. Final break with Jodl who is still attempting to transfer the main thrust exclusively towards south.

Entry of 27 August 1942 22.00 [hrs]

Worst crisis since 1941; F. is raging. In the evening unpleasant argument between Chief and Jodl, who tenaciously supports opinion of Kleist and List. We all have the impression that F. is faced with taking some decisive steps. Jodl has been under fire. [F. said] words had been put in his mouth, things would now change, he would make see to that, trust is gone, and he would therefore take upon himself the personal consequences. Night-time to Schmundt: 'I will be glad when I get rid of this loathsome jacket and ride roughshod.'

8 September 1942
(At Night)

I am simply no longer as quick on the uptake. I cannot get over the F.–Jodl collision, all the more so when I realise that quite unwittingly I may have been one of the causes of it. The files I brought on 3 September [*sic*] given me by von Kleist and Gyldenfeldt[418] about the difficulties of transportation and highway problems for Suchum and Tuapse had as their consequence Jodl's flight to Stalino. As I happened to overhear the whole altercation, I am able to imagine the extent of the breach. One gained the impression that F. was full of hate, and the unusual degree of agitation shown by Jodl did nothing to help lower the volume. The mood here is ghastly; the roots of F.'s rage and aggravation lie much deeper, and not just in the opposing opinions about whether the attack in the Caucasus should be towards Suchum or not. F. sees no end to it any more in Russia, particularly since none of the goals for summer 1942 have been achieved. He said himself how fearful he is of the winter which will soon be upon us. On the other hand, he will never retreat.

How long the business with H[alder] will carry on is a puzzle to me. At the conference with J. the outbursts against H. were so highly charged and hate-filled that one simply cannot repeat them. I will inform Heusinger tomorrow, for it is best if the Chief of the General Staff goes as quickly as possible of his own accord, rather than that he be booted out in the midst of another scene.

14 September 1942
F. – Schm. – Jodl (Seeckt)

F.'s distrust of generals and the officer corps has grown; attitude towards Jodl is icy, but officially correct once more. Jodl has given no ground and and responds in kind. Today there was sniping of a general sort against the generals, although J. and Halder were the targets. One observes in the F. his restrained fury, but also his uncertainty: 'What now?' Accused officer corps of poor judgement, lack of responsibility and a modicum of courage, as to their political convictions nothing was said. There was not a single person with whom he could have a political conversation. The last C-in-C (Brauchitsch) had occasionally asked some childishly naive questions; Ludendorff had done the same. Seeckt[419] at least had a clear political attitude, albeit the wrong one, and how pathetic his role had been as a deputy. He had to be grateful for Seeckt's brief interlude, for in retrospect the 1923 schism – exclusively Seeckt's doing – had been a blessing. He often wondered if the Russian principle of political commissars did not have a lot going for it. Two things certainly: it gave the commanders political pepper, and then they were also good organs of political control, for the danger of making armed political nonsense was always present. None of us said a word, Jodl's face an iron mask.

18 September 1942[+]

After the evening conference, which was as frosty again as everything else here, Schmundt and I had something else to report about. At the moment, F. seems determined to get rid of Keitel and Jodl.[420] Schmundt asked what successor he was thinking of. He mentioned Kesselring or Paulus; the only thing that held him back was the timing. Keitel, otherwise a good worker, was apparently under the influence of Jodl, and most of his opinions were not his own. The Chief of the General Staff would have to go beforehand, there was simply nothing more there. At the moment he trusted nobody amongst his generals, and he would promote a major to general and appoint him Chief of the General Staff if only he knew a good one. For the moment everything was repugnant to him. He was cursing himself that he had risked fighting a war with such generals, unable to take life and death decisions. Schmundt replied that one could not say that generally. Within a short time he would be in a position to provide him with a list of generals in whom he could place his trust. In contrast to Schmundt I have the impression that the F. is at the end of his tether with his nerves, and it is not only a question of personalities. Basically he hates everything in field-grey, irrespective of where it comes from, for today I heard again the oft-repeated expression that he longed 'for the day when he could cast off this jacket'.

24 September 1942

F. dismissed Chief of the General Staff in humiliating circumstances.[421] I did not hear about it from Schmundt until a little later and was summoned to look after him. Ha(lder) was completely taken aback, thanked me tearfully for coming and said: 'If you had gone through what I have just experienced you would understand how I feel to have you with me.' We raged against Keitel, who had conducted himself towards Halder in an unworthy and uncomradely manner.

26 September 1942

Schm. flew to Paris, fetched Zeitzler.[422] Latter with F., firing on all cylinders, promises him complete reorganisation of the General Staff. He will leave him alone to get on with it. Same old song: too old, too little experience at the front. Chief said he had a better impression from younger Gen(eral Staff) officers. [Engel 1959: This was a reference to Colonel i.G. Graf Stauffenberg, Organisation Division, who had often accompanied Halder to FHQ situation conferences and with Buhle frequently even made statements affecting decisions on operations.] From all this it is clear that the Reichsmarschall has been very active during the recent crises in stirring up sentiment against the Army and General Staff. Schm. is astonishingly optimistic; in the OKH opinions are very divided.

30 September 1942

F. had a long conversation with Schm(undt) and myself about a new Chief of the General Staff. Long discourse about duty of the General Staff. Since 1914 G(erman) General Staff had lost its way. Ludendorff had been its last dynamic force. Education by academics and theoreticians with 'royal box' privileges had been responsible for gradually separating these officers from their calling and duty. General Staff had turned into an institute for study in itself, its weapon was the pen and not the sword. He wanted young officers transferred from the front line into the General Staff to give the staff a new face. The new Chief had ideas: he had proved that in France. He had brought the post to life; he would doubtless sweep the High Command clean. Heusinger would definitely have to remain. He had adjusted things and had worked himself in. He also had the impression that Heusinger did not treat his ideas with the same reservation that Halder had.

1 October 1942

Long, unpleasant talk with Schm. who unfortunately did not apply the brakes yesterday with regard to the mistakes of the General Staff but stirred things up. Pleaded for abolition of the red leg stripes (even though he wears them himself!). The collar patches had to go, too; only a modest indication (coloured cord) should remain. I replied that at the moment I did not understand this struggle about the General Staff and uniform distinctions. It was right that young officers with front experience should join the staff, but it would not be much use if they lacked preparatory training. Certainly the Hirschberg instructors[423] had to be proven General Staff officers with front experience.

2 October 1942

Z(eitzler) reported that XIV Panzer Corps (was) on a broad front along the Volga and the river was barriered.[424] F. promised extensive destruction of the Russ(ian) supply system. Z. and even Jodl encouraged him to consider following up by capturing the city since this would free the forces tied up there. Reference to danger of high losses in house-to-house fighting. F. brusquely waved this aside and emphasised for the first time that capture of Stalingrad was an urgent necessity not only for operational reasons but also psychologically for world opinion and morale amongst Germany's allies.

3 October 1942

Situation report from Sixth Army read out by Z(eitzler). Spoke of heavy casualties in house-to-house fighting and a stiffening of Russ(ian) resistance. Question raised once more whether the attack on the city should not be abandoned in order to release forces for Army Group A and also with regard to the supply situation of A, which was extremely stretched. As before F. rejected this sharply with the observation that this was the typical half-measure which he expected from the Army.

10 October 1942

During course of situation conference, long discourse by F. about situation along the entire Eastern Front. F. considers Russian attacks on Army Group Centre and North not as a sign of strength, but weakness.[425] In his opinion they are diversionary tactics to draw away German forces from south. One should not believe everything the senior commanders reported. All reports had the tendency to prove as far as it was possible what needed to be done to look after number one. Enemy attacks and successes were accordingly coloured or dramatised to attract reinforcements, res(erves), art(illery) and aircraft. The only unselfish C-in-C was von Weichs, who had once lent forces to his neighbouring army to help it out of a predicament. Stalingrad had to broken from within, this would release our forces and deprive Communism of its sanctuary. Z. attempted to defend the C-in-C, spoke again of drain on forces, but is nevertheless on the whole optimistic.

18 October 1942

F. in high spirits today after fall of 'Red October'.[426] Believes all Stalingrad will soon be in our hands, saw from newsreels effect and value of the s.IG [infantry gun] in house-to-house fighting and is much encouraged; wants to increase production of the infantry gun. Reports of [Russian] troop assembly east of the Volga confirmed by long-range reconnaissance are interpreted by F. as intention to set up new defensive front line on the eastern bank of the Volga.

18 October 1942
Evening

Excited discussion F. and Jodl, who is utterly opposed to 'Special Measures' being taken against sabotage squads.[427] Spoke of consequences for 'Brandenburgers'[428] and SD people. F. expects to settle their hash by this form of intimidation. As before Keitel playing his pathetic role, stabbing Jodl in the back and fortifying F. in his resolve. Brought with him draft for Commando Order and got it copied. We very concerned about this order and got instructions from Jodl to make sure that C-in-Cs and commanders understand that it is to be handled in the same way as the Commissar Order. In conclusion F. utters strong words about Army's lack of enthusiasm for such deterrent measures. He knew very well that orders such as the Commissar Order had either not been acted upon or only with hesitation by the Army. The High Command was guilty of wanting to turn its soldiers into pastors if they could. If he did not have his SS, what sort of state would we be in now? Jodl replied that international agreements applied also in wartime, and for the benefit of one's own men.

19 October 1942

F. embarked again on a long dissertation about Halder. Once he had had a very good opinion and had hoped with [Halder] to have been able to banish Beck's ghost from the General Staff. Unfortunately he had succumbed to the foul air in the Bendlerstrasse and had become the puppet of his advisers. Lack of instinct for political necessities. H. was without doubt a good instructor at the academy but never a leader in battle. He had long hoped that [Halder] would draw the right conclusions for himself, but the question of a successor had always held him [F.] back. In the end he had bitten the bullet to demand the resignation of the man who had always done nothing but obstruct him. He had not envied Heusinger and the others who had had to work so closely with H(alder). He did not demand of any officer that he be a National Socialist, but enthusiasm to strike a blow, to fight, were pre-conditions for everything which followed.

22 October 1942

Z. reported again on the grave supply situation of [Army Group] South and requested increased air operations for supply purposes. Read reports from allied participants, mainly the Romanians, which complained of deficiencies in supply.[429] For the first time Z. broaches the question of transferring more troops from the West. Schm. and I laughed, since as Chief of Staff West he always had the opposite point of view. Christian[430] said he doubted that any more aircraft could be made available.

24 October 1942

(I) flew to see Tippelskirch[431] (German general with Italian Eighth Army) at Millerov.[432] Long talk with him and Gyldenfeldt.[433] 'Tippel' very depressed about morale, deployment, armament, discipline and fighting spirit of the Italians. Gen(eral) Messe[434] totally lacking and disinterested in overall situation. 'Tippel' demanded strong G(erman) res(erves) behind Ital(ian) sectors of front. These latter would not be able to contain any kind of serious threat. T. insistent that mixed fronts and German corps staffs were much better. After flight back reported at once to F. in presence of Keitel, Jodl and Schm. Repeated everything I had been told at Millerov. F. listened quietly, but did not view the position there so pessimistically. Defended single-race front[435] with Ger. reserves in support if need be. One could not (split up) Ital(ians) under division strength, in that way one would create gaps. Better heavy German counter-attacks.

27 October 1942

Am back from Voronezh.[436] OB [v. Salmuth of Second Army] provided me with assessment of the situation for F. Poorest opinion reserved for Hungarians;[437] he would not trust them with anything. Above all senior officers made a devastating impression and were quite candid that when the Russians attacked they would retire to 'previously prepared' positions to the rear. Second Army very concerned at poor armament of Hungarians: anti-tank guns mostly only 3.7 [cm], old tanks and not much heavy artillery. Second Army gravely worried at their having full responsibility for so broad a sector of the front, all the more so now that the present situation, the front being along the bend in the Don, was vulnerable to an offensive. I presented the assessment to F., added my own experience from Voronezh, where very strong Russian air activity and also heavy artillery barrages dictated battle tactics. F. not pleased by the report and assessment of the situation; had Schmundt report to him in detail about OB, but former spoke (of OB) in respectable terms. F. contradicted primarily the assessment of the Hungarians. He knew them better, they were good fighters when well led. Their officer corps was admittedly too weak and only lions in the officers' mess. F. did not believe in main Russian thrusts at Voronezh;[438] they could not attack everywhere, that had become a fixed idea amongst German commanders. At the moment they were all too worried. Nobody reported it all quiet in his sector. Appealed to Z. to bring his opinion to the attention of the army commanders.

6 November 1942

F. raged against military administration in France as the result of a report by SD and the Organisation Sauckel.[439] It was the worst foreign administration; they had dug themselves a nice little niche and were weak. If it were possible he would like to have all France under political control. The softness of the Army was responsible for the increase in the resistance movement and sabotage at the workplace. Very disappointed by Stülpnagel,[440] who in the opinion of the Reichsmarschall had always been a good National Socialist – insofar as one could speak of officers in such terms. Jews, French, you name it, slipped beneath the coats of these womanisers. And the Army was then so proud if they offered up an Our Father. (F.) finished with the words: 'Zeitzler, if I did not need you here, I would give you plenipotentiary powers to root out all the nonsense there.' Unfortunately Z. did not reply, and even Schmundt confirmed opinion of F. about occupation in French territories.

7 November 1942

For an assessment of Enemy Situation-East, Z. presented various OQuIV files: amongst other things it was now known for certain from many conferences that Stalin (had) emphasised the need for a major offensive in the south, and it had to be expected that the Russians would be assembling troops in the Don basin and east of Rostov. This pointed to intentions for an offensive. F. rejected this for the time being.[441] From experience one knew that the General Staff basically overestimated the enemy; Poland and France had been an embarrassment in this respect. All the more, therefore, should one persevere with the objective at Stalingrad, for Stalin could and would never abandon it. It was there that he would concentrate his defensive forces. The [offensive] forces spoken of were definitely moving up in this connection. The sooner Stalingrad was totally in our grasp the sooner we could reorganise our own forces and shuffle in the pact [allied] armies. Z put an opposing point of view, if rather timidly, mentioning the enormous capacity of the Russians for improvisation, which always brought its surprises. F. admitted this, but stuck to his assessment.

8 November 1942

Great excitement over the landings in West Africa [sic].[442] Wild outburst by F. against Luftwaffe, which just like the Army had been 'fooling around' with designs and now found itself without a long-range bomber.[443] We could have had the He 177 long ago, but with us everything had to be produced as the perfect design. The Luftwaffe had forced nothing through during the war. He would now himself take the designers in hand as he had done with the Army in 1939. Without him the Army would not have had the Panzer IV with the long 7.5 [cm gun] nor the 7.5 [cm] anti-tank gun, not to mention the self-propelled gun. At the situation conference itself, in comparison to others present (Foreign Office, Keitel and Jodl), F. was astonishingly well composed. A few worries about whether the French would abide by their agreement. Observation: 'One could possibly have offered them a better lure' but he had trusted only Pétain and Laval. All the others, even Darlan, played a double game. Jodl contradicted and was sharply put to rights with the words that soldiers were not always the best judges of men.

10 November 1942

Back from Mu(nich). Lively discussion amongst ourselves about F. speech at the Bürgerbräu.[444] Together with many others I was appalled that F. spoke in such optimistic terms with regard to his circle of listeners. Call from Sodenstern [Chief of Staff, Army Group B], how could one say that Stalingrad had already been taken. That would not be the case for ages. Schm. looked at it differently. Considered text completely correct and primarily aimed at the west(ern) Allies, also for the people, who needed motivation not least in view of the increase in air attacks.

14 November 1942[445]

Back from Stalingrad.[446] Reported my impressions and presented files. After landing at Kalatsch, went at once to commanding officer [Paulus], then 14th Division and 79th Infantry Division. Col-Gen. P(aulus) took me over the various sectors and we were able to discuss everything. Was surprised at Paulus's optimism about future developments. He is only worried about his neighbours right and left. Very big concern especially about the southern front, as there front is too thinly spread and not only amongst amongst allied armies, additionally no reserves to speak of. He did not represent the situation with XIV Panzer Corps as grave. He requested substantial res(erves) behind Italians and Romanians in the big bend of the River Don. Complained about supply and wants to see more aerial support. Believes that even the rem(aining) parts of Stalingrad can be taken slowly but surely. Nothing definite about enemy troop assemblies facing the front and on the east bank of the Volga. Should intelligence estimates of the enemy strength be correct and crises set in to the right and left of Sixth Army, then it would be crazy to hold on to Stalingrad. We did not have the necessary forces to do so. In the evening I reported all this to F., who in presence of Schmundt and Jodl heard me out quietly. He questioned Buhle closely about Romanian and Italian tanks and anti-tank weapons.

16 November 1942
F. – Schm. – Jodl

A grim, dark mood. F. had long conversation with Himmler, and then the atmosphere remained in keeping. After some time more thoughts about his age, life and slackening of his life energy. His 'own people' were making his life sour; he also knew very well what was afoot in the country. His enemies were growing stronger the longer the war went on. Groups were active to destroy him and his work and he also knew that people had aspirations for after his death, though up until now he had settled their hash. The sad thing was, these were not fanatical communists but mainly intellectuals, so-called priests and even high-ranking people in the military. He was considering what useful war-related job he could foist on these people, living in Germany with nothing to do, to stop them from doing stupid things and making others mad. One should not underestimate him, he knew more than many perhaps thought.

F. had received caviar and sweets from Marshal Antonescu which he ordered [to be] destroyed immediately.

19 November 1942

Bad evening situation conference. Apparently the Romanians have suffered a catastrophe. Still no clear picture. Col-Gen. v. W(eichs) addressed F. himself and requested free hand for Gen. Heim[447] (XXXXVIII Panzer Corps). Initially this was granted on Z(eitzler)'s recommendation but retracted after he spoke with Second Army and ordered push in different direction (to north-west).

Evening. One after another contradictory reports arrive from Antonescu, Harteneck and Winter. Z. unable to make sense of it and suggested to F., above all to hold Gen. Heim in check and not release him until the situation had clarified. Therefore detain Panzer corps. I reported to the Führer personally that Romanians were only equipped with Czech, French [tanks] and a few Pz III and IV of old design. Von W(eichs) reported during the night that Gen. Heim had pulled back behind the Tshirr sector and was at the disposal of army group.

20 November 1942

A typical situation conference. Total confusion about the Romanians. Everything revolves around Heim. F. is himself completely uncertain what to do next. Conflicting opinions and even OKH had no precise ideas to offer. Suggestion to leave decision to Jodl and v. W(eichs) was turned down. XXXXVIII Panzer Corps was supposed to do *everything*: help Sixth Army and then consolidate again to the north-west and mop up to the left.[448] Is bad that at the moment nobody has a clue where Heim is. There is no clear line in place. Is bad the continual butting-in by Keitel, who is confused through having no expert knowledge. In the evening I said to Schmundt, I wouldn't want to be in Heim's shoes.

21 November 1942

More and more reports straight from the Book of Job coming now from south of Stalingrad[449] as well. Similarly crisis there with the

Romanians. Jodl suggested Sixth Army should evacuate Volga front entirely since there was no longer any danger of attack there, and support the southern sector. On the other hand, encirclement of Stalingrad now only a matter of hours. F. said no with the well-worn arguments: it would do nothing to change the situation and the Russians would not be deceived. They were masters of house-to-house fighting and the Stalingrad territory would be lost again. Führer said again and again: 'No matter what happens we must hold it at all costs.'

24 November 1942

Ever more disquiet at the situation conference. Cause is the complete confusion about Army Gr. v. Weichs. F. continues to issue orders directly and over head of OKH about deployment of XXXXVIII Panzer Corps even though we remain ignorant of what it is doing and where it is. Heim's last report was that he had to break out to the south, since Igel could not be held. In the evening [I had a] conversation with Sodenstern, who really preferred to talk to Schm., but swore that he would work to put an end to the steady stream of intermediate orders coming from FHQ and OKH. It was impossible even for him to know what is going on. Heim had had to be given freedom to manoeuvre. He alone could judge his own fighting strength and that of the Romanians. This suggestion was dismissed brusquely by F. Strong words about Heim; in opinion of F. completely unsuitable to command a corps.[450] A grim mood prevailed. I told Schm. of Sodenstern's point of view. Schm. unfortunately did not share it. Said F. was completely right, even in crises the Führer had to impose strict leadership otherwise we would have a repetition of the Hoeppner business.[451] I really took him to task on this.

24 November 1942

Big debate about Gen. Paulus's signal. Wanted to pull back entire northern front because the situation had now become untenable. P. had written that he could not expand the southern front and hold the northern front. F. turned down suggestion out of hand even though Z. was in favour. Reason was that then everything would start moving. One knew how it looked. Z. emphasised unequivocally that the encirclement of Sixth Army was now becoming reality although, one hoped, only temporarily. F. promised to call up further units from the West [and] to examine [situation], and reiterated that St(alingrad) must not be given up in any circumstances. He was placing great hopes on H(oth), to whom he had entrusted mastering the situation at the bend in the Don.[452]

25 November 1942

Major discussion about air supply for Stalingrad.[453] Göring bound himself to supply Army. On the average one could manage 300 tonnes [illegible, might be 500 tonnes]. Everything would be thrown in, even the Ju 90s from the commercial runs. Z. was doubtful, thought that 300 (or 500) tonnes would not be enough, talked about the weather situation and losses. However, Reichsmarschall was enormously strong, said he would fly in *any* weather conditions. Demyansk and other cases had proved it possible. We were horrified at his optimism, which is not shared even by Luftwaffe General Staff. F. was enthusiastic about the Reichsmarschall, who would deliver the goods as he had done in the past. There was no chicken-heartedness with him as there was in many Army circles.

26 November 1942

Long discussion about v. M(anstein)'s assessment.[454] Suggestion: pull back Sixth Army. Considerations: pull back everything south of St(alingrad), perhaps even as far as the Dnieper, accumulate reserves, and then begin new flank operation from the north down to the sea (to the south). Case was presented by Z. factually but without expressing his own opinion. F. was, and remained, impassive but turned it all down. Reasons: everything would be seen as weakness, areas of utmost importance (would be) lost again, intolerable effect on Germany's allies, loss of time since one never knew what might not crop up next in the W(est), Africa or wherever. Von M(anstein) had good ideas operationally, but in view of the overall situation they were mere grey theory. As soon as the other senior commanders noticed that forces were being built up here or there, they would all be demanding the old recipe. In closing Z. requested that, in the case of emergency, Sixth Army should be given freedom to manoeuvre, and this F. spurned out of hand. Relief was the only thing in prospect, for which the bulk of Fourth Panzer Army was available.

26 November 1942

Heim has been relieved of command and ordered to report, apparently on account of his unauthorised move into the Tshirr sector, and repeated disobedience to orders. We are all of the opinion that he is the victim of bitter injustice. Unbelievable attitude of

K[eitel] who regularly intervenes as a sniper and behind whom, as is frequent is such cases, the Führer entrenches himself. It was he who also suggested to F. a court-martial. [I] had a long conversation with Schm. who was undecided about it and will talk to Heim when he arrives. Unfortunately everything Führer decides is sacrosanct for Schm. But it irks him all the same. Disappointing how little Z. intervened and (that) the army group no longer makes a case. Puma [Puttkamer] and I are in total agreement. In the evening I approached Schm. with another request for his help [regarding transfer to active unit].

26 November 1942

Christian's[455] great hour came. In presence of Jodl he stated grave reservations about assertions of Reichsmarschall; the promised quantity of supply was not possible. In his opinion in good weather conditions the best that can be hoped for is an average of 100 to 150 tonnes per day. F. rejected this after hearing him out in silence. Everything was just a question of time. An especially capable organiser would have to be appointed, with full plenipotentiary powers, if needed over the heads of the generals who were making difficulties for the air drop (v. Manstein, v. Richthofen?).

18 December 1942

Great disquiet again at the situation conference. LVII Panzer Corps not advancing, Russians throwing in new forces to oppose it, whole thing now looks defensive since no other forces available. Means that the attempt to relieve [Stalingrad] is coming to a halt 50–60 km from the Sixth Army front line.[456] Even worse with Army Group B. Apparently Italians have been breached, also Romanians with Army Detachment Hollidt.

Evening: v. M(anstein) again requested break-out by Sixth Army. Only way to maintain link to Stalingrad [*sic*] and so save the greater part of the army. Mood is depressed. F. turned down break-out once more despite desperate plea by Z. Very angry telephone calls from Busse[457] and also von M., since all have been directed to join Army Group B, now on the move, in order to plug the gap left by the Italians.

19 December 1942

Excited discussion, v. M. requested permission for break-out by Sixth Army again. F. was unbending, came out with same arguments as before. Does not believe army can be saved, found out somehow from Schm. that even Sixth Army considers break-out not possible under present circumstances. Von M. reported that if Sixth Army could not assist using its own forces, relief would be impossible.

19 December 1942
Work Theme

Major conference between F., Speer, Keitel and Fromm. Big discussion about increasing armament production, especially Panzers and ammunition. Fromm very heavily involved and complained bitterly about the disproportionate division of quotas for various Wehrmacht arms of service. Accused Reichsmarschall outright of giving preference to Luftwaffe at expense of Army; presented a report by Polte,[458] Magdeburg, complaining about shortage of labour and moreover being deprived of highly-qualified armaments workers. Speer admitted this and also did not dispute the assertion about Göring's arbitrariness in his capacity as head of the Four-Year Plan. Fr. came up with a suggestion, involved discussion about it followed, talked about making inmates in concentration camps and Jews in so-called 'containment areas'[459] available to the war economy, making them liable for war service and thus getting them into armaments. In this manner hundreds of thousands more workers could become available to the armaments industry. Speer seconded everything and said Fromm was right. Apparently the pair of them had got their heads together beforehand. Complaints were raised against SS-RSHA, which in most cases declined to provide statistics about the number of inmates, available camps and so-called group accumulations, this either by providing no figures, or false figures, or concealing information. It was also suggested involving female inmates in the industry, since women were specially suited for precision work. In this connection Speer complained about poor general standard of care in the armaments industry, especially towards prisoners of war and foreign workers. That would not do. If one wanted results, they had to be treated the same as German workers. F. listened to all this in silence and at first did not adopt much of a stance. Then he expressed his opinion. What was said about upkeep was correct, but one had to consider very carefully whom one was feeding. Consumers of food who were useless should not be permitted to enjoy it. Regarding the inmates, especially the Jewish ones, he would speak with Himmler. He shared the opinion that those under discussion could all be useful for the armaments industry. He was sharp with Fromm, denying that the various Wehrmacht branches received different treatment. He was keeping a sharp eye out for money being spent on playthings and idiocies. The war was too serious for fooling around, and even now he was not convinced that what they were up to in the Peenemünde[460] DIY workshops would be decisive for the war industry. 100 fighters and 500 Panzers seemed to him more important than a rocket fired upwards, and which generally did not come down where one wanted.

The really massive contribution of Fromm, and the help from the sidelines given by Speer, came as a surprise. Unfortunately no decisions were made. Keitel shone once more with a torrent of irrelevant blather.

20 December 1942
Strong words from Busse about attitude of Sixth Army staff at Stalingrad. Ic (Major Eismann, Manstein's No. 3 staff officer) brought bad news. Apparently [Paulus] and [his] Chief [of Staff] there were at odds, latter considered break-out impossible. Reported that Paulus no longer had control of his generals, for example Commanding General LI Panzer Corps[461] (v. Seydlitz) was openly defeatist.

28 December 1942
Here deepest depression. Nearly everybody had been hoping against hope that P. [Paulus] would take the risk and try to break out against his orders. He could have got out with the bulk of the men, albeit at a high cost in material. This evening Jodl spoke very seriously and one could see that even he was counting on Paulus acting independently. (Same view) definitely Chief of the General Staff and the Army Group. Nobody knows what should be done next at Stalingrad. F. very quiet and is almost never seen except at daily situation conference and to receive reports. What worries us most is that apparently discord rules within the encirclement and [Paulus] does not know how to proceed. In addition, air supply is getting worse.

28 December 1942
Christian reported again that in his opinion air drop not realistic. F. argued that this was only a question of rationalisation: if rubbish was being flown in, then that was so. One should get exporters to plan the job instead of lack-lustre administrative or General Staff officers.

Concentrates had to be got in, they were available and he would see to it personally.[462]

29 December 1942

Excited discussion between F. and Z., with Jodl supporting the latter. After initial resistance F. gave permission to pull back forces in the narrow Kuban bridgehead. Z. was overjoyed to have achieved this, as it is the first step towards saving the forces in the Caucasus.[463]

19 January 1943

Everything in chaos again after the Russians broke through the Hungarian lines.[464] All recommendations to pull back the n(orth) flank A(rmy) Group B and Second Army turned down by F.[465] Z. told F. that one had the impression latter did not appreciate the seriousness of the situation. It was nicely put. F. seized the opportunity, starting with von Blomberg and Fritsch, to launch another tirade against the Army, how they had disappointed him, how they had betrayed him. Verbatim F. said: 'If those who criticise me now had always recognised the seriousness, then I would not have had to fight against many things in the Army.'

1 February 1943

We are all imagining how it is ending at Stalingrad. F. was very depressed, looking everywhere for errors and negligence. Attempted to extenuate a report from Paulus addressed to himself,[466] and violently criticised Paulus's attitude. How can one avoid the road to eternity in such a situation? Faced with the heroism of the fighting man, how could one leave him in the lurch at the last moment? We had a very excited debate on the subject. Only Schmundt shared unreservedly the Führer's point of view – not ourselves, that is not we soldiers. Avoided conversing with others on this affair.

7 February 1943

At instigation of Schm., v. M(anstein) visited F. yesterday. It was a dour, icy talk, partially in a larger group, but mostly smaller circle. In a refreshing manner v. M. put forward clear demands: withdraw to the Mius, more units to the front, evacuate the Donetz region.[467]

To our astonishment F. listened to it passively. Afterwards a private talk. Schm. found out that v. M. touched on the subject of the Army High Command, requested a C-in-C East and a Wehrmacht Chief of the General Staff, this latter with the objective of finally getting Keitel

out of FHQ. Furthermore, freedom of manoeuvre for the army groups
in crisis situations, which could only be judged and decided upon on
the spot. In the operational respect v. M. was partially successful;
regarding the High Command as always he [Hitler] avoided the
question.

18 February 1943

(F. in) Zaporoshye.[468] M(anstein) had got tougher. (Said) literally: 'It
can't go on like this, mein Führer.' Made the old demands, (reported)
great danger at Kharkov, heavy attacks at the Mius. All conversations
were extremely unpleasant. We were being continually pressurised to
get F. away from the army group because v. M. needed to work
independently and enemy forces were threatening the airfield. On 19
February [written up following day] Field Marshal von Kl(eist) came.
Tough approach for decisions. I decided to fly to see Field Marshal v.
R(undstedt) on my return, as the crisis of confidence between F. and
commanders-in-chief was becoming ever more obvious.

22 February 1943
Paris

Flew to Paris, four-hour consultation at night with Field Marshal v.
R(undstedt) [Engel had been orderly officer with Rundstedt several
times]. Gave him the fullest report of recent events, holding nothing
back, and said that his intervention and demands were awaited. I told
him that F would definitely give ground if *he*[469] put himself forward
as spokesman for all field marshals. Result was deflating. Von R.
turned everything down with resignation and said literally: 'Why is it
me who has to mount this old donkey? Let v. M(anstein) and
v. K(luge) handle it.' He was too old and was sorry, but preferred not
to die plugging gaps in the dyke.

25 February 1943

K(luge) telephoned me. Was I in a position to arrange a private
meeting for him with F. on condition that neither K(eitel), Jodl,
Schmundt n(or) Z(eitzler) took part in it? I agreed to try, so long as he
could fly here as soon as he hung up.

27 February 1943

Called Army Group Centre and told them that Feldm(arschall) had to
be at FHQ Wolfsschanze[470] next morning. Favourable time, since K.
was in Berlin and Schm. was with Army Group North: Jodl was no

problem. When I made the request for the private meeting with
v. K(luge) since he had something on his mind, F. surprised me by
agreeing.

28 February 1943[471]
Fetched Field Marshal v. K(luge) from the airfield. He was determined
to resign his command if Army Command was not reshuffled to
incorporate new C-in-C East and remove Keitel. C-in-C was alone
with F. from 10.30 until 14.30 with a short break and for lunch: these
were also in privacy. I returned field marshal to the airfield and
enquired. Von Kl(uge) very depressed and thoughtful. Said he had
laid all his cards on the table and the Führer had heard him out in
silence. He was also in agreement with him about K(eitel). But then
F. had spoken convincingly about situation, possibilities and
requirements and appealed to his conscience to the extent that he
had not been able to go through with the final move. It was
devastating, but it was always like that.

Notes

Notes followed by ED are new to the English edition.

1. Hitler and his entourage, of which Captain Engel had formed part since becoming Army adjutant on 10 March 1938, set up HQ in the Hotel Imperial on the Kärntner Ring on 12 March. Lieutenant-General Guderian, who as Commdg. Gen. XVI Corps had taken part in the annexation of Austria, was also quartered there. (Information from Lieutenant-General Engel.)

2. Lieutenant-General Hans G., 1888–1954. Cmdg. Gen. Kommando der Panzertruppen February 1938 (April 1938 XVI Corps); General of Armoured Troops and Chef der Schneller Truppen November 1938; Cmdg. Gen. XIX Corps August 1939; Commander, Panzer Group Guderian June 1940; Colonel-General July 1940; Commander, Second Panzer Army October 1941; Führer-Reserve December 1941; General-Inspekteur der Panzertruppen February 1943; additionally July 1944–March 1945 Chief of the Army General Staff. Keilig 211/111.

3. Refers to the dismissal of Blomberg and Fritsch in January and February 1938 respectively (see Introduction). The intrigue which undermined Fritsch provided higher Army officers with constant cause for speculation on the now public differences of opinion existing between Hitler and the Army High Command.

4. Word in the shorthand version illegible.

5. Colonel-General Walther von Brauchitsch was successor to Fritsch as C-in-C from 4 February 1938 to 19 December 1941. Keilig 211/43.

6. In the original shorthand, word is 'Reichsmarschall'. Lieutenant-General Engel explained that either he misheard the term 'Field Marshal' or drafted it erroneously. [Göring was created Reichsmarschall on 19 July 1940. ED]

7. The meeting between Hitler and Innitzer took place on 15 March 1938. Regarding the attitude of the Catholic Church in Austria towards National Socialism see: Weinzierl-Fischer: *Österreichs Katholiken und der Nationalsozialismus 1933–1945*. Also Reimann: *Innitzer sowie Fried: Nationalsozialismus und katholische Kirche*.

8. Ludwig W., 1812–91. Osnabrück lawyer, 1848 appeal court judge at Celle, for several years Justice Minister in Kingdom of Hanover. After formation of Second Reich, leader of Centrist Party and as such organised the opposition to Bismarck during the cultural struggle.

9. Heinrich H., born 7 October 1900. Reichsführer-SS, 17 June 1936–May 1945; head of German police in Reich Interior Ministry, from 7 October 1939; additionally Reich Commissar for Consolidation of the German Race; following the attempted assassination of Hitler of 20 July 1944, commander-in-chief,

Ersatz Heer (Army of Reserve). Suicide by poison in British captivity, end May 1945. Archiv IfZ.

10. In the early hours of 13 March, in company with Gestapo and SD officials, members of the armed SS, and elements of the Austrian Legion formed in Germany, Himmler landed in Vienna and set up his HQ at the Hotel Metropol, later the first location of the Stapo-Leitstelle Wien (see: additionally IMT XVI, page 200; Eichstädt: *Von Dollfuss zu Hitler*, p. 421f; Schellenberg: *Memoiren*, p. 52). Himmler came for the purpose of applying all necessary measures to uphold law and order (per Article 2, para 1, Act of Reunification of Austria with the Reich, 18 March 1938 (for full text see Reichsgesetzblatt I, p. 262), the legal basis for all secret police activity in Austria. This involved the systematic rounding-up of 'anti-Reich elements' which began with the German invasion and afterwards the establishment of the Gestapo in Austria brought into effect in all former security centres and police stations in accordance with Hitler's edict of 18 March 1938 (RM BliV. 1938, No. 12) in pursuance of the terms of Article 2 of the aforementioned Act of Reunification.

11. Colonel-General Werner Freiherr von Fritsch. C-in-C from 1935 until dismissed in February 1938. On the Fritsch crisis see Krausnick: *Vorgeschichte*, pp. 283–305; Kielmannsegg: *Fritsch-Prozeß 1938*; Müller: *Heer*, chapter VI; also Hossbach: *Wehrmacht und Hitler*. pp. 86–97 and 105–26.

12. General of Artillery Franz H., 1884–1972. QM-General I at Army General Staff, from 1 March 1938; successor to Beck as Chief of Army General Staff 31 August 1938–24 September 1942; Colonel-General 19 July 1940. Keilig: 211/117. Notes relating to the same events (see following entry) are taken from respective parallel volumes, for which see Introduction.

13. Colonel-General von Fritsch.

14. Means the ousting of Fritsch on 4 February 1938, manipulations of personnel being used to disguise the proceedings. See note 11.

15. See note above.

16. Field Marshal Werner von Blomberg, 1876–1946. May 1935–end January 1938 Reich War Minister and C-in-C Wehrmacht. For the affair surrounding his marriage and ensuing fall from grace see Kielmannsegg: *Fritsch-Prozeß 1938*; Foertsch: *Schuld und Verhängnis*; Krausnick: *Vorgeschichte*, p. 282ff; Müller: *Heer*, chapter VI.

17. Rudolf Schm., 1896–1944. Reichswehr 9th Infantry Regiment, October 1920–May 1929; Lieutenant 1925; Staff, 1st Division October 1929; Captain 1931; 2nd Cavalry Regiment 1932; Army Organisational Dept (T2) in the Reichswehr Ministry 1933 (under departmental head Lt-Col Keitel); Major 1935; Staff 18th Division 1936; Senior Wehrmacht ADC to the Führer 29 January 1938 and (October) Lieutenant-Colonel; Colonel 1939; Major-General 1941; additionally Head of Army Personnel Office October 1942; Lieutenant-General April 1943; seriously wounded 20 July 1944 during assassination attempt on Hitler's life at Rastenburg and succumbed to his injuries 1 October 1944. Archiv IfZ. According to numerous reports the relationship between Schmundt and Engel during the first years of their collaboration was normal apart from the

occasional instance of friction such as was to be expected now and again between the respective representatives of the OKW and OKH. The gradually increasing and worsening differences of opinion may – apart from professional and political differences – be attributable to differences in temperament and character of the two men.

18. Frau Anneliese Schmundt, widow of Rudolf Schmundt, stated that this was 'improbable': oral declaration, 13 October 1972. A Führer Directive of 3 May 1938 introduced the Hitler salute for the entire Wehrmacht as the standard salute in Hitler's presence – see HVoBl. 20 [1938], page 154. Only after the assassination attempt of 20 July 1944 did the Hitler salute replace the standard military salute generally (see Allgemeine Heeresmitteilungen 11 [1944], p. 343; *Völkischer Beobachter*, 25 July 1944).

19. On the occasion of the military annexation of Austria.

20. 18th Division Staff, to which Schmundt was attached 1936–8, was at Liegnitz.

21. Location of 27th Infantry Regiment, from which Engel was detached to the *Adjutantur* (see Introduction).

22. Curt S., born 1899; Reichswehr, No. 1. Gen Staff Officer to C-in-C 1936; Lieutenant-Colonel 1939; Chief General Staff XXXVIII Corps 1941; Colonel 1941; Commander 58th Infantry Division 1943–5; Major-General 1943. Keilig: 211/318.

23. For Brauchitsch's personal situation see 18 October 1938; also Jodl: *Diary*, 1 February 1938 IMT XXVIII, p. 362; Krausnick: *Vorgeschichte*, p. 299; Müller: *Heer*, p. 268, and in connection with the latter Siewert: *Generale*, p. 86, where he revises his earlier details about the indemnity.

24. SS-Obergruppenführer and General der Waffen-SS Josef (Sepp) D., 1892–1966, from September 1933 commander, *Leibstandarte Adolf Hitler*.

25. The 'increase' of the Verfügungstruppe 'in this year' – per Himmler in a speech to SS-Gruppenführern on 8 November 1938 – was made on Hitler's order. The new unit, 4. Standarte *Der Führer*, stationed in Vienna and Klagenfurt, recruited mainly Austrians and made its public debut at the Party Convention 'Großdeutschland' in September 1938. See MA 312, sheet 2535–82; *Parteitag Großdeutschland*, p. 310; Stein: *Waffen-SS* at p. 17.

26. In order to eliminate the constant friction between the Army and SS-Verfügungstruppe, on 17 August 1938 in a secret document Hitler set out the tasks of the SS-Verfügungstruppe and defined the boundary where these differed from those of the Army. See 647-PS, IMT XXVI, p. 190ff. For the relationship between the Army and SS see Krausnick: *Vorgeschichte*, p. 235f; Müller: *Heer*, chapter IV; also ZS Doerr, p. 10; *Aufzeichnungen Fritsch*, p. 171.

27. This was Hitler's 49th birthday.

28. Blomberg's concern about the introduction of general conscription and the reoccupation of the Rhineland is described in Hossbach: *Wehrmacht*, pp. 95f and 98; also Müller: *Heer*, pp. 208f and 213.

29. Colonel-General von Fritsch is meant here.

30. As Kordt (*Akten*, p. 187) reports, Hitler decided shortly before his state visit to Italy at the beginning of May 1938 'to put his higher Foreign Office officials' into a kind of 'admiral's uniform' (see *Berliner Illustrierte* No. 19 of 12 May 1938.) In view of the impending meeting between the diplomatic officials of the German entourage and the suite of the Italian king and Mussolini's following – probably in view of the historicity of the Roman Empire-like scene – Hitler's wish to avoid presenting his Foreign Minister as an anonymous civilian is only too understandable in an era in which uniforms again played a role in politics. Ribbentrop's vanity, tied up with his weakness for expensive diplomatic uniforms, may have irritated Hitler sufficiently to provoke the remarks attributed to him by Engel.

Since diplomatic uniforms were abolished by the Weimar Republic, there had been no prescribed clothing requirement for the officials of the Foreign Ministry. Constant modification to uniforms in the Ribbentrop era makes a specific description difficult. In general one can say that the uniforms of officials of the higher level foreign service resembled those of ordinary officials but were black instead of blue. With respect to the former see *Handbuch des Auswärtigen Dienstes*, p. 34.

31. Diplomat Walter H., 1904–45. Head of Dienststelle Ribbentrop at Foreign Ministry 1937; Permanent Plenipotentiary of the Reich Minister for Foreign Affairs to the Führer March 1938; after 1 September 1939 in this role at FHQ.

32. General of Artillery Ludwig B., 1880–1944. Chief of Army General Staff, October 1933–31 October 1938; 1 November 1938 Colonel-General z V [Reserve of Officers]; formed part of military opposition and shot himself on 20 July 1944 after the failed attempt on Hitler's life. See Keilig: 211/18.

33. On 28 May 1938 at the Reich Chancellery. Participants in this conference were Göring, Ribbentrop, Neurath, Generals Brauchitsch, Beck and Keitel together with Admiral Raeder, C-in-C Navy. Under the influence of the Czech partial mobilisation on 20 May and the subsequent foreign press campaign against him ('Weekend Crisis'), Hitler revised his Plan Green for a military move against Czechoslovakia 'for the near future'. On the 'Weekend Crisis' see especially Celowsky: *Münchener Abkommen*, p. 220; also Weinberg: *May Crisis 1938*; Rönnefarth: *Sudetenkrise*, chapter 5. For the modification of Case Green especially 388-PS, IMT XXV; Jodl: *Diary*, 11 March 1938, JMT XXVIII p. 372; also Bullock: *Hitler*, p. 446ff; Foerster: *Beck*, p. 107; further extracts from Hitler's speech of 12 September 1938 in Domarus: *Hitler* I 2, p. 896; Kordt: *Akten*, p. 228.

34. Helena, daughter of King Nikolaus of Montenegro.

35. See 22 May 1938, first entry.

36. In this trial (September–October 1930) at the Reichsgericht Leipzig, Colonel Beck, regimental commander of 5th Fulda Artillery Regiment stationed at Ulm, appeared as a witness for former Lieutenants Scheringer and Ludin who were charged with treason. The officers had called upon their colleagues to adopt a neutral stance in the case of an attempt by the 'National Movement' to overthrow the government. Hitler used the opportunity to deliver under oath his

declaration regarding the legality of the NSDAP. See Vogelsang: *Reichswehr,* pp. 82f, 90ff, 416ff.

37. It remains uncertain which of the three known Beck memoranda from the period May–beginning of June 1938 is meant: Beck's response to Hitler's comments of 28 May was drafted the following day, his paper of 3 June was the reaction to an OKW report (No. 42/38 secret document, Chefsache [for service chiefs] L I), which had been distributed to the three Wehrmacht C-in-Cs on 30 May. If Beck was talking to Engel about his memorandum of 5 May ('Considerations as to the Military-Political Situation of Germany'), then Engel would have delivered the invitation to Beck at the beginning of May, thus before the Weekend Crisis, which is doubtful. For the consequences of the memoranda see Foerster: *Beck,* pp. 99–116.

38. Beck took down in brief phrases Hitler's observations of 28 May and drafted his response next day. See Foerster: *Beck,* pp. 107–13; Müller: *Heer,* p. 309.

39. In the shorthand version: 15 May 1938.

40. Fall 'Grün' – Case or Plan Green, the military plan for an attack on Czechoslovakia.

41. See additionally 388-PS, IMT XXV, p. 420f and pp. 427–32. The answer to Hitler's urgent enquiry about artillery to 'overcome fortress-like defenses' would not have given him much comfort: at the time of the preparations for the attack on Czechoslovakia, the Army had only twenty-three 21-cm mortars available and, of these, eight were in East Prussia.

42. For the development of the Panzer see Heiber: *Führerlage,* p. 61, note 1; Lusar: *Waffen,* pp. 31f and 57f; Senger and Etterlin: *Taschenbuch der Panzer,* p. 20; also Nehring: *Geschichte der deutschen Panzerwaffe*; Senff: *Entwicklung der Panzerwaffe.*

43. According to an explanation supplied by Lieutenant-General Engel, this was one of the numerous officers' mess incidents in which Army officers passed remarks denigrating the NSDAP. In this connection attention is drawn to a four-page report of the Bundesführer des Deutschen Reichskriegerbundes to the Reichsführer-SS of 29 January 1938 regarding criticisms of the SS and NSDAP by Army officers. See BA/NS 19/999.

44. Major-General Dr Richard Sp., Inspekteur der Westbefestigungen 1937–8. Keilig 211/321.

45. Unclear in the shorthand version, could also be 'last World War'.

46. General of Artillery Prof. Dr-Ing Karl B., Head of Army Weapons Office 1938–40. See Heiber: *Führerlage,* p. 126, notes 4 and 5.

47. However, see additionally 388-PS, IMT XXV, p. 429.

48. For technical details see Lusar: *Waffen* at p. 31.

49. Dr-Ing Fritz T., 1891–1942. As Inspector-General of the German Highways he laid the Reich autobahns. In 1938 he assembled a vast consortium of building firms under the umbrella known as 'Organisation Todt' for the purpose of pressing ahead with the western fortifications. In 1940 Hitler made him Minister for Arms and Ammunition. He was killed in February 1942 when his

personal He-111 aircraft crashed at Rastenburg during take-off. His successor in all offices was Albert Speer. For more about Todt see Milward: *Fritz Todt*.

50. General der Pioniere Otto F., 1933–8 Inspector of Engineers and Emplacements. See Keilig: 211/86; also Heiber: *Lagebesprechungen*, p. 135 note 1.

51. For Hitler's own thoughts on defensive emplacements see his comprehensive memorandum of 1 July 1938 (1801-PS and 1802-PS).

52. This was probably the second part of Beck's memorandum of 5 May 1938. Brauchitsch and Keitel had decided to show Hitler only this part for fear that he would suspend the discussion if he saw the first part (see Keitel: *Verbrecher oder Offizier*, p. 184). There is no mention of the French Mobile Guard, Police and Gendarmerie in the surviving document. Nothing in the archive material supports the theory, and if one discounts the hypothesis of an appendix to the memorandum respecting the fighting potential of possible opponents, then Beck's assertion that the French Army was the most powerful in Europe may have drawn forth Hitler's counter-argument in the form Engel mentions. The above-mentioned memorandum, with hand corrections to the text and endorsed '1. Reinentwurf' (No. 1. clean outline) is at BA/MA H 08-28/4; reproduced in text in Buchheit: *Beck*, pp. 133–8; with slight variations from the text in Förster: *Beck*, pp. 100–5. See also entries 24 July and 20 August 1938.

53. See note 52 above.

54. Because of the 100,000-man army imposed on Germany by the 1919 Versailles Treaty, most German males born in the period 1901–13 lacked military training. Hitler had stated – according to a file note in the OKW War Diary of 8 November 1939 – during a conversation with C-in-C Brauchitsch that for years he had been asking for this age-band, the so-called 'White Block', to be called up. (KTB OKW I, 1940–1, p. 951f). The War Minister (Blomberg) had been unable to comply with this demand on the grounds of a shortage of suitable instructors and training camps. At the time when war broke out, a small portion of the 'White Block' had received training, but only for a two- or three-month period.

55. Means Göring who, as Plenipotentiary for the Four-Year Plan, was responsible among other things for the distribution of raw materials to the three Wehrmacht services.

56. On 24 July Hitler attended the opening performance (*Tristan und Isolde*) of the 1938 Bayreuth Festival and was also present for the following: 25 July *Parsifal*, 27 July *Rheingold*, 28 July *Walküre*, 1 August *Götterdämmerung*. See *Völkischer Beobachter* of 25–8 July incl. and 3 August 1938.

57. Winifred W. née Williams, married 1916 Siegfried W., the son of Richard Wagner. After the death of her husband she ran the Bayreuth Festival.

58. See 18 July 1938 and note 72.

59. On 8 September 1939 Dr Todt appointed architect Siegfried Schmelcher (1911–91) to head a thirty-man team responsible for designing the Führer-HQs, and to some degree Schmelcher was involved in the planning and construction of all nineteen known locations. (geh. Rs 91/44 and 121/45, Bundesarchiv). The great secrecy surrounding the FHQs, and the fact that the Army ADC was under

orders not to divulge any information about them to the General Staff, is demonstrated by Engel's visit to FHQ Felsennest at Rodert south-west of Bonn on 27 January 1940 (see KTB FHQ No. 3, appendix, report of 31 March 1940). FHQ Felsennest was Hitler's HQ for the French campaign 10 May–6 June 1940. Halder was not aware of its existence until 24 February 1940 when FHQ Commandant Rommel rang him to ask how he wanted the telephone lines arranged.

60. The question of the Wehrmacht command structure and its jurisdiction, particularly in the event of war, seemed to have been resolved by Blomberg's dual role. As Reich War Minister he was responsible for the 'Organisation of the Fighting Nation', and as Wehrmacht commander-in-chief for the 'Organisation of the Fighting Forces'. OKH had set down in a memorandum, prepared by the Oberquartiermeister I, Major-General von Manstein, on the instructions of Fritsch, the functional difficulties by which the Reich War Minister was bound to be confronted in the exercise of his many-sided task. Fritsch wanted a separation of the ministerial and military functions. With reference to the uncontested supremacy of the Army within the Wehrmacht, he proposed that the Army should take over the military leadership and with it strategic and operational planning. For this purpose he foresaw the transfer of the 'Land Defence' and 'Abwehr' sectors to OKH from the Reich War Ministry while the office of C-in-C would combine with that of a Chief of the Reich (or Wehrmacht) General Staff. (See Fritsch memorandum copied in Keitel: *Verbrecher oder Offizier*, pp. 123–42). This August 1937 proposal was turned down by Blomberg. After his dismissal from office, Beck, Chief of the Army General Staff, concerned at Hitler's expansionist aims, revived talk about the command structure. He was hoping to force through the OKH suggestion and so strengthen the Army as to influence Hitler's foreign policy. Beck won over the new C-in-C, Brauchitsch, to his scheme, and the latter supplied a version of the memorandum of August 1937 to Hitler, who, after Blomberg's departure, exercised power of command over the entire Wehrmacht officially from 4 February 1938 (see Reichsgesetzblatt I, 1938, p. 111, also Jodl: *Diary*, 8 March 1938, IMT XXVIII p. 370). The renewed effort was unsuccessful. On the command structure see Müller: *Heer*, pp. 289–95; Manstein: *Soldatenleben* pp. 280–95; Warlimont: *Hauptquartier*, pp. 21–43; Keitel: *Verbrecher oder Offizier*, pp. 312–22; regarding development of command structure – Müller-Hillebrand: *Heer*, chapter IV.

61. Wilhelm K., 1882–1946. General of Artillery and head of Wehrmacht Office, October 1935; Cmmdg. Officer OKW Reich War Ministry, February 1938–May 1945; November 1938 Colonel-General; July 1940 Field Marshal. Keilig: 211/160.

62. See 20 April 1938 and note 28. The Army leadership had always feared that a large increase in the standing army might provoke foreign reaction. Accordingly Beck had been successful in opposing the suggestion of the Army General Office to increase Army size to 300,000 by 1 October 1934. See Foerster: *Beck*, p. 32; Müller: *Heer*, p. 208.

63. Martin B., born 17 June 1900, 1920–6 agricultural student, 1924 as

member of Rossbach Freikorps imprisoned for a political killing, 1928 Staff officer, Supreme SA-leadership, 1930–33 head of NSDAP Endowment Fund, July 1933 Reichsleiter and Chief of Staff, 'Führer's Representative'. From then on B. administered Hitler's private finances and his two properties at Berchtesgaden. 12 May 1941 (following Hess's flight to Britain) took over the office of 'Führer's Representative' and renamed it 'Party Chancellery'. In the later years of the war B. was included in Hitler's closest circle and exerted a decisive influence on him. Archiv IfZ.

64. Regarding spiritual care in the Wehrmacht see Messerschmidt: *Wehrmacht*, pp. 171–209; Schübel: *Soldatenseelsorge*; Scholder: *Die evangelische Kirche in der Sicht der nationalsozialistischen Führung bis zum Kriegsausbruch.*

65. Ludwig Müller, 1883–1945, evangelical theologian; former Wehrmacht pastor, Königsberg Wehrkreis; between 1933 and 1945 assumed the cloak of Reich Bishop of the 'German Evangelical Church'.

66. Major Henning von T., 1901–44. Belonged to the military resistance and shot himself after the failed attempt on Hitler's life, 20 July 1944. Keilig: 211/342. For Tresckow's role in the resistance movement see Scheurig: *Tresckow*; Hoffmann: *Widerstand*, p. 311; Leber: *Gewissen*, p. 158.

67. At the Party Conference 'For Freedom' 10–16 September 1935, held in Nuremberg coincident with the Reichstag session convened there, the 'Reich Flag Law', the 'Reich Citizen Law' and the 'Law for the Protection of German Blood and German Honour' were passed unanimously. The last prohibited marriage between any Jew and a 'Citizen of German or Related Blood'. See *Der Parteitag der Freiheit vom 10–16 September 1935*, pp. 254–67; also Reichsgesetzblatt 1935 I. pp. 1145–7.

68. That is, one Jewish and one 'Aryan' parent. One Jewish and one half-Jewish parent was 75 per cent mixed blood. ED

69. Dr Robert L., 1890–1945, chemist, head of German Arbeitsfront 1933–45. See *Der Grossdeutsche Reichstag*, p. 288.

70. Karl H., 1933–41 Propaganda Ministry; initially as Goebbels' personal assistant, later after departure of Walther Funk in January 1938, became his Secretary of State; Gauleiter of Lower Silesia 1941–5; died 1945. See Heiber: *Goebbels*, p. 143f.

71. See Introduction for Engel's supplementary duties in Wehrmacht racial matters.

72. According to former General Förster, in May 1938 a conference chaired by Göring enquired into the land fortifications, and all the western installations built hitherto came in for sharp criticism. For the discord between Hitler and the Fortifications Inspectorate see Förster: *Befestigungswesen*, pp. 41–51; also 1801-PS, 1802-PS.

73. See 18 July 1938 and note 52.

74. Near the Berlin Zoo at Kurfürstenstrasse 59.

75. Heinrich H., 1885-1987. NSDAP Reich photographer; 1938 Professor; Hitler's 'court photographer'. IfZ.

76. In connection with the C-in-C conference a conversation took place between Engel and Siewert.

77. See 18 July and 20 August 1938.

78. Date of Fritsch's dismissal. In this connection it means that the Army would have to reckon with further dismissals.

79. Since the first armed SS unit [*Leibstandarte Adolf Hitler* ED], formed with the approval of the Reichswehr Minister, came into existence in the summer of 1934, the Army felt its monopoly as the 'only weapon carrier of the Reich' compromised. Each increase in Waffen-SS strength was therefore viewed with justifiable apprehension. For the relationship between the Army and Waffen-SS units see Müller: *Heer*, pp. 147–82 and 345; Krausnick: *Vorgeschicht*, p. 248ff and Buchheim: *Die SS*, pp. 190–216.

80. After the meeting of the political leaders on the evening of 9 September on the Zeppelinwiese, there followed in the Hotel Deutscher Hof at Nuremberg a discussion respecting Plan Green (see 388-PS, IMT XXV, p. 464), at which besides the military adjutants only Hitler, Brauchitsch, Halder and Keitel were present. Jodl later described Keitel as 'shocked' that the C-in-C, for whose appointment he had fought, appeared to be such a disappointment and that he, Keitel, had not managed to prevent the disagreement which led to Brauchitsch and Halder being reproved by Hitler. (Jodl: *Diary*, 13 September 1938, IMT XXVIII, p. 378). For the controversy about Plan Green see Keitel, p. 190f. and 388-PS, IMT XXV, p. 464.

81. The *Leibstandarte Adolf Hitler* is meant here.

82. See 8 September 1938.

83. Colonel-General Gerd von R., 1875–1953. C-in-C Army Group 1 (Berlin) 1932–31 October 1938 (annexation Sudetenland GOC Second Army); in Polish campaign C-in-C Army Group South; in France C-in-C Army Group A; additionally from 25 October 1940 C-in-C West; Field Marshal 19 July 1940; C-in-C Army Group South Russian campaign until 3 December 1941; C-in-C West March 1942– July 1944. Keilig 211/281; Siegler: p. 135: NOKW – 141.

84. General of Artillery Walther v R., 1884–1942. C-in-C Army Group 4 (Leipzig) February 1938 (annexation Sudetenland. GOC Tenth Army); GOC Tenth Army 1 September 1939; Colonel-General 1 October 1939; GOC Sixth Army 20 October 1939; Field Marshal 19 July 1940; C-in-C Army Group South 1 December 1941. Keilig 211/264; Siegler; p. 134.

85. See 8 September and 16 October 1938.

86. Major-General Karl B., born 1890. December 1937, as colonel, head of ministerial office at Reich Air Ministry; additionally Permanent ObdL Liaison Officer to the Führer September 1939; General der Flieger January 1941; seriously hurt in assassination attempt of 20 July 1944. Heiber: *Führerlage*, p. 44.

87. That is, at the evening conference of 9 September 1938 about Plan Green. See 8 September 1938. note 80. According to a statement of General Bodenschatz on 14 February 1972, he was not present at the Deutscher Hof conference.

88. Hitler met Chamberlain for talks at 10.00 on the morning of 22 September 1938 at Bad Godesberg and flew back to Berlin on the afternoon of 24 September. See in confirmation, *Daten aus Notizbüchern*, p. 29.

89. Possibly about police tasks for the Sudeten-German Freikorps (SFK) on home territory and its subordination to the RF-SS. See also entry 28 September 1938: Broszat: *Das sudetendeutsche Freikorps* at p. 48; Groscurth: *Tagebücher*, 20 September 1938, p. 122 with note 111.

90. After Czech troops had withdrawn from the Sudetenland on the night of 21 September 1938 at the request of the western Powers, on Hitler's orders units of the SFK moved into the Ascher district the following evening. According to Jodl's diary entry of 25 September, they were followed, also at Hitler's order, by two SS-Totenkopf Sturmbanne. A Sturmbann was a unit of battalion strength. See ADAP II, Nos 563, 566 and 567; Jodl: *Diary*, 25 September 1938, IMT XXVIII, p. 386.

91. The border town of Asch had meanwhile become the seat of the Sudetendeutsche Partei leaders.

92. Respecting the formation, tasks and activities of the SFK see Broszat: *Das sudetendeutsche Freikorps*, pp. 30–9; regarding SFK weapons also Groscurth: *Tagebücher*, 19/20 September 1938, p. 121ff, with notes 108 and 111.

93. He means here concentration camp guard units, i.e. the SS-Totenkopf (Death's Head) units.

94. Meant here: SFK.

95. Underlined in the handwritten version.

96. Because the Army considered as imprudent the intended SFK provocations near the Sudeten border and its penetration – expressly ordered by Hitler – into the Sudetenland 'in the guise of terror groups' (see EC-366-1), the arming of the Freikorps by the German Army was handled with maximum slowness. See EC-366-2; NOKW-116; Jodl: *Diary*, 19 September 1938, IMT XXVIII, p. 381; Broszat: *Das Sudetendeutsche Freikorps*, pp. 37–43.

97. Engel's reports about Halder's state of mind are worthy of note. Under normal circumstances one would have expected Halder to have been relieved at the surprise news of the impending meeting in Munich. It would appear that Halder's nervous collapse must have been occasioned by the fact that the very far advanced plans for the putsch were wrecked at a stroke through the agreement to annexation of the Sudetenland. See Krausnick: *Vorgeschichte*, p. 368; Gisevius, *Ende*, p. 378, Müller: *Heer* at pp. 345–77.

98. Weizsäcker and Erich Kordt. See Kordt: *Akten*, p. 244.

99. Fritz W., 1891–1970. During the First World War captain and regimental adjutant, 16th Reserve Infantry Regiment, in which Hitler was a despatch carrier; Hitler's personal adjutant January 1935–January 1939; General Consul at San Francisco March 1939. Archiv IfZ.

100. Berlin Military District. The propaganda drive by 2nd Motorised Division on the evening of 27 September from Stettin to Saxony via Berlin was intended not only to convince the British and French diplomats of Hitler's determination

to resolve the Czech question by force but also to mobilise the fighting élan of the until then peaceable German people. Jodl: *Diary*, 27 September 1938, IMT XXVIII, p. 388; Krausnick: *Vorgeschichte*, p. 365; Kordt: *Akten*, p. 266ff; Domarus: *Hitler* I 2, p. 937.

101. Also known as 'brown birds' by virtue of the use of brown paper. This was a special service run by the Luftwaffe Research Office (Telephone Eavesdropping and Report Collation Centre) within the Air Ministry which passed on interesting material to Hitler, the Foreign Ministry and the Wehrmacht High Command.

102. Major-General Curt G.

103. Captain Friedrich-Wilhelm von M. [Rose to the rank of Major-General and wrote *Panzer Battles*, University of Oklahoma Press, 1956.]

104. Means the Panzer Training School stationed there. See Podzun: *Heer*, p. 818.

105. On 30 September 1938 Hitler invited Chamberlain for confidential talks at his Munich flat, during the course of which the British Prime Minister surprised him with a prepared German–British Peace Declaration, which both statesmen signed. Hitler's speech of 26 September on the theme of the peace declaration is reproduced in extracts in Domarus: *Hitler* I 2, pp. 924–32; also p. 946.

106. Hitler first mentioned his wishes with respect to the Danzig Corridor to the Polish ambassador on 20 September 1938 at Obersalzberg. See *Dokumente und Materialien*, I, p. 194. [The Corridor Question, a demand which Poland was not prepared to concede and which motivated the German invasion on 1 September 1939, involved an autobahn or railway line crossing Poland to link East Prussia and the German enclave of Danzig. This strip of road or railway would be sovereign German territory. ED]

107. According to information from Frau Alix von Reichenau, her husband was in China from May to October 1935, accompanied by his adjutant and Hans Klein, head of STAMAG (Steel and Machinery Co). During his visit, R. met Chinese politicians and military leaders, including Chiang Kai-Shek. As to the actual purpose of the visit Frau von Reichenau was not informed. (Reason may have been the projected German-Chinese cooperation in military and armaments field. See ADAP II, Serie C, No. 63, 89, 235, 262, 473.) [Original note states 1935 and not 1938. Hitler's remark about R. spoiling his 'Japan concept' suggests that R.'s meeting Chinese political and military leaders was unofficial. ED]

108. He had been sent to China in May 1936. Chiang Kai-shek was being advised by German officers, whom the Wehrmacht needed back. The Japanese, with whom Hitler had signed a pact in November 1936, were also resentful. ED

109. See 8 and 10 September 1938, also 388-PS, IMT XXV, pp. 464–9.

110. Major-General Friedrich (Fritz) F., 1888–1944. CO Army General Office 1934; General of Artillery 1 April 1939; GOC Ersatzheer (Reserve Army) and Head of Army Armaments 1 September 1939–20 July 1944; on account of his ambiguous attitude towards 20 July 1944 executed in March 1945. Keilig: 211/92. Himmler's criticism of Fromm, who was then head of the Army General Office, possibly resulted from the lassitude with which he complied with the

edict of 19 September to supply the Sudeten Freikorps with weapons. See EC-366-1, S.5 and EC-366-2, p. 4f.

111. In view of the increasing rivalry between Wehrmacht and SA at the beginning of 1934, and the recognisable fact in February of that year that Hitler was inclining towards the Reichswehr, Fritsch as Army C-in-C had decided to stay clear of the expected confrontation, and this may have been the reason why he supported the idea of setting up the SS *Leibstandarte*. For Fritsch's later attitude towards the SS see especially Beck's memorandum of 1 February 1938, BA/MA H 08-28/3 (Beck papers); also in IfZ F40; extracts in Hossbach, 1st edition, p. 68ff; Müller: *Heer*, pp. 88ff., 107, 109 and 142ff.

112. Reichsleiter Philipp B., 1899–1945, NSDAP Reichsgeschäftsführer [Head Manager] 1925–34; Head of Hitler's Chancellery October 1934–1945.

113. See 28 March 1938.

114. General of Artillery Dr-Ing Kurt W. Army Weapons Office Chief of Staff July 1937–March 1941; Chief of General Staff, LIII Corps, 25 January 1942; Chief of Staff, Eighteenth Army, 1 February 1942; Major-General and Head of Armaments Office, Ministry of Armaments and Munitions, November 1942. Keilig: 211/353.

115. An allusion to the assassination of Ernst vom Rath, Legation Secretary, German Embassy in Paris, by Herschel Feibel Grünspan on 7 November 1938. See Heiber: *Der Fall Grynspan*, pp. 133–72.

116. Captain Nikolaus v. B. Flight Training with DVS in Soviet Union 1928; Reichswehr (12th Infantry Regiment) 1929; 1932 2nd Lieutenant; 1933 transferred into Luftwaffe; Fliegergruppe Döberitz 1935; Staffelkapitän JG 134 'Horst Wessel' 1936; Luftwaffe adjutant to the Führer 1937–45; Major 1941; Lieutenant-Colonel 1943. Archiv IfZ.

117. Martin N., born 1892, evangelical clergyman. Sea cadet 1910; U-boat commander Imperial German Navy, 1918; theology student at Münster; Pastor, Berlin-Dahlem parish church 1931. Rejected National Socialism upon learning of its anti-Church intentions; September 1933 founded Pfarrernotbund [Pastors' Emergency League], the forerunner of the Bekennenden Kirche [Confessional Church]. His uncompromising attitude was occasionally criticised even from within his own ranks. Arrested July 1937 during police measures against members of the Bekennenden Kirche and charged with offences of deception, abuse of the pulpit and incitement to civil disobedience. Following findings of guilt on 2 February 1938 was taken by the Gestapo to Sachsenhausen concentration camp. In 1941 he was transferred to Dachau, where he spent the remainder of the war. See Niemöller, W: *Aus dem Leben eines Bekenntnis-pfarrers*; also Messerschmidt: *Wehrmacht im SS-Staat*, p. 187.

118. After Himmler's visit, which presumably resulted from a letter of complaint to Hitler from Niemöller's circle of acquaintances, Hitler's 'personal captive' received better nourishment and was treated by an ophthalmologist for sight problems caused by vitamin deficiency: information from Martin and Wilhelm Niemöller in letters dated 22 and 29 December 1973.

119. Following Germany's resignation from the League of Nations, various

Berlin Notbund pastors, amongst them Niemöller, sent a telegram of thanks to Hitler and promised 'a loyal following and intercessionary thoughts'. For the relationship of Niemöller towards National Socialism see especially Schmidt: *Niemöller im Kirchenkampf*, pp. 40–3. 119f, 131–6, 140–4; also D. Schmidt: Niemöller; also Niemöller: *Vom U-boot zur Kanzel*.

120. Admiral Erich Raeder, C-in-C German Navy, 1928–43.

121. Major-General Bodewin Keitel, Head of Army Personnel Office March 1938–September 1942; brother of Field Marshal Wilhelm Keitel, Chief of OKW.

122. Army Personnel Section 2

123. On 10 February 1939 at the Kroll Opera House, Hitler addressed senior commanders on 'Duties and Responsibilities of the Officer in the National Socialist State'. The text of this speech is not extant. See Domarus: *Hitler* II 3, p. 1075; also Kielmannsegg: *Fritsch-Prozeß*, p. 35; also report in *Völkischer Beobachter* of 11 February 1939; for the content of the speech see especially Müller: *Heer*, p. 383.

124. 'Italy Brings Order to Albania.' Under this headline, *Völkischer Beobachter* reported on 8 April 1939 on the landings in Albanian ports begun early the previous morning by Italian forces. Schultheiss: *Geschichtskalender, 1939*, p. 82f; Keesings Archiv 1939, p. 4017f, also VB of 9 and 10 April. On the long-held annexation intentions of the Italians see Ciano: *Tagebücher 1938-1943*, 14 February 1939, p. 39; Siebert: *Italiens Weg*, pp. 128–33.

125. Heinz L., adjutant of Reich Press Chief, representative of DNB [Deutschen Nachrichtenbüros] at FHQ.

126. HdK = Haus der Deutschen Kunst (House of German Art), in Munich's Prinzregentenstrasse.

127. 1883–1949; folk singer at the Munich 'Platzl'.

128. Will Sch., 1884–1962, stage actor and cabaret artiste, leader of the Berlin Cabaret of Comedians.

129. Female cabaret artiste on Berlin stage; born Gelsenkirchen 1884, died 1957.

130. Colonel Rudolf T., military attaché simultaneously at the Prague and Bucharest Embassies. Keilig: *Heer*, 211/341.

131. Not clear to whom this refers. ED

132. Lieutenant-General Friedrich von B., military attaché at the German Embassy in Washington from April 1933, and at the German consulate in Mexico from February 1938.

133. Gustav S., (doctorate in commerce), from 1931 Gauleiter of Koblenz-Trier (1942 Gauleiter of Mosel).

134. The Ordensburgen were three ideological training camps for Nazi Party cadres. Napola were Nazi elite schools. ED

135. The allusion is not clear, but it could be to the French practice of commissioning senior NCOs.

136. The SA was the natural rival of the SS. The SA politics of Brauchitsch were aimed at strengthening the SA's position by bringing it closer to the Wehrmacht.

Major Radke of the C-in-C's staff was Liaison Officer to the SA Chief of Staff (Lutze) and had a military-political portfolio. See Groscurth: *Tagebücher*, pp. 166 and 168.

137. See entry 11 August 1938.

138. The text implies Bormann. ED

139. See note 136. Groscurth was an Abwehr officer 1935–8, latterly Chief of Abt. II; company commander 49th Infantry Regiment at Breslau January–August 1939; at same time until beginning 1940 head of Verbindungsgruppe zbV (Liaison Group for Special Purposes) of the Abwehr at OKH.

140. All German warships in commission from light cruiser size upwards made calls to foreign ports in Europe and the Mediterranean pre-war. Occasionally Hitler would wait at the quayside for the returning ship to moor and then address the crews. Between 1933 and the end of 1938, the old battleship *Schlesien* and the light cruisers *Emden* and *Karlsruhe* made a number of world cruises with a complement of cadets. ED

141. Ernst Wilhelm B., 1903–60, doctorate in commerce. From 1933 Head of NSDAP Foreign Organisation (AO) in the rank of Gauleiter, 1937–41; at same time Secretary of State and Head of Foreign Organisation in the Foreign Ministry (Care of Reich-Germans Abroad). Archive IfZ; see NSDAP Organisation Book at p. 143.

142. Prince-Regent Paul of Yugoslavia and Princess Olga were guests of the Reich Government 1–5 June 1939. After the state visit they stayed over a few days privately in Germany, visiting Dresden amongst other places, and accepted an invitation from Göring to visit Karinhall. See *Völkischer Beobachter*, 1–6 June 1939.

143. Prince P. of Yugoslavia, born 1893 St Petersburg, Regent for Crown Prince Peter II 1934–41.

144. Princess Olga of Greece and Denmark, born 1903; married Prince Paul of Yugoslavia 1923.

145. Gerdy T., interior architect and decorator, widow of Ludwig T., designed the interior of the Haus der Kunst, furnished Hitler's private living quarters at the Reich Chancellery and at the Berghof. Archive IfZ.

146. Karl K., Director, Haus der Deutschen Kunst.

147. Paul Mathias P., 1903–84, painter.

148. In other words, Queen Victoria would prefer not to admit to having conceived and borne her children through the normal (indecent) process of human reproduction. ED

149. SS-Obergruppenführer and Waffen-SS General Karl W., born 1900. Head of the Personal Staff, RF-SS 1936; 'Liaison-Leader RF-SS to the Führer' 1939. SS personal file.

150. This means the so-called Heimwehr (Home Defence) Danzig, the formation of which had been approved by the City Senate and subordinated to the RF-SS. In June 1939 Himmler transferred from Berlin-Adlershof III SS-Sturmbann (identical with SS-Sturmbann *Götze*) of Totenkopfstandarte 4 which, once

established in Danzig, proceeded to recruit local volunteers. In the main the Heimwehr was composed of Germans from the Reich (two-thirds of the force). After being disbanded at the end of September 1939, the members of III SS-Sturmbann were absorbed into other *Totenkopf* units. See Klietmann: *Die Waffen-SS*, p. 419f; also Groscurth: *Tagebücher*, p. 183, note 379.

151. Lieutenant-Colonel K., Army General Office. Podzun: *Heer*, p. 22.

152. SS-Obergruppenführer and General der Waffen-SS Hans J, born 1894. Inspekteur der SS-Verfügungstruppe, 1936–9, as Standartenführer; Waffen-SS Kommando Amt 1940; Chief of Staff (later Head) SSFHA [SS Leadership Main Office] August 1940; SS-Gruppenführer 1941. SS-personal file.

153. Helmut Moritz Sch., evangelical theologian, member 'Jungreformatorische Bewegung'. See Bethge: *Bonhoeffer*, pp. 280, 331f, 629.

154. See 6 August 1938, note 61: as to the influence of Bormann on Wehrmacht spiritual care see Zipfel: *Kirchenkampf*, pp. 226,ff, 247.

155. D. Franz D., evangelical Bishop-in-the-field.

156. Commander Alwin A. Wehrmacht (Kriegsmarine) adjutant to the Führer, June 1938–June 1939; 30 June 1939 left naval service upon appointment to Hitler's personal *adjutantur*. For the Albrecht case see also Groscurth: *Tagebücher*, 24 August 1939, p. 179f.

157. Erich Sch-M., ObdM Chief of Staff January 1939–February 1944. Keilig: *Kriegsmarine*, 291/347.

158. Raeder had recently been promoted to this rank.

159. Hitler's guesthouse on the Obersalzberg.

160. The Tea House on the Obersalzberg, possibly designed by Hitler himself, is a stone pavilion, still standing today, perched on a rocky crag, the Mooslahner-kopf, and accessible by lift. ED

161. According to the Marriage Rules for Members of the Wehrmacht (HVOBl. 1936, p. 121), approval for a marriage petition could only be given if the bride-to-be was 'of German or German-related blood', of 'unobjectionable profession or calling' and was additionally 'deserving of respect and loyal to the state'.

162. Lady Unity Walkyrie M., supporter of National Socialism and admirer of Hitler; attempted suicide 3 September 1939 at Munich on outbreak of war between Germany and Great Britain; treated at Hitler's expense at the Universitätsklinik where visited by Hitler 10 September 1939 and 8 November 1939; repatriated via Switzerland April 1940; as a result of her suicide attempt died England 1948. Maser: *Hitler*, p. 320.

163. Lady Diana M., wife of British fascist leader Sir Oswald M.

164. Sir Winston Spencer Ch., 1874–1965. First Lord of the Admiralty, September 1939–May 1940; British Prime Minister May 1940–July 1945. [The Mitfords were not related to him. ED]

165. [Reichsärztführer = Head of Public Health.] After the death of Dr Gerhard Wagner in March 1939, Dr Leonardo Conti took over this office.

166. Professor Dr Karl B., born 1904, private physician to Hitler from 1934; General (later Reich-) Commissar for Hospitals and Health 1942. B. and Bouhler

were authorised by Hitler to carry out the euthanasia programme. Ärzteprozeß, Protokoll of 10 December 1945. p. 139f.

167. In 1935–6 the NSDAP Racial-Political Office produced three films for training purposes on the subject of euthanasia, but these were not widely released. The first propaganda film for Hitler's euthanasia programme was the 1941 drama *Ich klage an* (*'I accuse'*). See Wulf: *Theater und Film*, p. 353; Boberach: *Meldungen aus dem Reich*, pp. 207–11. About euthanasia see Mitscherlich: *Medizin ohne Menschlichkeit*, pp. 183–235; Platen-Hallermund: *Tötung Geisteskranker in Deutschland*; Henkys: *Gewaltverbrechen*, pp. 60–6; Dörner: *Nationalsozialismus und Lebensvernichtung*, pp. 121–52; Buchheim: *Euthenasieprogramm*, p. 60f.

168. Regarding Hitler's hours-long speech (with only a short pause at midday) of 22 August 1939 to senior commanders of the three Wehrmacht services, their chiefs of staff and the OKW departmental heads see particularly Greiner: *Wehrmachtführung*, pp. 38–43; Müller: *Heer*, pp. 409–11; also Groscurth: *Tagebücher*, p. 179f. and Bock Diary entry of 22 August 1939; also Hillgruber: *Strategie*, pp. 28ff., 207f. For content of the speech see the Nuremberg Documents: 798-PS, 1014-PS, Raeder 27 (Bde. IMT XXVI, pp. 338–44 and 523–4; XLI, pp. 16–27). Investigation critical of the source of the various version in Baumgart: *Ansprache Hitlers im August 1939*, pp. 120–49.

169. See 22 August 1939.

170. See additionally Groscurth: *Tagebücher*, 24 August 1939, p. 179.

171. See ADAP VII, no 271.

172. Halder's diary entry of 25 August 1939 makes no mention of a visit to the Reich Chancellery that day. [From 25 August 1939 the whole OKH was in the process of removing from the Bendlerstrasse in Berlin to the Zossen underground command centre 40 km south. The Army General Staff moved into bunker known as Maybach I at Zossen on 26 August 1939. Seidler & Zeigert: *Hitler's Secret Headquarters*. ED].

173. Pressurised by Mussolini's letter (see note 171) declining to involve Italy, handed to the German Foreign Ministry by Ambassador Attolico towards 1800 hrs, and the news of the signing of an Anglo–Polish treaty in London which preceded it (*Dokumente der Deutschen Politik*, Vol. 7, Part 1, p. 120), between 1930 and 2000 hrs Hitler cancelled the attack orders for all units along the eastern frontier. See KTB-FHQ No. 1, sheet 12 and Halder: *Diary* I, 25 August 1939, p. 31 with note 15. Respecting Hitler's reasons for this step: IMT X, p. 578; III, p. 280, XXXIX, 107.

174. Apparently Birger Dahlerus, a Swedish industrialist with extensive contacts in Britain and Germany, is meant here. On his own initiative in the summer of 1939, D. had acted as an intermediary between the two nations. After a long conversation with Hitler and Göring on 26 September (ADAP VIII, No. 138) in which Hitler had demanded 'a free hand with regard to Poland' as a precondition for peace talks, D. travelled to England for more discussions. In November 1939 he terminated his involvement at the request of the German government. See ADAP VI, No. 783; also Dahlerus: *Der Letzte Versuch*, and

Hillgruber: *Diplomaten* I, pp. 26–33.

175. See 25 August 1939. Amongst others is probably meant Ciano and Daladier.

176. That is, from Brauchitsch's point of view.

177. See 25 August 1939 with note 171.

178. See 25 August 1939 with note 174.

179. This opinion was not held solely by Hitler, for within the Army it was hoped, especially after Hitler's Reichstag speech of 28 April 1939 (Keesings Archiv, p. 4040), that 'the Polish Question' could 'somehow be resolved'. See Groscurth: *Tagebücher*, 18 April 1939, 5 June 1939, p. 173f with note 337, and p. 175.

180. See also Hillgruber: *Hitler's Strategie*, pp. 27–45. [The First Silesian War (1740–2) between Prussia and Austria developed into the War of Austrian Succession involving all the major European powers. ED]

181. After acquittal on proof of his innocence, Fritsch was appointed commanding officer of 12th Artillery Regiment. [He was killed two weeks later during fighting on the outskirts of Warsaw and on Hitler's order was accorded a state funeral at the Unter den Linden memorial in Berlin on 25 September 1939. See Seidler & Zeigert: *Hitler's Secret Headquarters*. ED]

182. See Halder: *Diary* I, 4 September 1939, p. 60; also War Diary OKW I, 1940/1941 p. 952.

183. See Hossbach: *Wehrmacht und Hitler*, p. 107f.

184. As reported in FHQ War Diary (No. 1, pp. 26 and 48) on 13 September Hitler flew from Nieder-Ellguth to the civilian aerodrome at Lodz, transferred with his entourage into cars and embarked on a so-called 'trip to the front' in company with General Blaskowitz, GOC Eighth Army, and the commanding generals of X and XIII Corps, Ulex and v. Weichs. The route was Pabjanice–Konstantinov– Aleksandrov–Zgierz–Lucmierz–Strykov–Bratoszewice.

185. Colonel-General Johannes Blaskowitz, 1883–1948. C-in-C Army Group 3 November 1938; GOC Eighth Army 1 September 1939; C-in-C East 20 October 1939.

186. That is, *Land* or provincial police.

187. The Führer-Directive for the formation of a Police division composed of militarily trained regular police officers was issued on 18 September 1939. See Tessin: *Ordnungspolizei*, p. 24.

188. As to the composition of SS divisions see Stein: *Waffen-SS*, p. 26f.

189. Magdeburger Recht: German city law applied to Silesia, Poland and Bohemia amongst other places.

190. Arthur G., 1897–1947. Deputy Gauleiter in Danzig and leader of NSDAP contingent in the Danzig Parliament, 1930–9; Inner Senator of Danzig 1933; President of Danzig Senate, November 1934–September 1939; Gauleiter and Reich Governor of the Wartheland Gau (province of Posen), October 1939.

191. Organisation of Germans living in the western parts of Poland.

192. Albert F., born 1902. Gauleiter in Danzig, October 1930; declared Head of State of the 'Free City of Danzig' by the Senate, August 1938; Reich Governor of Danzig-West Prussia, October 1939.

193. SS-Obergruppenführer Richard Hildebrandt held the office of SS and Polizeiführer (Vistula) based in Danzig October 1939–March 1943. For Hitler's Polish politics see Broszat: *Nationalsozialistische Polenpolitik* and Krausnick: *Hitlers Morde in Polen*, p. 196ff; also Groscurth: *Tagebücher* (October 1939); Halder: *Diary* I, 18 October 1939, p. 107.

194. Regarding Forster's comparatively humane enforced Germanisation programme, criticised by both Hitler and Himmler, see Broszat: *Polenpolitik*, pp. 127–31.

195. General of Artillery Walter H. Military commander Danzig-West Prussia, 12 September 1939; Cmmdg. Gen. VIII Corps, October 1939–January 1943. Keilig: 211/127.

196. Dr med. Karl Brandt. See 8 August 1939, note 166.

197. Cardinal Clemens August Graf von Galen, 1878–1946). Bishop of Münster; studied Innsbruck, Freiburg (Switzerland) and Münster; chaplain and priest at St Mathias Church, Berlin, 1906; priest at St Lambertus, Münster, 1929; appointed Bishop of Münster 1933. In 1941 preached openly against the 'destruction of valueless lives' and finally succeeded, together with the clergy of both confessions, in achieving Hitler's decision provisionally to curtail the euthanasia programme. See Grohmann: 'Ein Bischof stoppte die Euthanasie-aktion', in: *Freiheit und Recht*, Jg. 12 19, No. 3, p. 16ff; for text of Galen's sermon of 3 August 1941 see Neuhäusler: *Kreuz*, pp. 364–69; for Hitler's euthanasia programme see Buchheim: *Euthanasieprogramm*, p. 60f.

198. So far neither the existence of such an offer, nor a note in reply, has been confirmed.

199. Dr rer. pol. Otto D., 1897–1952, Reich Government Press Chief and State Secretary in Propaganda Ministry 1938–45.

200. Baldur von Sch., 1907–74. NSDAP Reich Youth leader, 1931–40; Deutsches Reich Youth Leader, 1933; Gauleiter and Governor of Vienna, 1940–45.

201. Hermann E., born 1900. Senior Editor of *Illustrierter Beobachter*, 1926–32; Bavarian State Minister for Economy, 1933–5; State Secretary in Propaganda Ministry, 1939.

202. Adolf W., 1890–1944. Gauleiter of Munich-Upper Bavaria, 1930; Bavarian State Interior Minister, 1933; additionally State Minister for Education and Culture and Deputy Minister President, 1936.

203. Wilhelm M., 1888–1945. Gauleiter of Württemberg, 1928; State President and Reich Governor in Württemberg, 1933.

204. Reports of similar steps appear in Groscurth: *Tagebücher*, p. 406f and 409ff, see also the work by Krausnick/Wilhelm on the Einsatzgruppen.

205. SS-Oberführer Ludolf von A. Senior ADC to RF-SS, 1938–41; leader of West-Prussian Home Guard, 1939; he did not become SS and Police Leader

(Crimea) until the end of 1941. SS personnel files.

206. During this conversation on 5 November Brauchitsch submitted the reservations he and the army commanders had regarding the imminent Western offensive and criticised the indiscipline of the troops. When Hitler became excited and demanded further details about the incidents and measures taken, the C-in-C was unable to answer, whereupon Hitler brusquely terminated the interview and considered dismissing Brauchitsch. See Groscurth: *Tagebücher*, p. 224f. and 305; War Diary OKW I 1940/1941, p. 951f. and Jacobsen: *Gelb*, p. 46f; also see 10 November 1939. For the consequences which this conversation had for the plans of the military opposition see Groscurth: *Tagebücher*, 5 November 1939, p. 224f.; Müller: *Heer*, chapter XI.

207. Colonel Eduard Wagner, 1894–1944. Head of Abt. 6, Army General Staff, 1936–40; Major-General August 1940; Army QM-General August 1940–July 1944; Lieutenant-General April 1942. Keilig: 211/353. Research to date (see Halder: *Diary*, I, 5 November 1939, p. 120 with note 4) has not confirmed that a memorandum from Wagner was submitted on 5 November. However, it is possible that the QM-General played a decisive role in the collation of the extracts for the C-in-C report. A report about the condition of the Army was prepared by Wagner's staff on the orders of the C-in-C on 8 November. This may be the document to which Engel referred, see 22 November 1939.

208. See 7 November 1939.

209. Presumably identical with the memorandum of 27 November 1939 (extracts reproduced in Groscurth: *Tagebücher*, p. 426): unabridged version at Bä/Military Archive. That there may have been an earlier memorandum from Blaskowitz (see Groscurth: *Tagebücher*, p. 80; Müller: *Heer*, p. 437) now seems unlikely in view of of the posterior nature of Engel's notes. Its existence in the literature of the subject may be founded on the allocation by the author of an incorrect date.

210. Kurt von Tippelskirch. Head of Abt. IV (OQuIV) in the Army General Staff, November 1938–January 1941; the departments Foreign Armies East and West were subordinate to him as well as the Attaché Group: GOC 30th Infantry Division, January–June 1942; German general with the Italian Army on the Eastern Front, August 1942–February 1943.

211. This visit of Guderian to Hitler (see Guderian: *Erinnerungen*, p. 76f) was a consequence of Hitler's address to commanding generals, army commanders and senior General Staff officers at the New Reich Chancellery on 23 November. The purpose of this 'forced reception' (see Jacobsen: *Gelb*, pp. 59–64) was to impress upon his 'reticent' generals the necessity for the Western offensive and to set aside the crisis of confidence existing between himself and Brauchitsch since 5 November. Since Hitler in his address of 23 November (for content of the speech see Groscurth: *Tagebücher*, pp. 414–18; also 789-PS, IMT XXVI, p. 327) had clearly belittled the achievements of the Army in comparison to those of the other two branches of service, which was considered an insult in view of the successful conclusion to the Polish campaign, and had brought to a head the crisis with the C-in-C during 23 November to the extent that Brauchitsch

petitioned to be relieved of his post, Guderian finally received the job of presenting to Hitler privately the 'mood of the generals'. See also Halder: *Diary* I, 23 November 1939, p. 131f.

212. This presumably relates to a report from Wagner's staff about the deficient state of the Army, which the C-in-C requested in justification of his stance following the altercation with Hitler on 5 November (see 7 November 1939). See also Groscurth: *Tagebücher*, p. 404.

213. Exactly when this conversation occurred cannot be determined. On 23 November 1939 at midday, Hitler addressed between 180 and 200 senior officers (commanders-in-chief and commanding generals): at 1330 hrs he continued his address and at 1800 hrs there ensued a conference with Brauchitsch and Halder. See Jodl: *Diary*, 23 November 39. WG 13 (1953) p. 59.

214. On 20 November, the proposed offensive was postponed to 3 December 1939. See Jacobsen: *Gelb*, p. 51.

215. OKL (Luftwaffe High Command) also demanded the extensive occupation of Holland. It was feared that the planned partial occupation might tempt the British to install airfields in the neutral zone for bomber attacks on the Ruhr. See Jacobsen: *Gelb*, pp. 54–9; Jodl: *Diary*, 31 October 39, WG 12 (1952), p. 284.

216. For the disagreement about the concentration of forces in attack-plan 'Gelb' [the initial plan for the invasion of France and the Low Countries ED] see Jacobsen: *Gelb* pp. 51–4 and 68–82; Halder: *Diary* I, several entries in the October–November period 1939: also particularly Manstein: *Siege*, chapter 5.

217. This refers to the disagreement between Hitler and Brauchitsch of 5 November 1939, as the result of which Hitler considered dismissing him. See 7 November 1939.

218. When the C-in-C offered his resignation of the evening of 23 November ('Spirit of Zossen', see Halder: *Diary* I, 23 November 1939, p. 132) it was rejected. See 3798-PS, p. 29; Bock *Diary*, 23 November 1939, p. 28.

219. General of Infantry Eugen Ritter von Sch., 1883–1941. Cmmdg. Gen. VII Corps, February 1938; GOC Eleventh Army, October 1940–September 1941. Keilig: *Heer*, 211/303.

220. As Tessin (*Geschichte der Ordnungspolizei*, Part II, p. 24) confirms, the Polizei-Division formed as the result of a Führer Directive of 18 September 1939 was not fully integrated into the Waffen-SS until 24 February 1942 [as 4th SS Panzer Grenadier Division].

221. In the original text a play on words: 'als Fahrer, aber nicht Pfarrer.' ED

222. Nevertheless there were SS men, even higher SS officers, who successfully defended their association with religious communities.

223. Hitler visited the Western Front for this purpose between 23 and 25 December 1939. See Domarus: *Hitler*, Vol. II 3, p. 1434, *Völkischer Beobachter* of 27 December 1939.

224. Originally 'Wachregiment Berlin' before its change of designation in the summer of 1939 (see HVOBl A, sheet 7, 1 July 1939). A company from this unit mounted the 'watch' before the *Ehrenmal* (monument to the fallen) on Unter den

Linden in Berlin. See *Panzer Großdeutschland*, pp. 35–46.

225. Incorrectly dated 1939 in the original.

226. Under Secretary of State in the US State Department, 1937–43. Sumner Welles visited European capitals at the instigation of the US President in order to discuss 'the possibilities of a lasting and secure peace in Europe' with the statesmen involved (for Welles's mission see Hull, C: *Memoirs*, p. 737ff). In early March he visited Berlin, conferred with Ribbentrop on 1 March (see ADAP VIII, No. 640: *Foreign Relations of the US* [FRUS] 1940, Vol. I, pp. 33–41) and Hitler the next day. For the protocol of envoy Schmidt regarding this conversation see: ADAP VIII, No. 649. Sumner Welles's report is in FRUS 1940, Vol. I, pp. 43–50. The text of this protocol appears in Hillgruber: *Staatsmänner*, pp. 68–76. On the third day of his Berlin visit S.W. engaged in full diplomatic activity, and had no less than four conferences: first with the Italian and Belgian ambassadors ('the most experienced members of the local Diplomatic Corps'), the opposition to Hitler and then Rudolf Hess (see FRUS 1940, Vol. I, p. 50), and finally drove to Karinhall for a conference of several hours with Göring (see ADAP VIII, No. 653, also FRUS 1940, Vol. I, pp. 51–6). After his return to Berlin he met Hjalmar Schacht who, amongst other things, remarked, with regard to the intentions of the opposition: 'It would take a few months perhaps, even if no offensive took place, before the conspirators would be ready to take action', or words to that effect (see FRUS 1940, Vol. I, p. 56f).

227. Franklin Delano Roosevelt, US President 1933–45.

228. As Halder makes clear, OQuIV, who had presumably been informed by the Foreign Office representative Etzdorf who was subordinate to him, reported twice (see 26 February and 2 March) about the Welles mission. Halder had also been informed personally by Etzdorf about the Welles–Hitler conversation.

229. Also see note 226.

230. HQ Army Group A.

231. Colonel-General von Rundstedt.

232. Chief of Staff Army Group A.

233. Colonel Günther B, No. 1 Staff Officer. Army Group A.

234. See also Manstein: *Siege*, p. 91ff and especially Jacobsen: *Gelb*, pp. 68–82, 111f with note 10 and pp. 114–18.

235. See note above.

236. Alexander Freiherr von D., Foreign Office envoy, Head of Protocol.

237. Dr jur. Hans F., 1900–46 (sentenced to death at Nuremberg, October 1946). Bavarian Minister of Justice, 1933; President of the 'Academy of German Law'; Governor-General of Poland, October 1939–1945. IfZ Archive.

238. Deportation and centralisation mainly into ghettos (Warsaw, Cracow, Radom, Lublin) was initially the fate of about three million Polish Jews. See Broszat: *Polenpolitik*, p. 65ff. As to the phases of the de-polandisation of the annexed eastern regions see Broszat: *Polenpolitik*, pp. 85–102.

239. For the relationship between military commanders and the civilian administration in the General Government of Poland see Groscurth: *Tagebücher*,

10 December 1939, p. 236; 17 January 1940, p. 242 and also Broszat: *Polen-politik*, pp. 74–9.

240. At Hitler's wish, the city of Linz, where he attended the Realschule for several years and for which he cherished an especial liking, was to be transformed into a European cultural centre. Hitler envisaged a portrait gallery as the hub of this endeavour, and he appointed the general manager of the Dresden Gallery, Hans Posse, to oversee the work officially. Of all the Linz projects, the collecting of works of art, which included weapons and coins, forged ahead the fastest, having Hitler's constant participation. Further in Brenner: *Die Kunstpolitik des Nationalsozialismus*, pp. 154–61. According to Engel, Frau A. was an expert of the first rank and administered the portrait gallery – consisting mostly of 'degraded art' – in the Party Chancellery building in Munich used by Hitler as a market place.

241. Not realised until after the first serious setbacks of the Russian campaign. Hitler considered the crisis before Moscow as 'a consequence of an as yet imperfect merging of soldiery and National Socialism' and after assuming personal control of the Army (20 December 1941) determined it to be his most important task 'to train the Army to be National Socialist'. For the training of the political soldier as an instrument of his ideological war leadership, his order of 22 December 1943 provided for NS-Leadership Staff at OKW, whose purpose was to ensure a unitary political–world political training for NS-Leadership Officers (NSFO). As regards the selection of the latter the NS-Leadership Staff would cooperate with the Party Chancellery in making recommendations for candidacy and hear appeals. Bormann's appointment as overall controller allowed for the first time an immediate NSDAP influence on the ideological leadership of the troops. See additionally the documentation in W. Besson: *Zur Geschichte des NSFO*, pp. 7–115: Messerschmidt: *Wehrmacht im NS-Staat*, pp. 441–80 and Demeter: *Das deutsche Offizierkorps*, p. 193f.

242. Of Prussia, 1880–1945, CO 230th Infantry Regiment, September 1939–March 1940, Major-General z.V., 1 March 1940. Keilig: 211/256. [His son, Prince Oskar, was killed in the opening days of the Polish campaign. ED]

243. Hitler's aversion to the contamination of internationalism found its expression later (19 May 1943) in a directive to distance men with international ties from important offices in state, Party and Wehrmacht. This applied to members of former royal houses, most of whom received a discharge from the Wehrmacht, also to those persons married or related to foreigners. IfZ Archive.

244. A form of document unknown in Church terminology (Information from the Kommission für Zeitgeschichte e.V., Bonn, on 14 December 1973, and from Father Dr L. Volk, SJ, Munich). Engel advised that these were sermon extracts sent to Wehrmacht members through the field post system. It cannot be ruled out that as the result of Bormann's delivery of forged 'pulpit letters' to Hitler, the clergy were forbidden to use field post numbers to supply Wehrmacht personnel with liturgical material.

245. Captain Deyhle, 1st General Staff Officer to Head of Wehrmacht Command Staff/Land Defence (i.e. Warlimont). In order to pre-empt the intended British

occupation of the Scandinavian coast, which unknown to the Germans was already under way, on 9 April German forces were landed in Norwegian and Danish harbours (Operation 'Weserübung').

246. See Jacobsen: *Der Zweite Weltkrieg*, p. 19ff.; for the Operation 'Weserübung' command structure see Warlimont: *Im Hauptquartier*, pp. 82–97.

247. General of Infantry Nikolaus von F., commanding operations against Norway and Denmark.

248. At the end of April 1940, RF-SS and Chief of the German Police ordered the deportation of about 2,500 gypsies near the western borders of Poland 'for security reasons'. A resettlement of gypsies scheduled for October that year was called off on the grounds that dealing with the gypsy question was to be postponed until after the war. It is possible that some confusion regarding the racial status of gypsies was responsible for the postponement. In an OKH directive of February 1941 gypsies or person of gypsy descent with 'striking gypsy-like features' were barred from Wehrmacht service; in July 1942 all full gypsies were discharged from the Wehrmacht. There were no exceptions. See Buchheim: *Zigeunerdeportation*, pp. 51–60; also Döring's investigation into the motive behind the gypsy deportation of May 1940.

249. See 2 May 1940.

250. Prinz Albrecht Strasse 8 was the seat of the SS-RSHA (Reich Main Security Office, the SS body in charge of the Security Service (SD), the Gestapo, and other departments).

251. The German offensive in the West began on 10 May 1940.

252. Major-General Hans J. Chief of the Luftwaffe General Staff, February 1939–August 1943; General der Flieger, July 1940.

253. The deployment of the infantry and the disposition of the mobile forces was undoubtedly agreed during the decisive discussions between Hitler and Colonel-General von Rundstedt, CO Army Group A, at the Charleville field HQ on 24 May 1940, but opinion on how the operations in Flanders should be brought to their conclusion wavered 'back and forth' and remained open. See Meier-Welcker, pp. 279–90 and the two investigations by von Jacobsen: *Dünkirchen*, and 'Dünkirchen 1940' in *Entscheidungsschlachten*, pp. 7–55.

254. Lieutenant-General Georg von S., Army Group A Chief of Staff.

255. FHQ Felsennest overlooking the village of Rodert near Bad Münstereifel was used between 10 May and 5 June 1940. According to Organisation Todt records and the FHQ War Diary, on 22 May 1940 Engel, in company with Lieutenant-Colonel Thomas, Schmundt and Dr Todt, inspected the village at Bruly de Pesche in Belgium soon to be converted into FHQ Wolfsschlucht and occupied up to 25 June 1940. ED

256. Reported differently in Domarus II 3, p. 1527 (who in a letter to the publisher dated 20 December 1973 gave an oral statement by General Hermann Balck as his source): after the conquest of Holland, Hitler left it up to Wilhelm II whether he wished to resume residence in Germany. Ilsemann (*Kaiser in Holland*, p. 345f.) reports on the isolation of Wilhelm II at Doorn in order to prevent the former Kaiser making contact with Wehrmacht personnel.

257. Mussolini informed Hitler on 30 May of his intention 'to step into the war', and on 2 June supplied details of his programme: 'On Monday 10 June declaration of war [from the balcony of the Palazzo Venezia], on the morning of 11 June hostilities commence.' See ADAP IX, No. 356 and 373. For more on the Italian entry into the war see Siebert: *Italiens Weg*.

258. The reference to Charles de Gaulle is curious. Hitler may have been aware of his prewar book *The Army of the Future* and perhaps that he had been made Deputy War Minister on 5 June 1940, but the comment implies that he knew much about de Gaulle, who did not make his first broadcast from Britain until 18 June. ED

259. OKH HQ was at Chimay, FHQ 'Wolfsschlucht' at Bruly de Pesche [misspelled by the author in the original as Peche ED] an abandoned village in Belgium 25 km north-west of Charleroi.

260. On 21 June the German conditions were presented to the French Armistice Commission at Compiègne, and the armistice signed the next day.

261. Arno B., born 1900, sculptor. Studied at the Düsseldorf Academy of Art and in Paris; from the end of 1933 lived in Berlin. Apart from monumental heroic works (Löwenplastiken at Maschsee near Hannover, 'der Wäger,' 'der Wager', both prepared for the new Reich Chancellery) in the main Breker turned out portrait busts – including Hitler.

262. Speer and the architect Hermann Giesler, whom Hitler had appointed Generalbaurat for the Capital of the Movement (Munich), were also summoned to FHQ in order to accompany Hitler on his tour of Paris on 23 June. So that they would merge in more satisfactorily with the military entourage, field-grey uniforms were provided for them. Speer: *Erinnerungen*, pp. 185–7.

263. As to the date of Hitler's visit and the duration of his stay in Paris the FHQ War Diary contains the following entry: '23 June 1940. 3.30 hr Führer flew to Paris. There short tour of city. 10.00 hr Führer returned from Paris.' For further on the Paris visit see also: *Daten aus Notizbüchern*. During his short stay, in pursuit of his special liking for the architecture of Garnier, Hitler visited the Grand Opera. He felt so much at home in this edifice, whose original scheme he had studied, that he took over the guided tour himself. He paused to visit the Eiffel Tower and – according to reports – spent a long period at Napoleon's sarcophagus in the Invalides. This was Hitler's only visit to Paris. Speer recalls Hitler's journey through the French capital in his *Memoiren*, p. 186ff. with photos. A pictorial account appeared in the *Illustierter Beobachter* of 4 July 1940.

264. Photographs show that both wore a smart field-grey uniform, if in all respects as per regulations remains uncertain.

265. On 17 June Wilhelm II sent Hitler a congratulatory telegram with the following text: 'Under the deeply moving impression of the armistice with France I congratulate you and the entire German Wehrmacht for the God-sent enormous victory with the words of Kaiser Wilhelm the Great in the year 1870: 'What turn of events through God's intervention!' In all German hearts resounds the chorale of Leuthen, which the victors of Leuthen, the soldiers of that great king, sang: Now thank we all our God!' See ADAP IX, No. 469. The Kaiser's wish

to return to Germany is not included in the text. However, it cannot be ruled out that the postcard contained a corresponding additional sentence. See also 28 May 1940 with note 241. As remarked in ADAP, Hitler thanked 'His Majesty' on 25 June. See Ilsemann: *Kaiser in Holland*, p. 345.

266. For the later situation of the former Kaiser at Doorn see Ilsemann: *op cit*, p. 345f.

267. Admiral Wilhelm C., 1887–1945 (executed at Flossenbürg concentration camp for complicity in plot of 20 July 1944). Chief of Abwehr (counter-intelligence) at Reichswehr Ministry, 1935; Chief of Office of Foreign Information and Abwehr, November 1938–June 1944. IfZ Archive.

268. That is, the prosecution of the war against Britain.

269. Meant here is HRH the Duke of Windsor, who abdicated the British throne as King Edward VIII to marry an American divorcée, Mrs Simpson. For a plot to kidnap the duke in the summer of 1940 see Schellenberg: *Memoiren*, pp. 108–18.

270. An allusion to the suicide attempt of Unity Mitford.

271. On 19 July 1940 Hitler addressed the Reichstag for several hours, which speech he concluded with an 'Appeal to England's Reason'. Text reproduced in Domarus II 3, pp. 1540–9.

272. On 19 July 1940 Hitler promoted twelve generals to field marshal. See *Völkischer Beobachter* for 20 July 1940.

273. See Halder: *Diary* II, 13 September 1940, p. 97.

274. Julius Sch., born 1898, pharmacist, from end of 1924 Hitler's personal adjutant.

275. Martin Bormann's brother was employed as Hitler's personal adjutant at the private chancellery (later Führer's Chancellery).

276. As commander of an army corps, in 1939 Guderian had seen Soviet armoured units during the capture of Brest-Litovsk. See Guderian: *Erinnerungen*, p. 73f.

277. Regarding the incorrect assessment of the Red Army not only by the German military see Halder's note of his conversations with Hitler on 5 December 1940; Reinhardt: *Wende*, pp. 18–25.

278. No such report appears to have been made in *The Times* of London. [Major Friedrich-Karl Schlichting, now commanding No. 2 Group, Kampfgeschwader (Bomber Group) 27 and Major Hans-Jürgen Brehmer of the Luftwaffe General Staff were shot down and captured while returning from a raid on Bristol during the night of 11/12 August. ED]

279. Field Marshal Erhard M. State Secretary for Aviation, 1933; General Inspector of the Luftwaffe, 1938; after Udet's death in 1941 Minister for Aircraft Production and Supply; head of Hilfsaktion für Stalingrad, 15 January–3 February 1943.

280. Hitler's 'last appeal' to Britain of 19 July (see 15 July 1940) was spurned by Lord Halifax in a radio broadcast on 22 July on the grounds that Hitler had given no indication that the offered terms were to be founded on justice, nor that other nations were entitled to the right of self-determination often demanded for

itself by Germany. Britain would fight on until its own independence, and that of the other nations, had been secured. See Schulthess: *1940*, p. 288f.

281. See 10 August 1940.

282. For the interpretation of Hitler's attack plan against the Soviet Union see Seraphim, Hillgruber: *Hitlers Entschluss*, pp. 240–9.

283. After Hitler had spoken with the French Deputy Minister-President Laval at Montoire on 22 October, he met Franco the following day at Hendaye in the hope of winning him over for an 'entire grand front against England'. However, Franco was not ready to accede to Hitler's wish that Spain should enter the war on Germany's side. See ADAP XI 1, Nos 220, 222 and p. 394f; regarding the course of the conversation in Hitler's saloon coach see also Schmidt: *Statist*, pp. 500–2; for Hitler's Gibraltar plan also see Detwiler: *Hitler, Franco und Gibraltar*.

284. Ribbentrop.

285. The Italian attack on Greece began from Albania on 28 October. See Ciano: *Diary*, 8 October 1940, pp. 262–82.

286. See Ciano, *op. cit.*, p. 277.

287. Major-General Enno von R., German military attaché in Rome, also German General at Italian HQ.

288. Hans-Georg von M., German ambassador at the Quirinal, 1938–43.

289. Present at this discussion, which preceded a brief meeting between von Brauchitsch and Halder, were, according to Halder (*Diary*, II, 4 November 1940 pp. 163–5) besides himself Keitel, Jodl, Deyhle, Schmundt, Engel and Brauchitsch. Engel's diary entry of 4 November needs to be complemented by Halder's record of Hitler's statement at the situation conference, since his broad observations on the overall balance of affairs after his foreign policy activity towards France and Spain and before the Molotov visit allow the historian to deduce that the decision in favour of striking East or West was, as before, open.

'14.30 hr Führer. (Present Keitel, Jodl, Deyhle, Schmundt, Engel, C-in-C and I).

1. Libya. Führer drew the following picture:
   a) More time than previously thought. It is not expected that Italians will make their attack on Mersa Matruh before the end of December. Then long-term preparations for water supply, highway construction etc. (3 months). Then hot weather begins. Nothing to do before autumn 1941.
   b) Italy has given notice that it requires Tripoli itself as a supply base and is forcing us to use Tunis for that purpose.
   c) Not much confidence in Italian commanders. Italy only wants us as 'blood-saver'.
   d) Operationally risky to ship troops across a sea we do not control and with an ally not prepared to use all means to keep this seaway open.

2. Spain. Franco has promised the Führer in a letter that he will in all seriousness fulfill the orally agreed promises, i.e. to come in on our side. Führer will now force Spain's entry into the war.

Possible British reactions: British establish themselves west coast of Africa. British establish themselves Morocco.

Spanish and Portuguese Islands.

France can and will defend its own territories. If necessary Spain must be helped defend its own islands.

3. Islands Question. Which islands [Canaries – Azores] should be occupied and by what means is being examined at the moment by OKW. OKH representative additional! (Heusinger).

4. Gibraltar.
a) When Spanish border is crossed, Luftwaffe must attack British Fleet in Gibraltar.
Bases must be set up beforehand.
b) Troops to be at readiness for advance into Portugal.
c) Get artillery soonest possible to south coast of Narrows [Strait of Gibraltar]!

5. Greece
a) British attempting to set up air bases on Lemnos and Salonika.
[British] AA units pushed up to Bulgaria's southern border.
Turkish attitude probably reserved. (Attempt by Russia to pressurise Turkey).
b) Army should prepare to support surprise invasion of Turkish Thrace. Suggestion to OKW (strengths, time required).
c) Luftwaffe to prepare to destroy Greek island bases.

6. Turkey. Russian problem developing. This question cannot be addressed until Russia is out of the picture. If Bulgaria driven south, with help of Russia Turkey can be kept quiet.

7. Russia. Remains the whole problem in Europe. Everything must be done to be ready for the grand reckoning.

8. America. If at all, [military involvement] not before 1942.

9. Sealion. Not before spring. Preparedness must be maintained. 'Improvement' indicated for our side.

10. France will be given help in the measure of what she does for us. Details of the newest agreements through Foreign Minister with Laval. First of all Swiss prisoners will be returned.'

Engel provided the following additional information:

1. The Luftwaffe will only be allowed as many 7.5-cm French guns as it can prove it needs. Org: 'What can we use them for? There are probably several hundred available.' (Note in margin).

2. Movements in East: (Transport Chief)
Danzig-West Prussia: 50,000–60,000 Bessarabian Germans
Zichenau (Government area) 40,000 from Lithuania
Warthegau-Posen: 60,000 Bessarabian Germans
Gouvernment: over 150,000–160,000 Poles and Jews from the regained territories.

Army will take no part in these movements, only know about them. Army will take no part in clearances, officers will be told that this movement will be terminated before war's end.'

Also see remarks in Hillgruber: *Strategie* as to the strategic and political possibilities open to Hitler in the summer and autumn of 1940.

290. See in this connection the two investigations by Jacobsen: *Dünkirchen* and 'Dünkirchen 1940' in *Entscheidungsschlachten*, pp. 7–55.

291. General of Infantry Kurt von Sch., 1882–1934. Reichswehr Minister, 1932; Reich Chancellor, December 1932–January 1933; murdered 30 June 1934 during 'Röhm Revolt' [Night of the Long Knives].

292. That is, Hindenburg.

293. The People's Commissar for Foreign Affairs, Vyacheslav Molotov, visited Berlin 12–14 November. For his conversations with Hitler and Ribbentrop see ADAP XI 1, Nos. 317, 325/6, 328/9. Halder: *Diary* II, 14 November 1940, p. 180 and 16 November 1940, p. 182f.

294. An entry appears in the FHQ War Diary for 10 March 1941 reporting a conference between FHQ-Commandant Lieutenant-Colonel Thomas and Colonel Schmundt at the Reich Chancellery when positions [of Army Groups] North, Centre and South were discussed. The following day Schmundt, Thomas and Engel travelled to a site conference at Rastenburg, where construction had begun during March under the supervision of an officer from Hitler's *Adjutantur*, who also monitored the work subsequently. On 14 June Standartenführer Rattenhuber of the Führer Begleitkommando, Major Momm (?) and a mosquito specialist joined the company, and Hitler took up residence ten days later, naming the complex FHQ Wolfsschanze [Wolf's Lair].

295. Instruction No. 21 dated 18 December 1940 for Operation 'Barbarossa' stipulated that the Wehrmacht should be *prepared*, even before the termination of hostilities against Britain, to overthrow Soviet Russia in a quick military campaign. For text see Hubatsch: *Führerweisungen*, pp. 84–8.

296. Lieutenant-General (from 1 October 1940 General of Cavalry) Ernst-August K., German military attaché in Moscow. At the beginning of September 1940, K. had given Halder a positive assurance about the Red Army (*Diary* II, 3 September 1940, p. 86. For Köstring's earlier assessment of the Red Army see Köstring: *Mittler*, pp. 181, 188f and 202ff.

297. See 15 November 1940.

298. See 10 August and 15 September 1940. To the Germans' surprise, in October 1941 the Russians deployed for the first time their T-34 tank, a machine of notable speed, good manoeuvrability over terrain and having in particular very strong armour resistant to the formerly adequate 3.7-cm anti-tank gun. On the deployment of the T-34 see Müller-Hillebrand: *Heer* III, p. 17f and Kissel: *Die ersten T-34*, pp. 130–2.

299. Whilst the official reason for Heinrich's visit was to deliver a report on the Finnish–Russian Winter War of 1939–40, the real purpose was a General Staff conference at OKH. See Halder: *Diary*, II, 30 January 1941, p. 264. Respecting the Finns' relationship with the Soviet Union see also ADAP XI2.

300. General of Infantry Rudolf G. Chief of Army General Staff Transport Division; Keilig: 211/98.

301. Halder mentions the OB [von Brauchitsch] as an additional participant in the conference (*Diary*, II. 1 February 1941, p. 265).

302. Major-General Hans Freiherr von F. Cmd 3rd Panzer Brigade, November 1940; GOC 5th Light Division, beginning 1941. Keilig: 211/93. Halder mentions his two-hour dialogue with Hitler (*Diary*, II, 1 February 1941, p. 265). After Mussolini requested Hitler on 20 December 1940 to send a German Panzer unit to Libya in the wake of severe setbacks in North Africa (see ADAP XI2, No. 541) Funck was sent there to assess the situation. On 25 January 1941 the German military attaché in Rome, General von Rintelen, sent the OKW a preliminary report by Funck (see War Diary OKW I, 1940/1941, p. 281) in which he stated that the envisaged force would not be large enough (see also Halder:*Diary*, II, 26 January 1941, p. 253). For further details of the German armoured assembly intended for Libya see Müller-Hillebrand: *Heer* II, p. 75, also War Diary OKW I, 1940–1, p. 321.

303. After the defeat of France, the Madagascar Plan was worked out by Rademacher, a senior diplomat at the Foreign Office (see ADAP X, No. 101). It proposed making the island into a 'Great Ghetto' inhabited exclusively by Jews (see Krausnick: *Judenverfolgung*, p. 354). In so far as one can interpret a remark to Raeder on 20 June 1940 in connection with a discussion about German colonial possessions in Africa, Hitler had already actually adopted Rademacher's Plan, if in a modified form. In 1937 Poland had investigated the settlement possibilities and living conditions on Madagascar for its Jewish population. No further action was taken following receipt of the report of the mixed Polish–Jewish Commission. See Ganther: *Die Juden in Deutschland*, p. 132.

304. Regarding the planned 'Major Justice Reform' see Weinkauff: *Justiz und Nationalsozialismus*, p. 150ff.

305. Dr h.c. Franz G., 1881–1941. Bavarian State Minister of Justice 1922–32 and Reich Justice Minister until his death. G. was responsible for engineering the reduction in the period of imprisonment to be served following Hitler's trial in 1924.

306. Professor Dr jur., Dr rer. pol. Franz Sch., 1876–1970. Secretary of State at the Reich Justice Ministry, 1931; joined NSDAP, 1938; from beginning 1941 until his departure in August 1942, chargé d'affaires at the Reich Justice Ministry.

307. Dr jur. Roland F., 1893–1945. Apparently converted to Communism as Russian PoW in WWI; lawyer 1923; from 1925 NSDAP member; Secretary of State at Reich Justice Ministry, 1934–42; President of People's Court, 1942–5.

308. For Soviet foreign policy see Beloff: *The Foreign Policy of Soviet Russia*, pp. 320–84; for German-Soviet relations see: *Das nationalsozialistische Deutschland und die Sowjet Union.*

309. The Protocol of Accession was signed at Schloss Belvedere in Vienna on 1 March by Ribbentrop, Ciano, Ambassador Oshima of Japan and Filoff, Bulgarian Minister-President. In connection hereto see Hitler's remarks to

Draganoff about the attitude of Bulgaria in the winter of 1940–1 in Hillgruber: *Diplomaten* II, p. 97.

310. For his efforts regarding Turkey see Hitler's declaration to the President of the Turkish Republic, Inönü, in which he gave assurances that the presence of some German soldiers in Turkey did not prejudice Turkey and that German units would remain clear of Turkey's borders. ADAP XII 1, No. 113.

311. See Halder: *Diary*, II, 14 February 1941, p. 281; respecting the military administration in Russia also Dallin: *Deutsche Herrschaft*, pp. 105–8.

312. SS-Gruppenführer and Lieutenant-General der Waffen-SS Karl W. Hitler's adjutant, 1933; Chief of RF-SS Personal Staff, 1936; RF-SS Liaison Officer to Führer, August 1939; SS-Obergruppenführer and General der Waffen-SS, 1942. IfZ Archive.

313. Julius St., 1885–1945, teacher. Gauleiter of Mittelfranken (from 1936 Franken), 1930–40; publisher of periodical *Der Stürmer*. Because of his many criminal acts and the affairs which were all the talk in Franconia, by edict of the Supreme Party Court Streicher (whose criminal prosecution Hitler waived) was suspended from office although he remained Gauleiter in name. Since he continued to exert influence on Gau policy making, he seems to have been put under some form of restraining order which confined him to his properties. Hitler's indebtedness to Streicher dated back to the abortive putsch at the Bürgerbräukeller in November 1923. After Hitler had collapsed and was no longer master of the situation, Streicher stepped in to handle the propaganda organisation the following morning. Streicher never mentioned this incident during his lifetime. See IMT XII, p. 340f. and Hofmann: *Hitlerputsch*, p. 201.

314. Dr Benno M., Nuremberg Police President.

315. After Greek troops had halted the Italian offensive and forced parts of the Italian forces over the border into Albania, and Britain had begun disembarking its troops at Greek ports, Hitler decided to assist his pressurised brothers-in-arms. Instruction No. 20 (Operation 'Marita') of 13 December 1940 contained the plan for the attack on Greece, which would proceed from southern Romania through Bulgaria. The Germans opened their offensive on 6 April 1941. See Hubatsch: *Weisungen für die Kriegführung*, p. 81; Müller-Hillebrand: *Heer* II, pp. 83–7 and Jacobsen: *Der Zweite Weltkrieg*, p. 29ff.

316. The Lend–Lease Law came into force on 11 March 1941. This legislation enabled the US President to lend or lease war materials to any state 'whose defence the President considers essential for the defence of the United States'. The Soviet Union was admitted into the Lend–Lease Programme in November 1941, and by the end of the war had received shipments in the value of $11 billion. The United States invested a total of $50 billion as the 'arsenal of democracy'. See Gruchmann: *Der Zweite Weltkrieg*, particularly pp. 137, 140, 142 and 518; also Jacobsen: *Der Zweite Weltkrieg*, pp. 222–6 (Lend–Lease Law).

317. The term appears in the original shorthand.

318. Legationsrat Dr jur. Karl Georg Pf., head of consular office at Memel; from mid-April 1941 at the German Embassy in Paris. IfZ Archive.

319. These were FHQ Askania Mitte, a railway tunnel, bunkers and barracks for

Hitler and OKH 40 km east of Lodz (Litzmannstadt) in the Tomasov Forest; and FHQ Askania Süd, a sheltered siding of concrete for Hitler's train located at Frysztak 20 km north of Krosno. They were intended as satellites of FHQ Wolfsschanze but used on only one night for their intended purpose because the German rate of advance into Russia was so swift. ED

320. Hitler's efforts to lure Yugoslavia into the Tripartite Pact met with success following the visit of Prince-Regent Paul to the Berghof (4 March 1941, no German transcript); the declaration of accession was signed at Schloss Belvedere, Vienna on 25 March (see *Völkischer Beobachter*, 26 March 1941). The protocol of the subsequent talk between Hitler and the Yugoslav Minister-President Cvetkovic appears in ADAP XII 1, No. 207.

321. This appears to be an afterthought inserted at the wrong date, since the *Bismarck* sinking occurred on 27 May 1941. ED

322. In the original misspelled as Heidrich.

323. In 1942 Himmler planned setting up the Reich school 'Marnix von Aldegonde' in Soestdijk. See his correspondence with the Reich Commissar for the Occupied Netherlands Territories, Seyss-Inquart, IfZ Archive, MA-328, 193-1713.

324. What he really means here is 'promote a new German generation'.

325. FHQ Frühlingssturm was a wooden railway platform close to a tunnel at Mönichkirchen on the single-track line between Wiener Neustadt and Markt Aspang and used between 11 and 26 April 1941 as sidings for Hitler's special train. ED

326. Franz v. P., 1879–1969. Consul (later ambassador) to Vienna, 1934–8; ambassador to Ankara, 1939–44. Papen visited FHQ on 19 April 1941: see *Daten aus Notizbüchern*.

327. British forces disembarked in the Iraqi port of Basra on 18 April. In breach of the undertaking given by the British ambassador that his troops would only exercise the right of passage enshrined in the mutual treaty (to support the front in Egypt), General Fraser set up a military base to handle further units being sent. Since he had not obtained the permission of the Iraqi government, fighting broke out in early May, during which the German government and others were asked for the immediate restoration of diplomatic relations (Grobba was then sent as ambassador) and arms shipments. Hitler decided upon 'activating German involvement in the Middle East' and sent two Luftwaffe Staffeln to Iraq. The stay of Grobba and the Luftwaffe was of short duration, for following the collapse of the regime and the internal chaos which succeeded it, a 'Commission for Internal Security' was set up which accepted the British armistice conditions. See: Grobba: *Orient*, pp. 220–48; ADAP XII 1, S. XLIV-XLVIII; War Diary OKW 1, 1940/1941 pp. 391–9.

328. Major Axel von B., son of the former Reich War Minister. Despatched to Iraq as OKW Liaison Officer, May 1941; killed there in air combat. See Grobba: *Orient*, p. 237. Blomberg's eldest son mentioned here fell in 1942 as the commander of a Panzer detachment in Tunisia.

329. Hadj Amin el-Husseini, Grand Mufti of Jerusalem.

330. Rashid Ali al-G., Minister-President of Iraq.

331. General of Infantry Hans von S. Chief of Staff Army Group North, 1 September 1939; Chief of Staff Army Group B, 25 October 1939; Cmmdg. Gen. XXX Corps, 10 May 1941.

332. The 'Guidelines for the Treatment of Political Commissars' belong among the complex of Führer-edicts dated 14 May 1941 respecting the exercise of courts-martial in the 'Barbarossa' territory. The final version of the Commissar Order was dated 6 June 1941. Its distribution was limited to army commanders and chiefs of the air fleets, and the contents were only to be passed down to the various command levels by word of mouth. Amongst other things it provided that political commissars fighting with Soviet forces 'are not recognised as soldiers and could not benefit from the protective regulations applying to PoWs. After segregation they are to be eliminated.' (Text in Jacobsen: *Kommissarbefehl*, p. 225ff.) These orders, which transformed Hitler's ideological outpourings to his generals of 30 March 1941 into a practical programme – ('We must' – in the imminent struggle against Bolshevism – 'from the standpoint of soldierly camaraderie turn our backs'), characterise his concept for the war against the Soviet Union. For Hitler's speech see Bock *Diary*, 30 March 1941: Halder: *Diary*, II, 30 March 1941, p. 337; Warlimont: *Hauptquartier*, pp. 175–8; for the Commissar Order see Jacobsen: *Kommissarbefehl*, pp. 163–279; Warlimont: *Hauptquartier*, pp. 166–87; for situation in law Betz: *OKW und Landkriegsvölkerrecht*, pp. 107–215.

333. Admiral Jean François D., Secretary of State for Navy, from February 1941 also acting Minister-President and Secretary of State for Foreign Affairs.

334. From Hitler's itinerary (see Hillgruber: *Strategie*, pp. 659–98), Darlan's visit lasted from 1530 to 1930 hrs. The (undated) protocol of the Hitler–Darlan talks runs to ten pages (ADAP XII 2, No. 491), text also in Hillgruber: *Diplomaten* I, pp. 536–49.

335. Baron Jacques B-M., permanent representative of the French ambassador in Berlin, from 25 February 1941 General Secretary, later (June 1941) Secretary of State in the office of the Vice-President of the French Ministerial Council.

336. Meant here is Professor Karl Haushofer, the principal protagonist of geopolitics in Germany. Hess had a close professional relationship with Haushofer and his son Albrecht.

337. After his arrest in Scotland, Hess established immediate contact with the Duke of Hamilton and proposed peace negotiations.

338. Means Karlheinz Pintsch, adjutant of Hess.

339. See Hitler's quoted remarks of 6 August 1938.

340. Günther von K. GOC Fourth Army, 1 September 1939; C-in-C Army Group Centre, December 1941–October 1943. Keilig 211/1686. Fourth Army was based at Warsaw.

341. See 10 May 1941. For Kluge's criticism of the Commissar Order see IMT XVII, p. 338.

342. Meant here are Einsatzkommandos of the security police and SD.

343. See additionally 16 October 1938.

344. Kurt Freiherr von Hammerstein-Equord had resigned as C-in-C of the Army in 1934.

345. Hitler's decision to conquer the economically productive southern regions (Ukraine and Don area, Donetz Basin and the Caucasus) were most clearly established in the study of 22 August 1941. See War Diary OKW I, 1940/1941, p. 1063.

346. This was 12th Infantry Division.

347. Ernst B., GOC Sixteenth Army, Army Group North.

348. Colonel Hans B-B., Chief of Staff, Sixteenth Army.

349. Regarding Hitler's uncertainty about the future – especially time-planned – prosecution of operations see Philippi, Heim: *Feldzug*, pp. 67–75; Reinhardt: *Wende*, p. 35. The Sixteenth Army War Diary contains an entry for 21 August 1941: '13.35 XXXIX.AK (Chief) reports: Colonel Schmundt visited the command centre in the forenoon and was informed as to the condition and readiness of the corps units.'

350. Field Marshal Carl Gustav Freiherr von M., 1867–1951, C-in-C Finnish armed forces; State President, 1944–6.

351. On 24 June 1941 Hitler arrived at his FHQ in Görlitz Forest east of Rastenburg to which he had given the code-name 'Wolfsschanze'. See FHQ War Diary, 24 June 1941.

352. Wilhelm Ritter von L., C-in-C Army Group North.

353. Mauerwald was the code name for the barrack encampment near Anger-burg in East Prussia which housed OKH HQ during the campaign against the Soviet Union. See Warlimont: *Hauptquartier*, p. 188 and Leyen: *Mauerwald*.

354. See 8 August 1941.

355. Since before the war Hitler had taken every opportunity which presented itself to denigrate the C-in-C's regulations for Army officers entitled 'Wahrung der Ehre' – Defending Honour – (No. 2500. 38PA [2]). He had demanded a revision of the antiquated rules and wanted personally to approve the new draft, but Engel confirmed to IfZ on 28 September 1973 that the regulations were never amended.

356. Probably refers to the case discussed in the entry for 19 January 1939. If so it is an indication of Hitler's prodigious memory.

357. Prinz August Wilhelm von Preußen, fourth son of Wilhelm II, is meant here. Per information from Engel (also supplied on 28 September 1973), Hitler used this pet name in recognition of August Wilhelm as one of the Party old guard.

358. With his Führer-Directive of 21 August 1941, Hitler put an end to discussion on the Army proposal for a reformation of the command structure dated 18 August (War Diary OKW I, 1940/1941, pp. 1051–9): 'The Army proposal . . . does not coincide with my intentions. I order the following: . . .' (Directive of 21 August reproduced in full in War Diary OKW I, 1940/1941, p. 1062f). Differences of opinion with his military advisers regarding the question of decisive points motivated Hitler in a 'Study' dated 22 August (War

Diary OKW I, 1940/1941, pp. 1063–8 and Halder: *Diary*, III, 22 August 1941, p. 193) 'to go over once more the fundamentals of this campaign', and sharply criticise the C-in-C while doing so. Regarding the crisis in Army leadership of summer 1941 see Halder: *Diary*, III, 22 August 1941, p. 206; Warlimont: *Hauptquartier*, pp. 196–207; Hillgruber: *Strategie*, pp. 547–9; Reinhardt: *Wende*, pp. 34–8; Philippi, Heim: *Feldzug*, pp. 67–74.

359. Of 21 August 1941. See entry of that date with note.

360. See Halder: *Diary*, III, 22 August 1941, p. 193.

361. Underlined in original. [Presumably refers to NSDAP. ED]

362. Written incorrectly in original as Heidrich. On this date Hitler received a report from H. regarding situation in Protectorate of Bohemia and Moravia.

363. Salonika, the 'Jewish Metropolis', had a Jewish population of 53,000 according to Hilberg, the largest Jewish community in Greece. Hilberg and Reitlinger agree that there were no special measures against the Jews in Greece prior to mid-1942. At Salonika in July that year forced labour was ordered for all Jewish men between the ages of 18 and 48. The deportation of Jews to Auschwitz, Lublin and Treblinka began in the spring of 1943. See additionally Hilberg: *Destruction*, pp. 442–8 and Reitlinger: *Endlösung*, pp. 420–9.

364. Both departments were subordinate to Fromm as Head of Army Armaments.

365. Mannerheim, the former CO of the Finnish Home Corps in the struggle for independence against the Russian revolutionary army (1917), was forced by Stalin to fight against his German former brothers-in-arms in 1944.

366. See entry of 6 August 1941.

367. Ironic nickname given to Hitler's advisers at military situation conferences. It was the title of a popular novel of the time by Werner Beumelburg.

368. Means the C-in-C.

369. Lieutenant-Colonel Heinz von G., Senior ADC to C-in-C.

370. Once Hitler had recognised that his original operational plan could not be kept to schedule (see Reinhardt: *Wende*, p. 35f) he adopted as his own, contrary to his directive of 21 August 1941 ('The essential goal to be achieved before the onset of winter is not the capture of Moscow . . .') the OKH concept, but without moving up sufficient forces to create a decisive thrust, and decided to gamble all on the 'Moscow trump card'. In his Directive No. 35 (of 6 September 1941: in full in Hubatsch: *Weisungen*, pp. 150–5) he ordered the destruction of the enemy forces protecting Moscow 'before the onset of the winter weather'. Regarding the scheduling see: War Diary OKW I, 1940/1941, p. 1056; also Halder: *Diary*, III, 5 September 1941, p. 215; especially also Warlimont: *Hauptquartier*, p. 207 with footnote 90; Hofmann: *Moskau 1941*, p. 144. As to the prosecution of the operation see Reinhardt: *Wende*, pp. 63–96, Halder: *Diary*, III, entries from 2 October 1941; also Warlimont: *Hauptquartier*, p. 207; Hofmann; *Moskau*, pp. 139–83; Philippi, Heim: *Feldzug*, p. 77.

371. According to Engel (communication to IfZ of 1 February 1973) who is talking here of a trough in morale, this sentence meant 'that Hitler made the

suggestion of carrying out feints with limited objectives away from the general direction of the offensive in order to tie down enemy forces and divert them from the real goals.'

372. Three words were deleted here at the request of the author.

373. Refers to the setting up of a new main effort in the Army Group Centre section towards Moscow after the successes in the Ukraine (the encirclement battles of Kiev and Gomel).

374. Field Marshal Fedor von B., from April 1941 until his illness in December that year, GOC Army Group Centre. His successor was the former GOC of Fourth Army, Field Marshal Günther von Kluge. Keilig: 211/3, 211/168. On the replacement of Bock see Reinhardt: *Wende*, p. 223f.

375. Father Josef T., 1939–45 Slovak State President.

376. Means here: the secret reason behind the success of the Catholic Church.

377. Underlined in the original.

378. The tense relationship between Hitler and Brauchitsch, which had been close to breaking point following Hitler's attacks on the C-in-C in the 'Study' of 22 August 1941 (Halder: *Diary*, III, 22 August 1941, p. 193 and War Diary, OKW I, 1940/1941, pp. 1063–8) did not survive the strain of the winter crisis of 1941. After Hitler had approved Brauchitsch's application to resign on 7 December 1941, he assumed command of the Army himself on 19th. See Lossberg: *Wehrmachtführungsstab*, p. 146ff; Halder: *Diary*, III, 19 December 1941, p. 354; on the consequences of Hitler's assuming command of the Army see Müller-Hillebrand III, pp. 37–40.

379. Field Marshal Albert K., Chief, Air Fleet 2 January 1940–Jun 1943.

380. This probably refers to the Austro-Hungarian Empire's method of keeping its Balkan territory under control.

381. Marshal Ion A., 1882–1946. War Minister, 1937–8; Romania's supreme Head of State (Conducatorul), 1940–41. For Hitler's relationship with Romania see Hillgruber: *Hitler, König Carol und Marschall Antonescu*.

382. Helene L. was the concubine of long standing of King Carol II of Romania. See: Easterman: *King Carol, Hitler and Lupescu*.

383. According to the itinerary (see Hillgruber: *Strategie*, p. 697,) Hitler was at FHQ Wolfsschanze from the 29th after attending the funeral of [the air ace ED] Colonel Mölders the day before. The Italian Foreign Minister addressed Hitler twice within a month – on 25 October at Wolfsschanze and on 28 November in Berlin. On both occasions he offered an increase in the number of Italian divisions on the Eastern Front. The shortage of food to which Ciano had referred at Wolfsschanze (Hillgruber: *Diplomaten* I, p. 634f) was supposed not to have been mentioned on the Berlin visit on Mussolini's order (Ciano: *Tagebücher*, 22 November 1941, p. 373). See Ciano, *op cit*, at p. 361ff and 373f, ADAP XIII 2, No. 424, 522; Hillgruber: *Diplomaten* I, pp. 626–38, 675–9.

384. For the reasons for the failure of the German offensive before Moscow see Philippi, Heim: *Feldzug*, pp. 94–106; Reinhardt: *Wende*, pp. 153–71.

385. During this discussion lasting several hours at FHQ on 20 December (see

Guderian: *Erinnerungen*, pp. 240–5 and Halder: *Diary*, III, 20 December 1941, p. 361) held at the initiative of Army Group Centre (see Reinhardt: *Wende*, p. 225, footnote 208), Guderian attempted, despite Hitler's 'stop order' (see War Diary, OKW I, p. 1085f) to obtain his consent to bring back Second Panzer Army and Second Army behind the Oka line. Regarding this, and the events leading to Guderian's departure on 25 December, Reinhardt: *Wende*, pp. 225–8; also Halder: *Diary*, III, 25 December 1941, p. 366.

386. The Oka–Susha defensive line is meant here.

387. Regarding the state of the troops see War Diary, Army Group Centre, 19 December 1941, reproduced in Reinhardt: *Wende*, p. 225.

388. During the Seven Years' War Frederick II held out in a fortified camp at B., a village north of Schweidnitz (Lower Silesia), from the middle of August until the Russian withdrawal on 9 September 1761, without the numerically superior Austro-Russian forces once having attacked it.

389. See 12 November 1941: after the departure of Brauchitsch, OKH Chief of Staff.

390. Hitler spoke at the Berlin Zeughaus on 15 March, Heroes' Remembrance Day.

391. Dr jur. Ernst K., 1903–1946. Secretary of State for Austria, 1938; as successor to Heydrich, (who was assassinated in June 1942), Head of Sicherheitspolizei and SD, from beginning 1943.

392. A section of the report 'Meldungen aus dem Reich' compiled by the Sicherheitspolizei and SD (Amt III, Deutsche Lebensgebiete).

393. Boris III, 1894–1943, King of Bulgaria. According to the itinerary for the king's visit to FHQ on 24 March 1942 (see Annexe to FHQ War Diary No. 6), Engel also formed part of the welcoming committee at Görlitz railway station.

394. Dr Walter D. Head of Army rocket development, 1936; head of Luftwaffe rocket development, 1939; Director of Army Test Institute for Rocketry at Peenemünde, 1943.

395. Wernher Freiherr von B. Head of development team for A4 rocket (later known as V-2) at Peenemünde from 1942.

396. In 1940, Hitler had held back the development of the rocket programme by depriving rockets of financial priority. Under the influence of Speer, and impressed by the team of scientific inventors at Peenemünde, as success at the various fronts began to dwindle in 1943 and he saw in large rockets the possibility of a wonder-weapon, Hitler approved the highest stage of priority for rocket production. Technical problems which continually manifested during the testing of such complicated flight bodies, the switch from single to series production, the problem of diverse completion programmes and not least the constant bottlenecks in supply ensured that operations were not ready to commence before late summer, 1944. For the development of rockets in Germany see Dornberger: *V-2*; Lusar: *Waffen und Geheimwaffen* at pp. 145–56; Klee and Merk, *Peenemünde*; Schneider: *Technik und Waffenentwicklung*, p. 236f; Bornemann: *Geheimprojekt Mittelbau*. pp 28–43; Speer: *Erinnerungen*, pp 375–8.

397. Several secret OKW and OKH reports are extant regarding the treatment in the Wehrmacht of persons of mixed race having 25 per cent and 50 per cent Jewish blood. According to these, half-Jews could only serve in Ersatzreserve II or Landwehr II, but quarter-Jews remained in the Wehrmacht and were also '*exceptionally during the war*' eligible for promotion. Similarly, it was possible for half-Jewish former officers, NCOs and officials to serve during wartime. These regulations also applied to all persons married to half- or quarter-Jews. (See OKW – 121 10-20 J [Ic] – No. 524/40 issued on 8 April 1940, IfZ Fd 44, sheet 18). All applications for exceptions – therefore the question of whether a half-Jewish person could remain in the Wehrmacht, where this was not covered by an earlier Führer-decision (OKW-WZ [II/J – No. 651/39 of 13 March 1939] Fd 44, sheet 18) – the promotion or employment or re-employment of quarter-Jews – required Hitler's personal approval (see OKH-No. 6840/41g PA2 [Ic] of 16 July 1941, Fd 44, sheet 19f.) Presumably in this decision the full-face and side profile photographs of the applicant played the decisive role. Had Hitler no objection based on the photographic criteria, the applicant would receive his 'document of approval'. By OKW decree of 25 September 1942, pursuant to 'the Führer's decision', there occurred a significant hardening in the treatment of half-Jewish members of the Wehrmacht. Applications for exception were abolished and those in the pipeline were returned to sender. Half-Jewish Wehrmacht members not in possession of a document evidencing Hitler's approval were discharged from the Wehrmacht forthwith. See: *Allg. Heeresmitteilungen*, 9 (1942), p. 501 and *Sammlung wehrrechtlicher Gutachten*, Vol. 4, p 72f.

398. This term is not found in the official texts of the regulations for the treatment of persons of part-Jewish blood in the Wehrmacht.

399. Presumably a member of the Personnel Group, Wehrmacht Central Department.

400. See note 397 above.

401. As is evident from the annexes to Second Army War Diary (29585/38, 22919/1), Col-Gen. Freiherr von Weichs was commanding officer Second Army (Army Group *Weichs*) until 14 July when General of Infantry Hans von Salmuth took over. On 9 July the army group received a query from Hitler as to whether it was possible to hold the bridgehead at Voronezh. Weichs's considered reply was: 'Bridge-head can not only be held, but absolutely must be.' (AOK 2/29585/33 and 22919/1). Regarding the situation at Voronezh also see Zwischenmeldung (Interim Report) for 19 October. and Tagesmeldung (Daily Report) at midnight of the Army Group *Weichs* Chief of Staff, Harteneck, of 9 July 1942 (War Diary AOK 2/ 29585/33) and Halder: *Diary*, III, 6 and 8 July 1942 at pp. 474, 477. Presumably the diary entry about the situation at Voronezh was written up some time later.

402. General of Armoured Troops Friedrich P. C-in-C Sixth Army, January 1942–January 1943.

403. Colonel-General Maximilian Freiherr von W., C-in-C Army Group B, July 1942–July 1943.

404. Colonel August Winter.

405. Formed from the SS Division (mot) *Germania*, later 5th SS Panzer Division *Wiking*.

406. Field Marshal Wilhelm L., C-in-C Army Group A, July–September 1942.

407. Colonel-General Ewald von K., C-in-C First Panzer Army, October 1941–November 1942.

408. Major-General Ernst Felix F., Chief of General Staff, First Panzer Army, April 1942–March 1943.

409. Probably means Wehrwolf, which in relevant period in 1942 was FHQ at Vinnitza, Ukraine, 16 July–1 October. FHQ Wolfsschlucht 1 in Belgium was used only in 1940. ED

410. For the situation of Army Group A see Philippi, Heim: *Feldzug*, pp. 147–55 and the pertinent entries between 21 August and 7 September in OKW War Diary II 1. 1942.

411. There occur here two interpolations dated 27 August 1942 at 1400 hrs and 2200 hrs referring to events which must have occurred after Jodl's visit to Army Group A – therefore at the earliest on 7 September (see note 417 below). The first interpolation is almost identical to the entry of 7 September 1942 and is discarded in this translation, the second is inserted following the diary entry of 7 September 1942. ED

412. The Hitler–List conversation took place on 31 August. For the content and atmosphere of the talk see Halder: *Diary*, III, 31 August 1942 with 'notes', p. 513f. and OKW War Diary II 1, 1942 p. 662.

413. See remark regarding Wolfsschlucht at 409 above.

414. According to the War Diary of Army Group A (31 August 1942) there '[took place] first of all [a] private conversation' to which were then joined the Reichsmarschall, Halder, Jodl and Jeschonnek. See excerpt reproduced in OKW War Diary II 1, 1942, p. 662.

415. Major-General Adolf H., Chief of Operations, Army General Staff, October 1940–October 1944.

416. Regarding the constantly deteriorating relationship between Hitler and Halder see Halder: *Diary*, III, 23 July, p. 489: 3 August, p. 496: 24 August, p. 510 and 11 September, p. 520, but especially 30 August, p. 513.

417. An almost identical entry was made with erroneous date for 27 August 1942 at 1400 hrs. The only significant difference between the two versions was that Hitler put blame on the Army C-in-C [*sic*] and not OKH in earlier note. On 5 September, GOC Army Group A invited Jodl to a conference at the Stalino field HQ to discuss the future deployment of XXXXIX Mountain Corps. This took place on 7 September on Hitler's order. It concluded that the planned offensive by 4th Mountain Division on Gudauti, a town north of Suchum on the Black Sea coast, would not proceed due to the difficult terrain (see diary entry 15 August 1942) and agreed to suggest to Hitler instead that, using the security of the mountain passes, the division be diverted to the Maikop area, from where it could be deployed against Tuapse. Regarding the situation in the Caucasus,

especially that of 4th Mountain Division, see Buchner: *Krisentage im Hoch-gebirge*, pp. 505–11, also Konrad, Rümler: *Kampf um den Kaukasus*. Jodl advocated the intended alternative plan to Hitler, who was in no doubt that it was completely opposed to his own understanding. See additionally OKW War Diary II 1, pp. 690ff, 695ff. As Warlimont elucidated in the explanation to Greiner's notes (OKW War Diary II 1, 1942 p. 697), the violent oral assault on Jodl was due much less to his support for an alternative strategy in the Caucasus than to his attempts to rebut Hitler's accusation that Field Marshal List had not followed his orders. Whilst doing so, Jodl had insinuated that Hitler himself bore responsibility for the allegedly erroneous measures ordered. As to the far-reaching consequences of this incident see OKW War Diary *op. cit.*, and also p. 12f.

418. See entries for 15 and 16 August 1942. Presumably the map material mentioned on 15 August is meant here.

419. Colonel-General Hans v. Seeckt, Head of Army Command, Reichswehr, 1920–6.

420. Apparently Schmundt later repaired the breach between Hitler and Jodl. See especially Warlimont's remarks at (3a) of his 'Erläuterungen', OKW War Diary II 1, 1942, p. 697.

421. No further details of the 'humiliating circumstances' have emerged. Tensions existed between Hitler and Halder since the Führer's decision to order a major attack in the southern sector had been made in July (see 4 September 1942, note 394). Hitler terminated the problem by dismissing his Chief of the General Staff on 24 September. Following the morning situation conference Hitler took his leave of Halder with the explanation that they had to part company because Halder was close to nervous exhaustion and his own nerves were no longer what they were. It was necessary for there to be inculcated into the General Staff a fanatical belief in the 'idea'. He was resolved to saturate even the Army with his Will. See Halder: *Diary*, III, 24 September 1942, p. 528; Bor: *Gespräche*, p. 226.

422. General of Infantry Kurt Z. Chief of Staff to C-in-C West, March 1942–September 1942; Chief of Army General Staff as Halder's successor, September 1942–July 1944. On Zeitzler's opportunity to use the relationship between Hitler and Jodl for the purpose of strengthening the position of the Chief of the Army General Staff and to put an end to the 'twin-tracked command structure in the east' see OKW War Diary II 1, 1942 p. 13: regarding the significance of Halder's dismissal for the Army leadership see Müller-Hillebrand: *Heer* III, p. 90f.

423. The War Academy was transferred initially from Berlin to Bad Salzbrunn, and then – presumably in the autumn of 1943 – to Hirschberg.

424. On 24 August 1942 XIV Panzer Corps reached the Volga at Rynok (north of Stalingrad). See OKW War Diary II 1, 1942, pp. 633, 635, also Paulus: *Befehl*, Sketch 5, p. 161.

425. Russian attacks above and beyond everyday occurrences experienced by the mentioned army groups cannot be identified in the OKH October situation

reports (see OKW War Diary II 2. 1942): on the other hand see OKW War Diary II 2, pp. 793 and 864f, also Philippi, Heim: *Feldzug*, p. 169.

426. After several days' fighting, the remaining areas of the 'Red October' metal plant fell to German forces on 28 October.

427. The successful British commando raid on the Glomfjord water plant in Norway (see Zaddach: *Kommandotruppen*, p. 75) which – as with a series of similar raids – had unpleasant consequences, was the motive for Hitler's 'Commando Order' of 18 October 1942 (see OKW War Diary II 2, 1942, p. 852). It provided that 'all enemy (squads) in action or fleeing from so-called commando operations [operations beyond the immediate theatre of fighting] are to be destroyed to the last man . . . bomb-, sabotage- or terrorist squads [landed from submarines or by parachute] . . . are under all circumstances to be utterly exterminated.' See Hubatsch: *Weisungen*, pp. 206–9; for Jodl's attitude to the Commando Order and its enforcement IMT IX, p. 240, as to amendments to the order IMT XXVI, 532-PS and 551-PS. The attitude of Canaris, who was concerned at the possibility of reprisals against Regiment 'Brandenburg' attached to the Abwehr (see note 428 below) is mentioned in Lahousen, ZS 658, IfZ Archive, sheets 13–16. Regarding the Commando Order under international law see: Betz: *Landkriegsvölkerrecht im Zweiten Weltkrieg*, pp. 216–52.

428. Lehrregiment Brandenburg zbV 800 (from end 1942/beginning 1943: Division Brandenburg) was attached to Abteilung II (Sabotage and Demoralisation; leader, Colonel Erwin Lahousen) at Amt Ausland/Abwehr (Foreign/Counter-Intelligence Office) and had commando operations as its main purpose. See: Brockdorff: *Geheimkommandos*; Kriegsheim: *'Brandenburger'*.

429. Presumably this meant the material presented by Zeitzler at the situation conference of 25 October resulting from his visit to Seventeenth Army at the front, see OKW War Diary II 2, 1942, p. 849 and 857.

430. Lieutenant-Colonel (later Major-General and Chief of Luftwaffe Command Staff) Eckhardt Ch., 1st General Staff officer to the Chief of the Luftwaffe Command Staff.

431. See 18 November 1939, note 210.

432. Italian Eighth Army HQ, where General Italo Gariboldi was C-in-C (June 1942–February 1943).

433. Major von G., former assistant to the German military attaché in Rome, General von Rintelen. See Halder: *Diary*, III, p. 437.

434. General Giovanni M. Cmmdg. Gen. Italian Expeditionary Corps, July 1941– November 1942; attached to Italian Eighth Army after its arrival on the Eastern Front (summer 1942) when renamed XXXV Army Corps. See Messe: *La Guerra al Fronte Russo*, p. 20ff., 180, 241.

435. To be understood here as the alternative to the 'mixed fronts' wanted by Tippelskirch.

436. According to the diaries of FHQ-architect Leo Müller (see Seidler & Zeigert, *Hitler's Secret Headquarters*), Engel attended a conference with Müller and other Organisation Todt architects on 25 October 1942 to discuss the new FHQ, W2, near Soissons in France, and arrived at Saint-Rimay next day to inspect the

railway tunnel in which FHQ W3 was to be set up. On 27 October Engel flew to Berlin with the Organisation Todt group. His visit to Voronezh in Russia must have taken place later than the date of the diary entry. ED

437. The Hungarian Second Army was south of the German Second Army. Regarding the participation of the Hungarian allies in the 1942 offensive see Hillgruber: *Einbau der verbündeten Armeen*, pp. 670–4.

438. The OKH situation report (OKW War Diary II 2, 1942, p. 842) of 18 October reported heavy enemy artillery fire in the southern sector of the Voronezh bridgehead.

439. Fritz S., 1894–1946, executed as war criminal. Reich Governor of Thuringia, 1933: Reich Defence Commissar for Wehrkreis X (Kassel), September 1939; General Plenipotentiary for Forced Labour, March 1942.

440. Carl-Heinrich von St. Military Governor, France, February 1942–21 July 1944. Executed in connection with assassination attempt of 20 July 1944.

441. In contrast see Greiner's notes on the situation reports of 2 and 7 October, OKW War Diary II 2, 1942, pp. 864, 868.

442. Means the Allied landings in Morocco and Algeria on 7–8 November 1942.

443. For use in attacking the infrastructure set up by the Allies in support of their operations in the Mediterranean.

444. Published verbatim in the 9 November 1942 edition of the *Völkischer Beobachter* (Munich edition): slightly abridged version in Domarus: *Hitler* II 4, pp. 1933–44.

445. Since no exact historical representation of the battle can be presented at the time of writing, observations regarding the events at Stalingrad have been limited to corrected and confirmed amendments to Engels' notes for the period 14–26 November 1942. These rely – for the most part from oral enquiries – on a critical assessment of Engel's notes for the period for which Lieutenant-Colonel Dr M. Kehrig was engaged at IfZ invitation: the publisher is greatly indebted to him. On the basis of sources not previously subjected to analysis and personal interviews, Dr Kehrig, an assistant at the Militärgeschichtlichen Forschungs-amtes at Freiburg/Breisgau, has produced a comprehensive work: *Stalingrad, Analyse und Dokumentation einer Schlacht*, Stuttgart 1974.

446. The entry in the Sixth Army HQ War Diary for 17 October 1942 reads: 'During the morning the adjutant to the Führer, Major Engel, visited the army in order to gather personal impressions of the Battle for Stalingrad. He accompanied the Chief of the Army General Staff to the forward command post at Gumrak where he was given an opportunity to observe the fighting from a forward battle position in the presence of the Chief of the Army General Staff and the Commander-in-Chief. He left on the morning of 18 October. He was supplied with a sketch map of the attack plan at Stalingrad, a schedule of the successes and losses in the battle for the city and the proposal for the intended winter division of forces.'

The schedule listing the gains and losses of Sixth Army for the time in question appears in an annexe to the War Diary, but the two sketches are absent. In neither the Sixth Army War Diary for the period to 19 November 1942 nor its annexes does there appear any mention of an additional visit by Major Engel to Sixth Army at Globinskaya in November. Kehrig considers improbable the reported optimistic frame of mind attributed to Paulus and discusses the point at length in his cited publication.

447. Lieutenant-General Ferdinand H. GOC XXXXVIII Panzer Corps, 1 November 1942. This unit was stationed from 9 November 1942 to the rear of Third Romanian Army as Army Group B reserve. From the Panzer corps war diary and files it is unequivocally clear that it was only to be deployed with permission of Army Group B. There is no mention anywhere of an earlier release from Hitler personally or the OKH, and according to Colonel Winter this was never the topic of a discussion. Entries in the Panzer corps war diary show that a situation developed such that 22nd and 14th German Panzer Divisions, and 1st Romanian Armoured Division were all alerted about 0900 on 19 November 1942 by the GOC, Lieutenant-General Heim, and prepared for a movement to the north-east. A little later Heim was present at a conference between Colonel-General von Weichs and the GOC Third Romanian Army at which the army group released XXXXVIII Panzer Corps for a counter-attack to the north-east. At about 0930, however, the German liaison staff commander notified Third Romanian Army that the thrust to the north-east had been called off, and that army group had issued a new order which would arrive shortly. From this it was apparent that the push to the north-east was not to be made with the entire Panzer corps, but that the corps was to concentrate for the counter-attack towards Bolshoi, which was north-west. Colonel Winter has confirmed that the change of direction was ordered on Zeitzler's intervention. What factors were decisive for Zeitzler in ordering this change of direction are not clear, but that it was based on a talk with Second Army positioned 400 kilometres away seems highly improbable. The Chief of the Second Army General Staff, General Harteneck, has stated that he does not recall any discussion with Zeitzler at that juncture and rejects utterly the possibility that there was one. According to Doerr (*Feldzug*, p. 64) XXXXVIII Panzer Corps (Romanian 1st Armoured Division, 22nd Panzer Division) had run frontally into the attacking Russian Fifth Tank Army, was thick in the melee on on 20 November and was fighting off attacks from all sides.

That night Army Group B ordered the Panzer corps to disengage, but not until 26 November did the corps finally manage to extricate itself and withdraw behind the Tshirr defensive line.

448. As Doerr (*Feldzug*, p. 64) mentions, radio signals from FHQ ordered the Panzer corps to attack to the north, then to the north-east, then to set up an all-round defence. None of these orders could be carried out because the corps was still grappling with the enemy.

449. On 20 November 1942 Soviet forces to the south of Stalingrad joined the offensive against Fourth Panzer Army, which at the time was composed of IV German Army Corps with two German and one Romanian infantry divisions, and of VI and VII Romanian Army Corps. The latter had two good cavalry divisions. Engel's diary entry of 21 November 1942 portrays in abridged form the events involving Fourth Panzer Army on 20 November 1942. The other

observations he makes cannot be confirmed from existing documentation. See Kehrig, *op. cit.*

450. It cannot be ruled out that on 24 November Hitler criticised the lieutenant-general's command of the corps and condemned Heim himself as completely unsuitable; however, Heim was not relieved of command until 29 November 1942.

451. Col-Gen. Erich Hoeppner was sacked from command of Fourth Panzer Army in January 1942 for withdrawing against Hitler's orders so as to prevent his army from being encircled.

452. This observation arose from the midday situation conference of 24 November 1942 and on the whole is correctly reported. On that day Colonel-General Hoth was given the task of assembling an armoured group in the Kotelnikov area, to head north-east towards Sixth Army and so re-establish contact with it. Neither in this order, nor in any other addressed to Hoth, is there mention of Hoth mopping-up the situation in the Don Bend.

453. This note cannot be confirmed from the archive material. Regarding the air supply to Stalingrad see: J. Fischer; *Zahlenangaben bei Görlitz: Stalingrad,* pp. 274–7.

454. M. assumed command of the newly formed Army Group Don on 27 November. Previously (on 24 November) he had been instructed on the situation by von Weichs at Army Group B HQ at Stavobelsk. Whereas Weichs was of the opinion at the latest at 1700 hrs on 23 November 1942 that the situation could only be saved by a full operational decision to withdraw Sixth Army from Stalingrad, in an assessment of the situation sent to OKH on 24 November 1942, Manstein stated that Sixth Army could remain in Stalingrad provided an adequate supply of fuel and ammunition was guaranteed. This was therefore in direct contradiction of the situation assessment of Weichs. Manstein's opinion of 24 November 1942 was apparently – to go by Engel's entry – discussed at FHQ in the morning or noon situation conference of 26 November, but none of the points coincides with the notes for that day. If Zeitzler actually did request on 26 November that Sixth Army be permitted to extricate itself from Stalingrad this is not clearly confirmed by the archive material.

455. It is substantiated that on this day, probably after the evening situation conference, Lieutenant-Colonel Christian, Wehrmacht Command Staff, elaborated in the presence of Jodl his grave doubts about Göring's assertions regarding the supply of Stalingrad from the air. Who supplied Christian with the statistics, and who possibly urged him to speak out, remain a mystery.

456. As regards the following entries reflecting the plight of Sixth Army see Manstein: *Siege*, chapter 12.

457. Colonel Theodor B., on 27 November 1942 No. 1 Staff Officer, General Staff, Army Group Don.

458. A factory which manufactured armatures, machinery and metalware: during the war turned over to armaments production.

459. This presumably means the ghettos at Warsaw, Cracow, Chenstochau, Radom and Lublin.

460. See 5 May 1942

461. LI Corps was an Army Corps, not Panzer: (see OKW War Diary II 2, 1942, pp. 1386, 1393.)

462. See OKW War Diary II 2, 1942, p. 1200.

463. See OKW War Diary II 2, 1942, p. 1200f; Philippi, Heim: *Feldzug*, p. 202.

464. The Hungarian Second Army on the north flank of Army Group B is meant here. See OKW War Diary III 1, 1943, pp. 44, 47, 51, 54, 56, 58.

465. See additionally Philippi, Heim: *Feldzug*, p. 203.

466. According to Engel, Major Coelestin von Zitzewitz, OKH Liaison Officer to Sixth Army, who had been flown out of the encirclement at Stalingrad on 20 January, handed this report to Hitler at a situation conference. Von Zitzewitz himself does not mention presenting a report in his unpublished memoir ('Am Wendepunkt des 2. Weltkrieges – Als Verbindungsoffizier beim AOK 6 in Stalingrad vom 25 November 1942 bis 20 January 1943'). Latter reported by Lt-Col Kehrig on 21 May 1974. For situation report by Z. see Paulus: *Befehl*, p. 92.

467. See additionally Manstein's report (*Siege*, pp. 437–44) about the four-hour conversation with Hitler on 6 February 1943.

468. [According to Domarus: *Hitler – Reden und Proklamationen, 1932–45*, Wiesbaden, 1973, Vol. IV at p. 1989, Hitler arrived by air at Zaporoshye at 0600 on 17 February 1943. On that day, Russian forces broke through at Ssilsinikov railway station, and Hitler could hear their artillery and machine-gun fire. ED] Regarding Hitler's visit to HQ Army Group Don/South, also see Manstein: *Siege*, pp. 454–9.

469. Underlined in original.

470. All major sources have Hitler at FHQ Wehrwolf (Vinnitza, Ukraine) from 19 February until 13 March 1943. ED

471. Engel left the *Adjutantur* at the end of March 1943 in the rank of lieutenant-colonel. After several command courses he took over 27th Infantry Regiment, his former Rostock regiment, and was given command of 12th Infantry Regiment at the end of June 1944. At the cessation of hostilities, Lieutenant-General Engel was an Oak-Leaves holder and commanding the 'Ulrich von Hutten' Division. [According to the diaries of Dipl. Architect and OT-Oberbauleiter Leo Müller, acting head of FHQ construction, on 20 March 1943 Engel and FHQ-Commandant Streve attended a conference with Organisation Todt in Berlin to discuss two new FHQs under construction in France, W2 near Rheims and W3 in a railway tunnel near St-Rimay. On 4 April 1943 Engel took part in further discussions with OT at Obersalzberg. Engel makes no reference anywhere to his duties with respect to FHQ, but appears to have been retained on the staff of the *Adjutantur* for a period of at least four days beyond the official date of termination. See: Seidler & Zeigert: *Hitler's Secret Headquarters*. ED]

Appendix 1
Armed Forces High Command (OKW), 1941–42

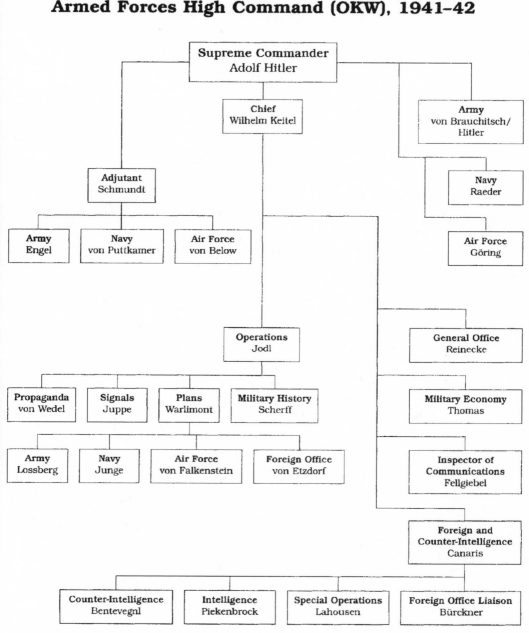

Appendix 2
Army High Command (OKH), 1941–42

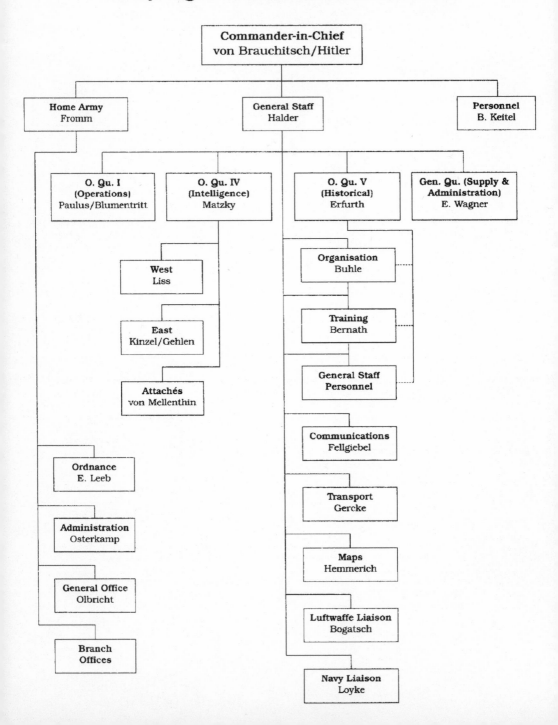

Commander-in-Chief
von Brauchitsch/Hitler

Home Army
Fromm

General Staff
Halder

Personnel
B. Keitel

O. Qu. I
(Operations)
Paulus/Blumentritt

O. Qu. IV
(Intelligence)
Matzky

O. Qu. V
(Historical)
Erfurth

Gen. Qu. (Supply &
Administration)
E. Wagner

West
Liss

Organisation
Buhle

East
Kinzel/Gehlen

Training
Bernath

Attachés
von Mellenthin

General Staff
Personnel

Communications
Fellgiebel

Ordnance
E. Leeb

Transport
Gercke

Administration
Osterkamp

Maps
Hemmerich

General Office
Olbricht

Luftwaffe Liaison
Bogatsch

Branch
Offices

Navy Liaison
Loyke

Bibliography

1. Unpublished Documents

Bundesarchiv, Koblenz
Akten der Wehrmachtadjutantur beim Führer. NS 10/6
Persönlicher Stab RFSS/Feldkommandostelle. NS 19/neu 1558 =
 T 175 Rolle 126; auch IfZ/MA-328
Persönlicher Stab RFSS/Schriftgutverwaltung. NS 19/999; NS 19 HR/5 = T
 175 Rolle 90; auch IfZ/MA-312

Bundesarchiv/Militärarchiv, Freiburg im Breisgau
Kriegstagebücher der Führerhauptquartiers. KTB Nr. 1–6. RH 47/
 v. 4–9
Kriegstagebüch Nr. 8 der 1. Pz.Armee vom 1. 4.–31. 7. 42 und
 vom 1. 8.–31. 10. 42. 24906/1a und 24906/1b
Kriegstagebüch AOK 6/Führungsabteilung. 1. Band der Zweitschrift vom 6.
 Oktober 1942–11 November 1942 mit Anlageband. 30155-33 und 30155-11
Das Fernschreiben Mansteins vom 24. November 1942 befindet sich in der
 Akte RH 19 VI/30 (früher Heeresgruppe Don 39694/3a)

Bundesarchiv/Zentralnachweisstelle, Kornelimünster
Sammlung Wehrrechlicher Gutachten und Vorschriften, Heft 4, bearbeitet von
 Rudolf Absolon 1966 (als Manuskript gedruckt)

Institut für Zeitgeschichte, München
Adam, Wilhelm. ZS 6
Aktenstücke zur Geschichte der Wehrmacht 1938–1945. Fd 44
Nachlaß Beck. F 40
Bock, Fedor von: Tagebuech 1939–1940. F 91
Daten aus alten Notizbüchern 30. 1. 34–30. 6. 43 (sog. Itinerar Hitlers), MA3/$_1$
 (Hitler's Daily Acitivities, Library of Congress)
Doerr, Hans. ZS 28
Förster, Otto. ZS 1133
Persönliche Dokumente. Fritsch. F 10
Hitler: "Denkschrift zur Frage unserer Festungsanlagen" [vom 1. Juli 1938]
 1801-PS, 1802-PS
Aufzeichnungen General d. Inf. a. D. Curt Liebmann 1922–1959. ED 1
Rundstedt, Gerd von. ZS 129
Siewert, Curt. ZS 148

Ferner folgende Dokumente aus den Nürnberger Serien

EC-366(1) Bericht Oberstlt. Köchling über die Tätigkeit als Verbindungsoffizier des OKW zum sudetendeutschen Freikorps.

EC 366(2) Auszug aus den Tagebuchnotizen der 2. Abt. Gen.Stb. d. H. über Entstehung und Tätigkeit des Sudetendeutschen Freikorps.

NOKW- 141 Personalbogen von Offizieren.

3037-PS Erklärung von Fritz Wiedemann über die Führerbesprechung vom 20. Mai 1938.

3798-PS Gemeinsame Erklärung von Brauchitsch, Manstein, Halder, Warlimont, und Westphal über die deutsche Wehrmacht.

4005-PS Rede von GL Rainer am 11. 3. 42 über "Der Nationalsozialismus in Österreich von 1934 bis 1938".

2. Published Documents, Articles and Books

Adonyi-Naredy, Franz v.: *Ungarns Armee im Zweiten Weltkrieg*, Neckargemünd 1971

Akten zur deutschen Auswärtigen Politik 1918–1945. Aus dem Archiv des Auswärtigen Amts. (ADAP)
  Serie D (1937–45), Bd. 1–12, Baden-Baden 1950–6, Frankfurt am Main 1961–4, Göttingen 1969–70; Serie C (1933–7), Bd. 2, Göttingen 1973

Baumgart, Winfried: 'Zur Ansprache Hitlers vor den Führern der Wehrmacht am 22. August 1939. Eine quellenkritische Untersuchung'. In: *VfZ 16* (1968), pp. 120–49

Beloff, Max: *The Foreign Policy of Soviet Russia 1929–1941*, London 1949

Besson, Waldemar: 'Zur Geschichte des nationalsozialistischen Führungsoffiziers'. In: *VfZ 9* (1961), pp. 76–115

Bethge, Eberhard: *Dietrich Bonhoeffer*, München 1967

Betz, Hermann Dieter: 'Das OKW und seine Haltung zum Landkriegsvölkerrecht im Zweiten Weltkrieg', jur. Diss. Würzburg 1970

Bidlingmaier, Gerhard: 'Erfolg und Ende des Schlachtschiffes "Bismarck"'. In: *Wehr-wiss. Rundschau* 9 (1959), pp. 261–81

Boberach, Heinz (Hrsg.): *Meldungen aus dem Reich*, Neuwied und Berlin 1965

Bor, Peter: *Gespräche mit Halder*, Wiesbaden 1950

Brenner, Hildegard: *Die Kunstpolitik des Nationalsozialismus*, Hamburg 1963

Brockdorff, Werner: *Geheimkommandos des Zweiten Weltkrieges*, München-Wels 1967

Broszat, Martin: *Nationalsozialistische Polenpolitik 1939–1945*, Stuttgart 1961. Schriftenreihe der Vierteljahrshefte für Zeitgeschichte, Nr. 2

Buchheim, Hans: 'Das Euthanasieprogramm'. In: *Gutachten des Instituts für Zeitgeschichte*, Bd. I, München 1958, pp. 60f.

Buchheim, Hans: 'Zigeunerdeportation'. In: *Gutachten des Instituts für Zeitgeschichte*, Bd. I, München 1958, pp. 51–60

Buchner, Alex: 'Krisentage im Hochgebirge'. In: *Wehrkunde* 9 (1960), pp. 505-11

Buck, Gerhard: 'Das Führerhauptquartier'. In: *Jahresbibliographie der Bibliothek für Zeitgeschichte*, Stuttgart 38 (1966), pp. 549-66

Bullock, Alan: Hitler. *Eine Studie über Tyrannei*, Düsseldorf 1953

Ciano, Conte Galeazzo: *Tagebücher 1939-1943*, Bern 1947

Dahlerus, Birger: *Der letzte Versuch*, München 1948, 1973

Dallin, Alexander: *Deutsche Herrschaft in Rußland*, Düsseldorf 1958

Demeter, Karl: *Das deutsche Offizierkorps in Gesellschaft und Staat 1650-1945*, Frankfurt am Main 1962

Detwiler, Donald: *Hitler, Franco und Gibraltar*, Wiesbaden 1962

Deuerlein, E. (Hrsg.): *Quellen zur Konferenz der "Grollen Drei"*, München 1963

Das nationalsozialistische Deutschland und die Sowjetunion 1939-1941. Akten aus dem Archiv des Deutschen Auswärtigen Amtes. Deutsche Ausgabe von Eber Malcolm Carrol und Fritz Epstein, Berlin 1948

Dörner, Klaus: 'Nationalsozialismus und Lebensvernichtung'. In: *VfZ 15* (1967), pp. 121-52

Doerr, Hans: *Der Feldzug nach Stalingrad. Versuch eines operativen Überblickes*, Darmstadt 1955

Domarus, Max: *Hitler. Reden und Proklamationen 1932-1945*. 2 Bde., München 1965

Dornberger, *Walter: V 2 - Der Schuß ins Weltall. Geschichte emer großen Erfindung*, Eßlingen 1952

Eichstadt, Ulrich: *Von Dollfuß zu Hitler. Geschichte des Anschlusses Österreichs 1933-1938*, Wiesbaden 1955

Erfurth, Waldemar: *Die Geschichte des deutschen Generalstabes von 1918-1945*, Göttingen, Berlin, Frankfurt 1957

Fischer, Johannes: 'Über den Entschluß zur Luftversorgung Stalingrads. Ein Beitrag zur militarischen Führung im Dritten Reich'. In: *Militärgeschichtliche Mitteilungen* 2 (1969), pp. 7-68

Förster, Jürgen: 'Die Auswirkungen der Schlacht von Stalingrad 1942/43 auf die europäischen Verbündeten Deutschlands und die Türkei', phil. Diss. Köln 1974

Förster, Wilhelm: *Das Befestigungswesen*, Neckargemünd 1960

Foerster, Wolfgang: *Generaloberst Ludwig Beck. Sein Kampf gegen den Krieg*, München 1953

Foreign Relations of the United States (FRUS). Diplomatic Papers: The Conference of Berlin (The Potsdam Conference), Vol. I, Washington 1960

Ganther, Heinz (Hrsg.): *Die Juden in Deutschland. Ein Almanach*, Hamburg n.d.

Die Geschichte des Panzerkorps Großdeutschland. Gesammelt und zusammengestellt von Helmuth Spaeter, Bd. 1, Duisburg 1958

Gisevius, Hans-Bernd: *Bis zum bitteren Ende*, Hamburg n.d.

Görlitz, Walter: *Der deutsche Generalstab. Geschichte und Gestalt. 1657–1945*,
Frankfurt am Main n.d.

Görlitz, Walter: 'Die Schlacht um Stalingrad 1942–1943'. In: *Entscheidungsschlachten des Zweiten Weltkrieges.* Hrsg. von Hans-Adolf Jacobsen und
Jürgen Rohwer, Frankfurt am Main 1960

Greiner, Helmuth: *Die oberste Wehrmachtführung 1939–1943*, Wiesbaden 1951

Grenfell, Russel: *Jagd auf die Bismarck*, Tübingen 1953

Grobba, Fritz: *Männer und Mächte im Orient*, Göttingen 1967

Groscurth, Helmuth: *Aus den Tagebüchern eines Abwehroffiziers 1938–1940.*
Hrsg. von Helmut Krausnick und Harold C. Deutsch, Stuttgart 1970

Gruchmann, Lothar: *Der Zweite Weltkrieg*, München 1967

Guderian, Heinz: *Erinnerungen eines Soldaten*, Heidelberg 1950

Handbuch des Auswärtigen Dienstes. Auf Veranlassung des Auswärtigen Amts
bearbeitet von Dr. Erich Kraske, Halle an der Saale 1939

Das deutsche Heer 1939, hrsg. von H.-H. Podzun, Bad Nauheim 1953

Heeres-Verordnungblatt
  Jg. 15 (1933), Jg. 17 (1935), Jg. 18 (1936), Jg. 20 (1938) Teil C

Heiber, Helmut: *Joseph Goebbels*, Berlin 1962

Heiber, Helmut (Hrsg.): *Hitlers Lagebesprechungen. Die Protokollfragmente
seiner militärischen Konferenzen*, Stuttgart 1962

Heiber, Helmut: 'Der Fall Grünspan'. In: *VfZ* 5 (1957), pp. 133–72

Helmert, Heinz und Helmut Otto: 'Zur Koalitionskriegführung Hitler-
Deutschlands im zweiten Weltkrieg am Beispiel des Einsatzes der
ungarischen 2. Armee'. In: *Zeitschrift für Militärgeschichte* 2 (1963),
pp. 320–39

Henkys, Reinhard: *Die nationalsozialistischen Gewaltverbrechen*, Berlin 1964

Hilberg, Raul: *The Destruction of the European Jews*, Chicago 1961

Hillgruber, Andreas: 'Das deutsch-ungarische Verhältnis im letzten Kriegsjahr'.
In: *Wehrwissenschaftl. Rundschau* 10 (1960), pp. 78–104

Hillgruber, Andreas (Hrsg.): *Staatsmänner und Diplomaten bei Hitler*, Frankfurt
am Main 1967

Hillgruber, Andreas (Hrsg.): *Staatsmänner und Diplomaten bei Hitler.* Zweiter
Teil, Frankfurt am Main 1970

Hillgruber, Andreas: 'Der Einbau der verbündeten Armeen in die deutsche
Ostfront 1941–1944'. In: *Wehrwiss. Rundschau* 10 (1960), pp. 659–82

Hillgruber, Andreas: *Hitlers Strategie. Politik und Kriegführung 1940–1941*,
Frankfurt am Main 1965

Hoffmann, Peter: *Widerstand, Staatsstreich, Attentat*, Müuchen 1969, 1970

Hofmann, Hanns Hubert: *Der Hitlerputsch. Krisenjahre deutscher Geschichte
1920–1924*, München 1961

Hofmann, Rudolf: 'Die Schlacht von Moskau 1941'. In: *Entscheidungs-schlachten des Zweiten Weltkrieges*. Hrsg. von Hans-Adolf Jacobsen und Jürgen Rohwer, Frankfurt am Main 1960

Hoßbach, Friedrich: *Zwischen Wehrmacht und Hitler, 1934–1938*, Wolfenbüttel und Hannover 1949, 1965

Hubatsch, Walter: *Hitlers Weisungen für die Kriegführung 1939–1945*, Frankfurt am Main 1962

Huck, *see* Neufeldt, Huck, Tessin

Illustrierter Beobachter 1940

Ilsemann, Sigurd von: *Der Kaiser in Holland. Aufzeichnungen des letzten Flügeladjutanten Kaiser Wilhelms II.* Hrsg. von Harald von Königswald. Bd. 2. *Monarchie und Nationalsozialismus 1924–1941*. München 1968

Jacobsen, Hans-Adolf: *Dünkirchen*, Neckargemünd 1958

Jacobsen, Hans-Adolf: 'Dünkirchen 1940'. In: *Entscheidungsschlachten des Zweiten Weltkrieges*. Hrsg. von Hans-Adolf Jacobsen und Jürgen Rohwer, Frankfurt am Main 1960

Jacobsen, Hans-Adolf: *1939–1945. Der Zweite Weltkrieg in Chronik und Dokumentation*, Wiesbaden 1961

Jacobsen, Hans-Adolf: *Zur Vorgeschichte des Westfeldzugs*, Göttingen 1956

Jacobsen, Hans-Adolf: 'Kommissarbefehl und Massenexekutionen sowjetischer Kriegsgefangener'. In: *Anatomie des SS-Staates*, Bd. II, Olten und Freiburg im Breisgau 1965

Jodl, Alfred: 'Das dienstliche Tagebuch des Chefs des Wehrmachtführungs-amtes im OKW fur die Zeit vom 13. Oktober 1939 bis zum 30. Januar 1940'. Hrsg. von Walter Hubatsch. In: *Die Welt als Geschichte* 12 (1952), pp. 274–87; 13 (1953), pp. 58–71

Kalinow, Kyrill: *Sowjetmarschälle haben das Wort*, Hamburg 1950

Kehrig, Manfred: *Stalingrad. Analyse und Dokumentation einer Schlacht*, Stuttgart 1974

Kempner, Robert: *Eichmann und Komplizen*, Zurich 1961

Kielmannsegg, Johann Adolf Graf: *Der Fritsch-Prozeß 1938. Ablauf und Hintergründe*, Hamburg 1949

Kissel, Hans: *Panzerschlachten in der Pußta*, Neckargemünd 1960

Kissel, Hans: 'Die ersten T 34'. In: *Wehrwissenschaftl. Rundschau* 5 (1955), pp. 130ff.

Klee, Ernst und Otto Merk: *Damals in Peenemünde*, Oldenburg u. Hamburg 1963

General Ernst Köstring. *Der militärische Mittler zwischen dem Deutschen Reich und der Sowjetunion 1921–1941*. Bearbeitet von Hermann Teske, Frankfurt am Main 1965

Konrad, R. und E. W. Rümler: *Kampf um den Kaukasus*, München n.d.

Krausnick, Helmut: 'Vorgeschichte und Beginn des militlärlichen Widerstandes gegen Hitler'. In: *Vollmacht des Gewissens*, Bd. I, Frankfurt am Main, Berlin 1960

Krausnick, Helmut: 'Judenverfolgung'. In: *Anatosnie des SS-Staates*, Bd. II, Olten und Freiburg im Breisgau 1965

Krausnick, Helmut: 'Hitler und die Morde in Polen'. In: *VfZ 11* (1963), pp. 196–209

Kriegsheim, Herbert: *Getarnt, getäuscht und doch getreu. Die geheimnisvollen "Brandenburger"*, Berlin 1958

V. Loßberg, Bernhard: *Im Wehrmachtführungsstab. Bericht eines Generalstabsoffiziers*, Hamburg 1949

Lusar, Rudolf: *Die deutschen Waffen und Geheimwaffen des 2. Weltkrieges und ihre Weiterentwicklung*, München 1956

Mannerheim; G.: *Erinnerungen*, Zürich 1952

Manstein, Erich von: *Aus einem Soldatenleben. 1887–1939*, Bonn 1958

Manstein, Erich von: *Verlorene Siege*, Bonn 1955

Maser, Werner: *Adolf Hitler. Legende, Mythos, Wirklichkeit*, München und Eßlingen 1971

Meier-Welcker, Hans: 'Der Entschluß zum Anhalten der deutschen Panzertruppen in Flandern'. In: *VfZ 2* (1954), pp. 274–90

Mellenthin, Friedrich Wilhelm von: *Panzerschlachten. Eine Studie über den Einsatz von Panzerverbänden im Zweiten Weltkrieg*, Neckargemünd 1963

Messe, Giovanni: *La Guerra al Fronte Russo*, Rom 1947

Messerschmidt, Manfred: *Die Wehrmacht im NS-Staat. Zeit der Indoktrination*, Hamburg 1969

Ministerial-Blatt des Reichs- und Preußischen Ministeriums des Innern. Ausg. A. 1938

Mitscherlich, Alexander und Fred Mielke (Hrsg.): *Medizin ohne Menschlichkeit*, Frankfurt am Main 1960

Model, Hansgeorg: *Der deutsche Generalstabsoffizier. Seine Auswahl und Ausbildung in Reichswehr, Wehrmacht und Bundeswehr*, Frankfurt am Main 1968

Muller, Klaus-Jürgen: *Das Heer und Hitler. Armee und nationalsozialistisches Regime 1933–1940*, Stuttgart 1969

Muller-Hillebrand, Burkhart: *Das Heer 1933–1945*. Bd. I. *Das Heer bis zum Kriegsbeginn*. Darmstadt 1954

Nehring, Walter: *Geschichte der deutschen Panzerwaffe*, Berlin 1969

Neufeldt, Huck, Tessin: *Zur Geschichte der Ordnungspolizei 1936–1945*. Schriften des Bundesarchivs (3). Koblenz 1957

Der Oberbefehlshaber des Heeres (Hrsg.): Wahrung der Ehre. Nr. 2500.38 PA (2). Neudruck 1938

Der Parteitag der Freiheit 1935. Offizieller Bericht über den Verlauf des Reichsparteitages mit sämtlichen Kongreßreden, München 1936

Der Parteitag Großdeutschland 1938. Offizieller Bericht über den Verlauf des Reichsparteitages mit sämtlichen Kongreßreden, München 1938

Philippi, Alfred und Ferdinand Heim: *Der Feldzug gegen Sowjetrußland 1941 bis 1945*, Stuttgart 1962

Picker, Henry: *Hitlers Tischgespräche im Fuhrerhauptquartier 1941–1942*, eingeleitet u. veröffentlicht von Gerhard Ritter, Bonn 1951

Picker, Henry und Heinrich Hoffmann: *Hitlers Tischgespräche im Bild* (hrsg. von Jochen von Lang), Oldenburg u. Hamburg 1969

Platen-Hallermund, Alice: *Die Tötung Geisteskranker in Deutschland*, Frankfurt am Main 1948

Der Prozeß gegen die Hauptkriegsverbrecher vor dem Internationalen Militärgerichtshof (IMT), 42 Bde., Nurnberg 1947–1949

Reinhardt, Klaus: *Die Wende vor Moskau. Das Scheitern der Strategie Hitlers im Winter 1941/42*, Stuttgart 1972

Reitlinger, Gerald: *Die Endlösung*, Berlin 1960

Schellenberg, Walter: *Memoiren*, Köln 1956

Scheurig, Bodo: *Henning von Tresckow*, Hamburg und Oldenburg 1973

Schmidt, Dietmar: *Martin Niemöller*, Hamburg 1959

Schmidt, Jürgen: *Martin Niemöller im Kirchenkampf*, Hamburg 1971

Schmidt, Paul: *Statist auf diplomatischer Bühne*, Bonn 1949

Scholder, Klaus: 'Die evangelische Kirche in der Sicht der nationalsozialistischen Führung bis zum Kriegsausbruch'. In: *VfZ 16* (1968), pp. 15–35

Schramm, P. E. (Hrsg.): *Kriegstagebuch des Oberkommandos der Wehrmacht (Wehrmachtführungsstab)*

    Bd. I. 1. August 1940–31. Dezember 1941, zusammengestellt und erläutert von Hans-Adolf Jacobsen, Frankfurt am Main 1965

    Bd. II 1. 2. 1. Januar 1942–31. Dezember 1942, zusammengestellt und erläutert von Andreas Hillgruber, Frankfurt am Main 1963

Schröter, Heinz: *Stalingrad ". . . bis zur letzten Patrone"*, Osnabrück [1954]

Senff, Hubertus: *Die Entwicklung der Panzerwaffe im deutschen Heer zwischen den beiden Weltkriegen*, Frankfurt 1969

Senger und Etterlin, Dr. F. M. von: *Taschenbuch der Panzer 1943–1954*, München 1954

Seraphim, Hans-Günther und Andreas Hillgruber: 'Hitlers Entschluß zum Angriff auf Rußland'. In: *VfZ 2* (1954), pp. 240–54

Siebert, Ferdinand: *Italiens Weg in den Zweiten Weltkrieg*, Frankfurt am Main, Bonn 1962

Siegler, Fritz Frhr. von: *Die höheren Dienststellen der deutschen Wehrmacht 1933–1945*, München 1953

Siewert, Curt: *Schuldig? Die Generale unter Hitler*, Bad Nauheim 1968

Stein, George H.: *Geschichte der Waffen-SS*, Düsseldorf 1967

Tessin, *see* Neufeldt, Huck, Tessin

Trevor-Roper, H. R.: *Hitler's Table Talk 1941–1944*, London 1953

Warlimont, Walter: *Im Hauptquartier der deutschen Wehrmacht 1939–1945*, Frankfurt 1962

Weinberg, Gerhard L.: 'The May Crisis, 1938'. In: *The Journal of Modern History* 29 (1957), pp. 213ff.

Weinkauff, Hermann: *Die deutsche Justiz und der Nationalsozialismus*, Stuttgart 1968

Weinzierl-Fischer, Erika: 'Österreichs Katholiken und der Nationalsozialismus'. In: *Wort und Wahrheit* 18 (1963) 2. Halbbd., pp. 417–39, 493–526; 20 (1965) 2. Halbbd., pp. 777–804

Wiener, Fritz: 'Die deutsche Panzertruppe 1939–1945'. In: *Feldgrau*, 5 (1957), pp. 109–12; 135–8; 173–4

Wulf, Joseph: *Theater und Film im Dritten Reich. Eine Dokumentation*, Gütersloh 1964

Zaddach, Frank-Helmut: *Britische Kommandotruppen und Kommando-unternehmen im Zweiten Weltkrieg*, Darmstadt 1963

Zipfel, Friedrich: *Kirchenkampf in Deutschland 1933–1945*, Berlin 1965

3. Select English Bibliography

Barnett, Correlli ed., *Hitler's Generals*, Weidenfeld & Nicolson, London, and Grove Press, New York 1989

Beevor, Antony, *Stalingrad*, Viking, London and New York 1998

Below, Nicolaus von, *At Hitler's Side: The Memoirs of Hitler's Luftwaffe Adjutant 1937–1945*, Greenhill, London 2001

Cooper, Matthew, *The German Army 1933–1945: Its Political and Military Failure*, Macdonald and Jane's, London, and Stein and Day, New York 1978

Deutsch, Harold Charles, *Hitler and his Generals: The Hidden Crisis January–June 1938*, University of Minnesota Press, Minneapolis 1974

Halder, Franz, *The Halder War Diary 1939–1942*, Greenhill, London 1988

Heiber, Helmut & Glantz, David M., eds., *Hitler and His Generals: Military Conferences 1942–1945*, Enigma Books, New York 2002

Kershaw, Ian, *Hitler: 1889–1936 Hubris*, Allen Lane, London, and Norton, New York 1998

Kershaw, Ian, *Hitler: 1936–1945 Nemesis* Allen Lane, London, and Norton, New York 2000

Manstein, Erich von, *Lost Victories*, Methuen, London 1958

Müller, Klaus-Jürgen, *The Army, Politics and Society in Germany 1933–45: Studies in the Army's Relation to Nazism*, Manchester University Press 1987

Messenger, Charles, *The Last Prussian: A Biography of Field Marshal Gerd von Rundstedt 1875–1953*, Brassey's, London and New York 1991

Seaton, Albert, *The Russo-German War 1941–1945*, Praeger, Westport Conn 1971

Seaton, Albert, *The German Army 1933–45*, Weidenfeld & Nicolson, London 1982

Seidler, Franz W. and Zeigert, Dieter, *Hitler's Secret Headquarters*, Greenhill Books, London 2004

Stahlberg, Alexander, *Bounden Duty: The Memoirs of a German Officer 1932–1945*, Brassey's, London and New York 1990

Warlimont, Walter, *Inside Hitler's Headquarters 1939–45*, Weidenfeld & Nicolson, London, and Praeger, New York 1964

Wheeler-Bennett, John, W. *The Nemesis of Power: The German Army in Politics 1918–1945*, Macmillan, London, and St Martin's Press, New York 1954

Index